ISRAEL AND JORDAN IN THE
SHADOW OF WAR

Also by Adam Garfinkle

WESTERN EUROPE'S MIDDLE EAST DIPLOMACY AND THE UNITED
STATES
THE POLITICS OF THE NUCLEAR FREEZE
FRIENDLY TYRANTS (*coeditor with Daniel Pipes*)

Israel and Jordan in the Shadow of War

Functional Ties and Futile Diplomacy in a Small Place

Adam Garfinkle
Coordinator of Political Studies
Foreign Policy Research Institute, Philadelphia

St. Martin's Press   New York

First published in the United States of America in 1992

Printed in Hong Kong

ISBN 0-312-04899-8

Library of Congress Cataloging-in-Publication Data
Garfinkle, Adam M.
Israel and Jordan in the shadow of war/Adam Garfinkle.
p. cm.
Includes bibliographical references and index.
ISBN 0-312-04899-8
1. Israel—Foreign relations—Jordan. 2. Jordan—Foreign
relations. 3. Jewish–Arab relations—1917– 4. Israel–Arab
conflicts. 5. West Bank—History—20th century. I. Title.
DS119.8.J67G37 1992
327.569405695—dc20   91-11987
                                                           CIP

This book is dedicated to the honored memories of Samir al-Rifai and Reuven Shiloah, two men who did what they could, two men of peace.

Contents

Contents

Preface: Project History and Methods

This book studies the significance of functional contacts in the mediation of political change, using the relationship between Jordan and Israel within the broader canvas of the Arab–Israeli conflict as a case in point. In truth, my interests are less those concerning the theory of functionalism than its application to the particulars of this fascinating case. Academics looking for new insights into the work of David Mitrany, Ernst Haas, and others will not find them here. But the case is important both for its own sake, and for what it might mean more generally to what is wistfully called the Arab–Israeli peace process. If the case reflects back on theory, too—as I believe it does—so much the better for those who take that interest especially to heart.

The theory of functionalism, in its most basic form, argues that apolitical associations often have or can be made to have benign political spillovers. The more such apolitical associations that exist, then, the more benign spillovers one should expect. This is intuitively reasonable, particularly for those people reared in a culture that honors empiricism and imagines that post-Enlightenment European definitions of reason are universal. But it is not always true that the more people get to know one another, the less enmity they hold for one another. History is replete with examples of just the opposite taking place and that is because the Golden Rule is not normally operative in relations between states; as George Bernard Shaw put it in a different context: "Do not do unto others as you would they should do unto you. Their tastes may not be the same."[1]

The most prominent generic form of thinking based on functionalist premises is the belief that the more any two countries trade, the less likely they are to go to war with each other.[2] This is just not true, however. The most dramatic contrary example, perhaps, is that as German tanks were advancing toward the Soviet border in preparation for their surprise attack on the Soviet Union in 1941, Soviet trucks were busy carrying foodstuffs and raw materials into the German zone of Poland in the spirit of Rapallo and the Nazi–Soviet Non-Aggression Pact of 1939.

A related functionalist notion, common to most Americans and many others too, concerns not trading but talking. Arms control negotiations, in particular, are thought good even if agreements are not reached because one does not go to war as long as one is talking with the potential adversary. But anyone who remembers or knows that Japanese diplomats were still in the United States when Pearl Harbor was bombed understands enough to doubt that.

Functionalism seems to appeal particularly to Americans who, more than most peoples, engage in the Calvinist-influenced presumption that there is always some level of material incentive or threat that can succeed in getting one's opponents either to do or not do things inimical to one's interests, as the case may be. In the pages that follow, we will have recourse to describe the Johnston Plan of the early 1950s, a functionalist-inspired project if ever there was one. The belief in the political power of material incentives is the flip-side of sorts to the American penchant to call for and to put stock in the efficacy of economic sanctions as a tool of foreign policy—despite repeated evidence that sanctions rarely work as intended and are more often than not embarrassingly counter-productive.

In virtually all of its various forms, functionalism as positive or normative theory has always struck me as so much wishful thinking; what it expects to be the case—whether having to do with trade, talk, economic coercion or what-have-you—rarely has been the case in normal historical circumstances. But that is the key—*normality*. Relations between Israel and its Arab neighbors are not normal. Therefore, applying the law of reciprocal paradox, I wondered whether a theory normally distinguished for its being mistaken might, in abnormal circumstances, prove to be insightfully correct. One is reminded of O'Henry's famous story, "The Gift of the Magi," where she sells her beautiful long hair to buy him a watch-chain, and he sells his watch to

buy her combs and barrettes for her beautiful long hair. The
result: good intentions, wrong theory, bad results, but a
happy ending just the same. That is the motive, or better
perhaps, the hunch, that beckons me to look at functional
contacts between Israel and Jordan.

Given the hazy image of Jordanian–Israeli ties deliberately
concocted for protection's sake by both protagonists and
occasional mediators, the subject matter is more recalcitrant
than most to typical academic research. The main problem
concerns data. Israeli–Jordanian functional ties are so
shrouded in deliberate mutual discretions that many are the
mysteries and evasive is the evidence at hand. It generally
helps to be both native to the region and very patient in doing
research, all the more so in this case. A native I am not, but I
have been patient: my pursuit of the data represented here has
gone on for the better part of a decade. So tedious and slow
has this process been that, for all the time spent collecting for
and thinking about the project, this is on balance a rather
short book.

What follows here is a description of Israeli–Jordanian
relations "below the line of sight," so to speak, and an
analysis of what they mean, and could mean, in the context of
"high" politics in the region. The organization of the book is
fairly simple. Chapter 1 is broadly historical and appropriately brief. It sums up the history of Zionist–Hashemite
contacts and offers explanations for its curiously calm nature
amid other, more pandemonic Israeli–Arab relationships.
There is an enormous amount of history here, much of
which has been covered in recent years (in Hebrew) in books
by Moshe Zak and Dan Schueftan,[3] and more lately in
English by Uri Bar-Joseph, Avi Shlaim, Mary Wilson, and
the team of Yossi Melman and Dan Raviv.[4] There is no
reason to repeat all of this and I have no intention of trying. I
only wish to provide enough of it to give some sense of the
development of Israeli–Jordanian relations before the June
1967 war.

Chapter 2 picks up the parable and describes what occurred
in Israeli–Jordanian ties in the years after the June 1967 war.
Obviously, as nearly 700 000 Jordanian citizens came under
Israeli occupation,[5] and as hundreds of thousands of

Palestinian Arabs made their way across the river into Jordan, much changed. As is often the case in politics, the broad picture was no one's particular vision, but rather an unplanned evolution over many years that nevertheless reflected both a certain geopolitical reality and the inexorable needs of social relations in a tight place.

Chapter 3 describes the Israeli–Jordanian diplomacy of the 1984–87 period in some detail, and specifies the role played by the array of low-level contacts that functioned between Israel and Jordan. This period stands as perhaps the best existing example of an effort "from above" to use functional contacts to move, influence, and sustain "high" diplomatic agendas. In particular, the narrative here illustrates that the visible diplomacy of this period, which involved the United States, Israel, Jordan, the Soviet Union, Egypt, Syria, the Palestine Liberation Organization, and key Arab notables on the West Bank, was unintelligible beyond a certain level of sophistication without knowledge of the invisible diplomacy going on concerning functional questions between Israel and Jordan, with occasional American intercession.

Again, I have not tried fully to exhaust the high diplomacy of this period. The series of discussions between Yasir Arafat and King Hussein during this period, for example, were extraordinarily complex. My aim is not to fully chronicle them—and indeed I have not done so here. I only wish to describe them in as much detail as necessary to shed light on the role or functional contacts in the diplomacy of the period.

Chapter 4 describes in brief what happened in the area from the beginning of the *intifada* in December 1987, through Jordan's surprise "disengagement" from the West Bank in the summer of 1988, and to the Persian Gulf crisis of August 1990, insofar as it bears on the significance and direction of low-level personal contacts. Jordan's alteration of its relationship with the West Bank changed some things on the ground in the region but not others. Quite aside from the disengagement, there have been other changes in Jordan that have affected its ties with Israel. The American mediative role remained after the *intifada* as well, and took noteworthy new directions into the first half of 1990.

Chapter 5 reflects briefly on what the future has to offer and reflects briefly on the utility of functional cooperation to advance or sustain explicit diplomatic agendas and aspirations.

What emerges from all of this, at the very least, is a calculus upon which the careful observation of daily and monthly events can be analyzed in a fuller context. That alone should be worth something.

I used essentially four kinds of sources in writing this book. First were interviews and conversations—the difference between the two depending less on content than on the air, the locale, and the circumstances—with Israelis, Jordanians, Palestinians, Americans, Soviets, and Europeans of assorted description. In the course of pursuing this study, I have travelled to both Israel and Jordan in past years: in 1986, I spent many weeks researching and interviewing on the topic in Israel, courtesy of a Fulbright Fellowship. A few delicate and somewhat peripheral discussions took place with Soviet academicians in Moscow, that trip enabled by a condominium of the Foreign Policy Research Institute and the Institute for the Study of the USA and Canada of the Soviet Academy of Sciences, brokered by the International Research Exchange Board (IREX).

Second, there were secondary sources—books and articles. The former kind of secondary source was useful only for general background, of which there is some below, but only as much as is required for the main themes of the narrative to proceed. The magazine cache was also very sparse in reliable information. I am especially grateful to Mr Mark Barnhart, formerly of the Fels Center of Government at the University of Pennsylvania, for chasing down much of this obscure material, and for not only seeking, but finding, quite a few sharp needles amidst a formless and unenticing literary haystack.

Third was the local media in Israel as well as Foreign Broadcast Information Service transcripts of radio and periodical materials from the region, translated from Hebrew and Arabic. These turned out to be very valuable sources indeed. Although they are not usually finished analytical products, and they are not always completely reliable, one can learn to read between the lines of such material with reasonable competence over time. Still, even the skilful use of such sources hardly amounts to an exact science.

Finally, communication with other scholars working on related subjects, or having background knowledge in related subjects, has also been of use. Thus far, I can thank in print Daniel Pipes, Asher Susser, Avraham Sela and Moshe Zak for their help.

The sparseness of the resources, and their occasional nature, has counselled me to write the essay that follows with a special kind of care. Much of the information I gathered, being anecdotal, is either of dubious or uncheckable reliability. Some of it appears to be lies for fun and profit of various kinds. Jordanians, in their discussions with outsiders, tend to minimize contacts with Israel, even if they know or suspect otherwise. Israelis, to the contrary, have an incentive to exaggerate the level and nature of such contacts because it makes Israel seem less like a regional pariah than it is. Some of this exaggeration is designed as propaganda, gentle though it may be. Some of it is illusion, wishful thinking, and little else.

Non-Israelis who have sympathy for Israel have also at times exaggerated the closeness of Israeli–Jordanian ties. For example, David Pryce-Jones once claimed: "In more than one crunch, Israeli supplied vital arms and fuel to the King."[6] He offered no evidence, however, and this assertion is, to the best of my knowledge, quite wrong. It does point up, however, a temptation to exaggerate if only because that which is covert often communicates special excitement and momentuous significance to most outside observers.

This being the case, there is a special premium on data that can be corroborated. Some information can be triangulated from multiple sources and, when this has been the case, I have been firmer in my language. But most cannot. Much of what I heard was gossip and rumor, once, twice and thrice removed from the original source. Clearly it is not always possible to track down such rumors, nor is it always practical to try. In normal research endeavors one discounts stories that cannot be directly confirmed and trusts other sources. The problem here is that there are not very many other sources. Thus one must to some extent trust one's intuition and general sense of the state of play.

And there is another imbalance. Israelis talk (and talk) and the Israeli press leaks (and leaks). But those interviewed on the Arab side have tended to be circumlocutious about naming names and saying anything specific. The Arabic press leaks but less and not in the same way. Besides, if one can imagine that one of the qualities of a press is that it has a volume, then there is simply a lot less of the relevant Arabic press to leak. In sum, things assumed to be common knowledge among those in the know, or who think they are in the know, sometimes turned out to be true, sometimes false, as best I could tell. But much of the time, I could not tell for sure.

Jordanians have always been reluctant to speak openly about their contacts with Israel and Israelis, but this reluctance has become even more pointed since the November 1989 elections in Jordan ushered in the age of Jordan's experiment in the democratic process. This is rather ironic if one stops to think about it. In essence, the opening up in Jordan that has taken place since November 1989 has allowed bitterly anti-Israel and anti-US sentiments to frighten into silence those Jordanians who had straddled the line between public distance and private contact with Israel that has developed over the years. The outpouring of resentment against the United States for deploying forces to Saudi Arabia only made things worse in this regard.

Most important, the security of discreet ties between those on opposite sides of a political conflict can be jeopardized by publicity, and this of course works directly against the basic purpose of field research. There are many places where, in a typical academic presentation, one would expect to see a footnote. Here, the reader will find either an unsatisfactorily vague remark or nothing at all. This is because I respect the need in many cases to protect the general political insulation of many of the processes I am trying to describe. This is sometimes difficult to do; all things being equal, I would like nothing better than to name names, for example in chapter 4 where I detail US mediation in 1989–90 between Israel and

Jordan on the problem of riparian rights to use the Yarmouk River waters. But I should not, so I name very few.

In some respects, then, this project is not finished, and in others it is not finishable. For these reasons this little volume is perhaps best thought of as an analytical prolegomenon rather than as an inclusive or final treatment of the topic. Such a final treatment, if it is ever written, will almost certainly not be contemporary but historical analysis, and neither I nor those of you whose eyes pass over these lines in this year (1991) are likely to be around to behold it.

All the same, such imperfections and deviations notwith-standing, the narrative below should provide some satisfaction to those genuinely interested in the nuts-and-bolts details of the Arab–Israeli conflict and its amelioration. To my knowledge there is nothing in the open literature that presents the breadth of description of low-level Israeli–Jordanian contacts provided here.

That raises a last prefatory curiosity. At first blush it is surprising that so little effort has been made to study Israeli–Jordanian low-level contacts. But on reflection it is not so surprising after all. Israeli scholars are not wont to focus on such matters for fear of jeopardizing them—or at least when they have written on them, they have not written in English. Some Jordanians have similar concerns plus the additional one of fear at being labelled a defeatist and of being punished for it by the PLO, Islamic militants, or Syrian intelligence operatives.

American scholars have been uninterested, it seems, for three possible reasons. First, American diplomacy has concentrated for so long on the public and formal/legal aspects of Middle East peace negotiations that most scholars have failed to develop a concept of such a study. Even those scholars who are interested in informal diplomacy seem more interested in studying what outside powers can do to facilitate contact than in studying what contact already exists.

Second, it is not a subject that can be easily researched from secondary sources: travel and interviews are absolutely essential and many scholars lack the time and resources to do what is necessary.

Third, and hopefully least important, there is a growing bias within American Middle Eastern studies toward pro-Arab and vaguely pro-Third World agendas. The Middle East Studies Association breaks out in a sweat of umbrage should any of its members accept funding from the Central Intelligence Agency or maintain official liaison with Israeli organizations, but it encounters no insuperable problems when its members are showered with funds from the Libyan or Saudi governments, or maintain liaison with the Palestine Information Office in New York City. This general atmosphere tends to render interest in studying real peace with Israel on the level of human beings face-to-face with other human beings unpopular.

This is unfortunate because Americans are in a good position to do the work. The United States has good relations with both Israel and Jordan, the United States government has mediated frequently between the two countries over a variety of topics, and an American scholar is probably capable of a greater level of emotional distance than any local actor. Yet, as a good bibliographical search indicates, very little if anything has been done by American scholars to study low level Israeli–Jordanian contacts.[7]

Finally, it is perhaps worth noting, too, if only in passing, what is not included in this book. What Israel and Jordan do below the line of sight may be singular, but it is certainly not altogether unique. There are other places around the globe where political enmity defined according to formal political boundaries and personal animosities along those same borders are not parallel. There can be many reasons for this. One is the non-overlap of political boundaries with ethno-linguistic ones, such that Somalia and Ethiopia can be at war, but ethnic Somalis on different sides of the border not. The same can be said, albeit in a more complex way, about Kurds in Iran and Iraq during the Gulf War, or about Tamils in India and Sri Lanka, again in a fashion unique to local circumstances. Divided nations like Korea and Germany (between 1945 and 1990) are special cases of a different kind because they are based on political and ideological cleavages larger than their national similitudes and which, as ought to be clear, can change considerably over time as those larger cleavages change. And then there is the example of South Africa's dealings with the black Front Line states, where economic dependencies play a major role in blunting the inclusiveness of state-to-state hostility. And notwithstanding the tensions between Cambodia and Thailand, and between hostile Muslim *mujahidin* in Afghanistan and Russians in Central Asia, the mere fact of long or otherwise porous borders has facilitated personal penetrations both hostile and accidental that have had occasionally interesting consequences.

Useful as a comparative perspective on low-level functional contacts between formal adversaries might be, nothing of it is included below. That awaits a far more ambitious—and probably a collective—effort.

This study was supported in part by a grant from the United States Institute of Peace (#004). My interest in the topic began long ago and has extended beyond the grant period specified by that Institute. Of course, nothing in this essay shall be construed as representing the views of the United States Institute of Peace, its board, or any of its constituent representatives.

ADAM GARFINKLE

Notes

1. From *Maxims for Revolutionists*, quoted in *Stevenson's Home Book of Quotations* (New York: Dodd, Mead & Co., 1967) p. 804.
2. Functionalism is an established theory within international relations. One of its classical expressions is David Mitrany's "The Functional Approach to World Organization," *International Affairs*, July 1948.
3. Zak's book is not available in English. If and when it is, it will offer a most impressive collection of materials, and there is a good reason why that is so. Zak was for many years Editor-in-Chief of the Israeli daily *Ma'ariv*. From the looks of his office, I feel confident in saying that he is the sort of person who keeps everything, and he has retained original dispatches from

Ma'ariv correspondents before newspaper copy was submitted
to the military censors for their perusal. Hence he is his own
archive. For a hint of what he knows, see his "A Survey of
Israel's Contacts With Jordan," in Itamar Rabinovich and
Judah Reinharz, eds, *Israel in the Middle East* (New York:
Oxford University Press, 1984). As for Shueftan, see his *Yahase
Yarden—Ashaf B'shelav Hadash* (Tel Aviv: Yad Tabenkin,
1985).
4. Uri Bar-Joseph, *The Best of Enemies: Israel and Transjordan in
the War of 1948* (London: Frank Cass, 1987); Avi Shlaim,
Collusion Across the Jordan (New York: Columbia University
Press, 1988); Mary C. Wilson, *King Abdallah, Great Britain and
the Making of Jordan* (New York: Cambridge University Press,
1988); and Yossi Melman and Dan Raviv, *Behind the Uprising:
Israelis, Jordanians, and Palestinians* (New York: Greenwood
Press, 1989).
5. More than 700 000 Arabs came under occupation after the June
1967 war—around a million—but Gazan Arabs were legally
stateless at that time, having never been granted Egyptian
citizenship.
6. David Pryce-Jones, "The Timid King," *The New Republic*,
Year-End Issue, 1982, p. 19.
7. A brief exception is Daniel Pipes, "The Unacknowledged
Partnership," *The National Interest*, No. 10, Winter 1987/88,
pp. 95–98.

Introduction

Extensive informal arrangements between Jordan and Israel have evolved over the last forty years despite the absence of a formal document of peace between the two governments. The two countries have developed a workable *modus vivendi* that has endured through strained periods, and that in fairer times has exhibited even a certain discreet warmth. The existence of these informal ties has not yet propelled Israel and Jordan toward a full or a public peace, and by themselves are unlikely ever to do so. But on a number of occasions, the Israeli–Jordanian *modus vivendi* has contributed to limiting regional violence and has affected regional balances in crisis, most notably in September 1970.

Some of the arrangements worked out between Israel and Jordan over the years have been either initiated or sanctioned and negotiated at the highest level. In Israeli intelligence files the amount of information, including the actual transcripts of conversations between King Hussein and other high Jordanian officials on the one hand and Israeli officials on the other over the years, fill many file cabinets. One confidential estimate holds that there is approximately 500 hours of reading therein.

Other connections between the two countries, which have been dubbed by one writer "the best of enemies,"[1] have emerged from the needs of day-to-day relations between people living in a small area. Still others are more or less accidental and incidental, such as when radio and television waves stumble across political borders without anyone necessarily meaning them to do so.

Many of the evolved arrangements between Jordan and Israel are best described as combinations of the accidental and the deliberate. High level and low level contacts have often been mutually reinforcing, the former sanctioning the latter and the latter advancing the former. Functional cooperation became more important to both countries after the June 1967

1

War, and particularly after hope for a comprehensive settlement diminished, leaving practical matters on the ground the only thing left to do. But on at least one occasion, during the 1984–86 period (discussed below in chapter 3), the Israeli government sought to use a range of functional contacts with Jordan and the prospects for expanding them in pursuit of an explicit and important diplomatic agenda. That agenda involved not only Israel, Jordan and the Palestinians but, at different levels and in different ways, also the United States, the Soviet Union and other regional actors.

The range of issues on which functional contact and cooperation exists, between Israel and Jordan is surprisingly large to those unacquainted with the particulars of local reality. The list includes: agricultural development, pest control, water conservation and allocation, pollution control, intelligence, navigation, air traffic control, mining, utilities management, banking and commerce policy, scientific and technical exchange, and more besides.

This does not mean that all is well between Israel and Jordan, or that their public hostility, especially on the Jordanian side, is just a public relations charade. Although deliberate public relations fuzzing has occurred, both countries do cause each other considerable trouble. Jordan is the logical gathering point of any Arab war coalition on Israel's eastern front, and so is of constant concern to Israeli military planners. Jordan refuses to make peace or negotiate directly with Israel in public, contributing to Israel's ostracization in the region and in the world at large. Jordan has in the past allowed Palestinian groups to operate from Jordanian soil against Israel, and it propagandizes the Palestinian cause in its press and at world forums.

On the other hand, Israel is stronger economically and militarily than Jordan and has defeated it both times the two armies have met on the field of battle, in 1948 and in 1967. In between those years, and through the fall of 1970, Israeli cross-border reprisals humiliated, pained, and weakened the Hashemite regime. More important these days, there are many Israeli politicians on the far right who view Jordan as illegitimate, and hope that the Palestinian problem will one day be solved at Hashemite Jordan's expense.[2] This view, that "Jordan is Palestine," seems to be growing in Israel, and it has already caused no small amount of anxiety, even alarm, among the Jordanian political élite.

This alarm appeared to turn into something bordering on panic in early 1990 when King Hussein seemed to worry that the arrival in Israel of many thousands of Soviet Jews would be the catalyst for the mass expulsion of Palestinians into the east bank. With the outbreak of the Kuwait crisis in August 1990 the prospect that Israel would exploit the upheaval temporarily to seize part of the east bank and expel Palestinians into it by the tens of thousands rose even higher in the minds of many Jordanians. Surely these fears contributed to Jordan's acute equivocation during the early weeks of the crisis.

In fact, the Israeli government had no plans to attack Jordan or expel masses of Palestinians across the river, either before, during or after the Kuwait crisis. But even short of that, political forces in Israel that support or are quietly sympathetic to the idea, euphemistically called "transfer," have been ambivalent about the quiet relationship with Jordan. They have been inclined to tolerate only the sort of cooperation that is wholly tacit, coinciding interests being allowed to run a parallel course without special encouragement or contact. They certainly have not sought to broaden or deepen the relationship.

In addition, Jordanian weaknesses sometimes put it in a vise between wishing to keep proper relations with Israel, and being pressed by other Arab parties to work in a way that irritates decent relations. For example, when Jordan finds it in its interest to work toward water-sharing arrangements with Israel, it often if not always involves Syria, which has always disdained the very notion. The relationship, then, is fluid, unpredictable at least at its margins, and subject to various kinds of political pressures from both sides.

Nevertheless the contrast between Israeli–Jordanian ties and either Israeli–Egyptian or Israeli–Syrian relations is quite striking. In the first case, there is a formal document of peace in effect, the strategic and psychological value of which is not to be minimized. But there is little personal texture in Israeli–

Egyptian relations even after more than a full decade of formal peaceful relations; hence the epithet "the cold peace" by which it has come to be known in Israel and in the United States. The Egyptians have the luxury of wanting simply to be left alone from dealings with Israel and they have largely had their way on that score. Peace or no peace, for the Hashemite Kingdom of Jordan and the Palestinians that live within it, detachment of that sort is not an option.

As for Syria, its relations with Israel have been hostile and vituperative; for a variety of reasons, Syria has much less of an inclination to develop a positive *modus vivendi* with Israel. There is nevertheless a form of tacit understanding over certain regional security matters between Damascus and Jerusalem, and there is quite likely a secret side agreement between Israel and Syria as part of the U.S.-brokered 1974 Golan disengagement accords that specifies this *modus vivendi*, and implies penalties for breaking it, in more detail.[3]

Still, the Israeli–Jordanian case is unique in the region. The intensity and breadth of low-level contacts is larger and longer-lived than in any other case by far. As noted above, this relationship has not evolved into something more public or legal, yet, in a region where patterns of separation have been dominant and stereotypical images of the adversary have grown up and remain strong,[4] there is some justification for hoping that personal contacts can be of positive value in the struggle for peace and normal relations. Two reasons stand forth.

First, while apolitical, technical cooperation by itself is unlikely to precipitate major political change for the better, it may provide a buffer against a major worsening of relations. Israel and Jordan cooperate not because they love and admire each other but because it suits their interests to do so. They are, so to speak, locked in a cold embrace. Such a mutuality can guard against a rapid and unpredictable unraveling of relations in an area known for producing surprises of the melancholy sort. As illustrated below, aspects of Israeli–Jordanian behavior during the Palestinian *intifada* bear this out.

Second, low level contacts can be deliberately expanded "from above," either between the two parties themselves or with the help of a third country, in this case meaning in particular the United States. As such, low-level contacts represent a signalling repertoire that can be used instrumentally in the tense, early stages of a political dialogue or, as we shall see below, at other stages as well. The greater the range of such a signalling repertoire, the greater the flexibility that the two sides could have in taking marginal risks, the availability of which is in turn conducive to negotiating progress.[5]

In the Middle East in particular negotiations, whether secret or open, must be understood as part of a broader political process, which rests in turn in an even broader social environment. Peace between governments can never be secure unless reinforced at the social level by reconciliation between peoples. It simply makes common sense to tend to all these dimensions simultaneously in so far as that is possible.[6] Put slightly differently, such low level contacts represent a pre-existing personal texture to an improved political relationship. One can think of it as a reservoir of "normalization" held in escrow against the day that political progress on higher levels might be made.

In addition to giving a new and fragile peace relationship more texture—a critical ingredient in having a peace "stick" against the forces that would seek to hew it into pieces—low level contacts are some protection against the erosion of the relationship in the more distant future. Things change. Sovereign countries that choose to make peace can, under new circumstances or new leadership, also choose to make war. But if an environment can be created from functional contacts that leads to more than casual contact, a web of interlocking interests may evolve that will give more people a stake in the preservation of peace. People do not live by bread alone, it is true, and economic conditions do not dictate political ones in any simple way. But elemental logic suggests that fewer people are willing to risk their lives and the lives of those they love in pursuit of a rarified ideological goal when their personal futures look bright than when they look bleak. This is, not entirely incidentally, the logic behind the Hashemite monarchy's attempts over the years to integrate Jordan's Palestinian population in the east bank.

Many observers would question the relevance of Israeli–Jordanian relations to Arab–Israeli peace these days. According to many, including many Israelis, Israel's relationships with the Arab countries, however important, are secondary to the Palestinian issue, the struggle between two national movements, the Jewish and Palestinian Arab, for the same piece of land. The focus of most discussion about peace nowadays is not on a Jordanian "option" or role, as was the case in the period directly after the June 1967 war, but rather on whether or not there should be an independent Palestinian state, what limitations on its sovereignty, if any, there should be, and within what borders it should be sited.

The Jordanian government's "disengagement" from the West Bank in the summer of 1988 added to the perception of Jordan's relative marginality to the peace process, to the extent that some writers assume the inevitability of an independent Palestinian state and the permanent irrelevance of Jordanian influence and power west of the Jordan river. Graham E. Fuller of the RAND Corporation, and formerly of the Central Intelligence Agency, wrote in a much noted study that "the ultimate establishment of a Palestinian state on the West Bank and Gaza is now inevitable."[7] He also wrote: "The United States finally abandoned the long and fruitless task that led it through various versions of a 'Jordanian option' . . . Only when Jordanian King Hussein finally and formally disavowed such a non-starter in 1988 did the United States finally drop this quest."[8] But then, in seeming contradiction, Jordan, he said, "under almost any circumstances" is "likely to be closely involved in future West Bank events."[9] If there is no Jordanian option, what is meant by close involvement? If Jordan is closely involved, does that imply that possible limitations on the sovereignty of an "inevitable" independent Palestinian state will be at Jordan's behest as well as Israel's? If so, then how can an Israeli–Palestinian negotiation be imagined that does not involve Jordan?

It is, of course, true that the pure, original conception of the Jordanian option—the restoration of the political and territorial status quo ante of 5 June 1967—has been out of the question for a long time. Jordan's United Kingdom proposal of March 1972 recognized that. Since 1972 there have been further devaluations of Jordan's aspirations for direct influence in the West Bank (and by extension in Gaza). The 1974 Rabat Summit empowered the Palestine Liberation Organization as the sole, legitimate representative of the Palestinian people. Jordan had no choice but to accede to such a decision in public, but in private it struggled mightily against it, with some success. The 1976 elections in the occupied territories, which so favored the PLO, further reduced Jordan's leverage and popularity. The coming of the Likud government, after May 1977, had the effect of galvanizing local Palestinian nationalism as the Israeli occupation took on a different tone and ideological cast. The war in Lebanon in 1982 and the displacement of the PLO from Lebanon further stimulated the coalescence of Palestinian nationalism in the territories which, with the further passage of time, eroded Jordan's residual presence yet further. And with the explosion of the *intifada* in December 1987, most commentators were quick to pronounce the Jordanian role dead and buried, an impression sealed and cemented by Jordan's own disengagement some months later.

But it is not so simple. Things are not always what they seem in the Middle East, and elsewhere too. There is a perduring logic to a Jordanian role in the peace process, even if it is a lesser and more complicated role than that envisaged in the late 1960s. That is, possibly, what Fuller meant by Jordan's close involvement; it is, in any event what he should have meant. Of what does the logic of a Jordanian role consist? It consists of three elements: *procedural, protective,* and *practical.*

Procedural. As anyone who follows the peripeties of the peace process knows, arranging direct negotiations between the parties has proven to be extraordinarily difficult. Since the middle 1970s Israel, under every government it has had, has refused to negotiate with the PLO. This refusal is enshrined in particular in a side letter between the United States and Israel concerning the PLO's role in a settlement, attached to the second Sinai disengagement agreement of September 1975. But the Arab states as a group, and the Palestinian people, too, have either been unwilling or unable to bless a negotiating process that did not include the PLO. Hence there have been no direct Israeli–Palestinian negotiations. The efforts that have been made by the United States as mediator, and by many of the local protagonists, to get around this problem have been numerous, clever, inventive, occasionally devious— but all have one thing in common and that is failure.

On numerous occasions a Jordanian role as a way to finesse if not solve the problem of the venue of Palestinian participation has been raised, not least by Jordan itself. And it is logical that it be raised. Jordan has a good relationship with the United States. It is part of the Arab League and the Arab state system. It is on good terms with Egypt, which has had a formal document of peace with Israel since March 1979. It has, as everyone in the region knows, an extensive private relationship with Israel. It is, everyone also knows, the preferred negotiating partner for peace of the Israeli Labor Party which has led the Israeli government for much of the post-1967 period. By some legal definitions, too, including what United Nations Security Council Resolution 242 clearly implied about Jordan's role at the time, Jordan's rule of the West Bank from 1948 through 1967 gives it certain rights and a certain status. In other words, because of Jordan's history and various superpower, regional and Israeli connections, the easiest path to undoing most or all of the Israeli occupation of the West Bank leads through Amman.

This, at least, is what most observers have long believed and that is why US policy has held out an important role for Jordan. US policy since 1967 has opposed both an independent Palestinian state and permanent Israeli occupation or annexation. So, by the way, has the Israeli Labor party—a not insignificant datum. No matter how you look at it, that leaves Jordan in one capacity or another as a central player.

A negotiation that starts by dint of a joint Palestinian–Jordanian negotiation, in which the role of the PLO is implied but never stated, might not end with a prominent Jordanian role inscribed in the conflict's resolution. Then again, it certainly might. Even under the worst of circumstances for Jordan, solving the procedural issue through Jordan gets Amman's foot in the door, whereupon it can proceed to protect its interests. And its interests, mainly aimed at defending itself against the predations of radical Palestinian nationalism, are many.

Hashemite Jordan and the PLO compete for the fealty of Palestinians in the West Bank and even in the east bank. Hashemite Jordan must compete because, if it loses that battle, it stands to lose all. Jordan's population on the east bank is more than half Palestinian and its loyalty to the regime, while estimable under the circumstances, is fragile and subject to reversal. Jordan cannot afford to ignore what goes on in the West Bank, because it invariably affects what will go on in the east bank. No matter what it says, the monarchy has no more lost interest in the future of the West Bank than a tree that sheds its leaves in winter is necessarily dead.

The question of which side would emerge the stronger from a temporary Jordanian–Palestinian political condominium aimed at getting Israel out of the territories is therefore of crucial importance. This question has never gone away and probably never will. As of the summer of 1990, Jordan was quietly re-engaging in the West Bank; for example, it aided a putsch within the Democratic Front for the Liberation of Palestine by releasing DFLP members from Jordanian jails. Jordan still has many advantages in the struggle with the PLO over the West Bank: international legitimacy, access to the territories thanks to Israel, administrative experience and skill, the blessing of the United States and Israel (under some circumstances but not others), and a residual local patronage network. The PLO lacks all of this, but Jordan lacks one important thing that the PLO does have: ideological legitimacy to Palestinians. Thus Jordan and the PLO size each other up and warily circle in the ring like two boxers, each one hoping to give up as little of its advantage as possible, and to gain as many assets from its adversary as possible.

Hence Jordan's willingness to carry the PLO into a negotiation with Israel has always carried a price that the PLO, in the end, has always refused to pay: ultimate subservience to Hashemite desiderata in foreign and security policy, and a downward revision of PLO positions so as to ensure a stable settlement with Israel (no post-settlement Palestinian irredentism) and between the Hashemite monarchy and its own Palestinian citizens (no PLO claim, with a

West Bank entity, to the loyalty of east bank Palestinians).
Arafat's unwillingness or inability to make these concessions
is what destroyed the attempt to build a PLO–Jordanian
political compact in the 1984–1986 period, and limits its
construction today.

On the other hand Jordan cannot walk into a negotiation
with Israel by itself, even if it wanted to do so. It needs the
seal of PLO approval, particularly if territorial concessions to
Israel in a final settlement are necessary—and almost
certainly they are. If the regime lacks such approval, it may
not be able to protect itself from its Arab neighbors or from
its own Palestinian citizens; the volatility of this combination,
in case anyone needed reminding, was proved once again by
the Kuwait crisis of August 1990, wherein the King found
himself squeezed between a resentful population and an Iraqi
menace on one side and his natural Arab allies and the United
States on the other. At least until it is finally destroyed or
destroys itself, the PLO and its Arab supporters hold a
negative veto on what Jordan ideally wishes to do—make a
separate peace with Israel on its own terms.

So, put simply, no negotiation over the future of the West
Bank and Gaza can begin that does not feature a Jordanian
role, for Israel will not allow it. No Israeli political party will
bargain directly with the PLO, and a Likud-led government
will not bargain at all if giving up territory is implied in the
negotiation. But in the foreseeable future, at least, there
cannot be a Jordanian role unless, skillfully packed into it
somewhere, is a PLO role. For Jordan to make peace with
Israel, it must first make an adequately protective arrangement (if not peace) with Palestinian nationalism. The necessity
for a PLO role insures that, if there is a settlement resulting
from the negotiations, a Palestinian entity of some kind in the
West Bank and Gaza will come into existence—to call it a
state, as Fuller chooses to do, is in this instance not an
analytically precise term because different states (the United
States, Austria, Lesotho) have in fact different levels of
sovereign prerogative. The necessity of a Jordanian role
insures that any future Palestinian entity will not be fully
sovereign, and that objective interests shared by Israel and
Jordan in limiting the fuller expression of Palestinian nation-

alism will be operative in such a settlement. Obvious, then, is it not, how the legacy of discreet Israeli–Jordanian ties could come into play in such a circumstance?

Protective. Suppose for a moment that a joint Jordanian–Palestinian (read PLO) delegation were able to enter into a negotiation with a Labor Party-led Israel under the auspices of American mediation. Suppose further that Egypt supported the negotiation, and that the Soviet Union was too distracted and Syria too isolated or too weak or just disinclined effectively to derail it. Finally, suppose that the negotiation produced a phased settlement that included the eventual evacuation of the Israeli army from most of the territories occupied in 1967 in the West Bank and Gaza, and the creation of a Palestinian "state" with most of the accoutrements of sovereignty, yet a state still compatible with basic Hashemite security interests. What would be the fate of such a bargain, especially if it took some years to implement in full?

Almost certainly some Arab states would oppose such a settlement—Syria and/or Iraq being the most important. Also many Palestinians would oppose it, arguing that too many historical concessions were made to obtain it. This young Palestinian state would, as a result, find itself liable to becoming a new Lebanon, ripped to pieces by internal factions, each competitively supported by outside powers. It would, that is, unless it were protected from such a fate by an Arab state (self-)interested in its placidity. And that state is Jordan.

Put simply, not only is Jordan necessary to the process of negotiating peace, it is also crucial to having any agreed settlement implemented and preserved in a dangerous regional environment. Israel, too, would take an interest in protecting a negotiated outcome but Israel would not be in a position to shelter a Palestinian political entity in the same way that Jordan could. Israel could implicitly provide a military umbrella to protect such a semi-sovereign entity from invasion by Syria or possibly Iraq, but it could not commune intimately with such a state politically as could Jordan. Even Egypt, because it is farther away, less self-interested in the result, and taken up with its own domestic problems, could not do as well as Jordan. For Jordan, its domestic problems are anyway inseparable from things Palestinian.

Here again, should the peace process ever get this far, Israeli and Jordanian interests would coincide in protecting compromises so painfully reached. And again the legacy of predictability and even trust invested in functional ties in years past could play a role in consolidating a new mutuality of interests.

Practical. If a semi-sovereign Palestinian state comes into existence, the practical problems that exist today in everything from water shortages to agricultural quotas, to killing flies and mosquitoes, to facilitating pilgrimage to Mecca for Palestinian Muslims are not going to go away. It will still be a small, dry, ecologically fragile area, and the problems then as now will transcend political boundaries. It is noteworthy that not even the most radical Palestinian nationalists in the *intifada* are prepared unequivocally to demand closed borders with Israel if a Palestinian state should come into being in reality and not just on paper. By now the Israeli and proto-Palestinian economies are too well linked to be severed easily. Jordan's economy is in many ways linked to Israel's through the Palestinians and the West Bank. Peace or not peace, settlement or not settlement, even the politically unkempt process of muddling through will continue to require practical cooperation on many levels. Blood, it is said, is thicker than water. Money is sometimes thicker than blood, especially if dire poverty is a looming possibility. The private ties across the river, especially those evolved since 1967, are simply part of the fabric of local realities these days. Whether "high" politics change or not, there is a new reality on the ground. There may not be a formal or coextensive Israeli–Jordanian condominium over the West Bank and Gaza, but reality resembles that more than it resembles the symbolic lines of negative political absolutisms one finds in most speeches and official statements.

For all these reasons—procedural, protective, practical—it is much too soon to count Jordan out of the picture. If one takes the trouble to look beyond the rhetoric into the reality, one discovers soon enough that the pure options discussed in

Western parlors and some foreign ministries—like that of a fully independent Palestinian state—are bound to stay in those parlors and ministries pretty near forever. Indeed, if the conflict in its essence moves toward resolution in the years ahead, Jordan's role will grow in importance even if not in its public profile. And the significance of Jordan's relationship with Israel will grow with it.

Notes

1. Uri Bar-Joseph, *The Best of Enemies: Israel and Transjordan in the War of 1948* (London: Frank Cass, 1987).
2. Ariel Sharon makes this argument whenever he can. See his political autobiography, *Warrior* (New York: Simon and Schuster, 1989), especially pp. 244–247. For a critical analysis of the idea, see Daniel Pipes and Adam Garfinkle, "Is Jordan Palestine?" *Commentary*, October 1988.
3. Here see Yair Evron, *War and Intervention in Lebanon: The Israeli–Syrian Deterrence Dialogue* (Baltimore and London: Johns Hopkins University Press, 1987), especially chapters 2 and 6. It might also be noted that the possibility of direct and discreet military staff meetings, designed to prevent accidental encounters in Lebanon and elsewhere, should not be discounted.
4. Here see Daniel Pipes, "Two Bus Lines to Bethlehem," *The National Interest*, No. 6, Winter 1986/87.
5. This is the argument usually given for what is called Track Two diplomacy. See here John W. McDonald, Jr, and Diane B. Bendahmane, eds., *Conflict Resolution: Track Two Diplomacy* (Washington: Foreign Service Institute, US Department of State, May 1987).
6. Here see the comments of Harold Saunders, former Assistant Secretary of State for the Near East and South Asia, in *Mediation in Middle East Conflicts*: Maxwell Summer Lecture Series, 1986 (Syracuse: Syracuse University, 1986) pp. 44–5.
7. Graham E. Fuller, "The Palestinians: The Decisive Year?" *Current History*, February 1990, p. 53.
8. Ibid., p. 55.
9. Ibid., p. 46.

1   A Short History of Zionist–Hashemite Ties

Dean Acheson once said that things are not always as they seem, but sometimes they are. This unintentionally profound remark applies quite well to the history of Israeli–Jordanian ties. It is true, just as it seems, that Hashemite Jordan and Zionist Israel have been, and remain, enemies. A state of war exists between them, their mutual border is fortified on both sides, and their militaries plan strategies directed at the other. Their statesmen criticize, warn, and threaten one another like adversaries typically do, and common people on both sides of the frontier fear the common people on the other side. Israel and Jordan have gone to war twice (1948, 1967) and for all anyone knows, they may do so again.

But there is another side to the relationship that is more complex, nuanced—and very much less well known. Below the line of sight, so to speak, the formal public absolutism of no recognition, no negotiation and no peace sheds its skin. Jordanian and Israeli leaders have met, in the region and outside it, on numerous occasions. They have given each other gifts, developed personal relationships and even a degree of mutual trust. Less exalted Israeli and Jordanian officials have met, too, on even more numerous occasions and they still do so. When they meet to plan water allocation, for example, they sit at a picnic table, joke, trade cigarettes, and greet each other by first names. Here there are no declarations of war, no defiant absolutisms, no "high" politics, no fear. Limited though they are, these personal relationships come close to being normal. Overall these relationships give lie to the vulgar image that Arab–Israeli relations are implacably hostile from top to bottom, and they also give the lie to some extreme occidental presumptions that Middle Easterners are all and always fanatical, unreconcilable, and irrational. In fact many aspects of Israeli–Jordanian cooperation resemble

15

typical Western organizations or corporations that compete, but that compete within understood limits.

The sources of both of these sides to the Israeli–Jordanian relationship—the hostile and the regular—are historical, resting on precedent, accident, and the power of both ideas and personalities. It is to a brief survey of that history we now turn.

THE ACCIDENTAL ALLIANCE

Contact between Hashemite and Zionist began only in this century, around the time of the First World War. Although it may be hard for some unfamiliar with this history to accept, the Zionists in Palestine and around the world, and the Hashemites, then in the Hejaz, were mutually unaffiliated allies of Great Britain in that war. It is a familiar story. Based in part on a distended estimation of the power of world Jewry, the British government sought to enlist the help of the Zionist movement in its war against Germany. Some Englishmen of the time, perhaps encouraged by the sly desperation of Chaim Weizmann, the head of the Zionist Executive, believed that European Jewry could become a fifth column working against Wilhelmine Germany and aiding Britain. This hope, and the equally fervent Christian Zionist education of the British upper classes in those days, led to the Balfour Declaration of November 1917.

At the same time the British sought to cultivate a fifth column in their campaign against the Ottoman Empire. British officials, particularly in India, recognized at least dimly that the reforms and modernizations undertaken in Turkish imperial domains since the Revolution of 1908 had greatly antagonized the Arabs, for whom these administrative reforms meant mainly more police, more taxes, and more trouble. More important, Turks toyed with European nationalist ideas, thus breaking the age-old link between Islamic faith and political identity. It was the development of the rudiments of modern Turkish nationalism that led the Arabs to question more pointedly and purposefully their own status within the Ottoman Empire.

Just months before the war, the Emir Abdallah of Mecca was sent by his father, Sharif Hussein, to London to tell England that the Arabs would ally with Britain against the Turks if London pledged support for Arab independence under Hashemite rule. Abdallah, 34 years old at the time, told his story to Lord Kitchener, His Majesty's Consul General and Agent in Egypt. Kitchener listened but refused to promise military aid or anything else. Abdallah returned home disappointed.

But by 1915 war had come and Abdallah's trip was recalled. Considering both the distance of the Hejaz from the imperial center in Istanbul, and a general rambunctiousness among the Arabs, the British government now hoped for a revolt against the Turks led by the Hashemite clan of Mecca. In late 1915 it commenced secret negotiations with the Hashemite, the Sharif of Mecca, Hussein ibn Ali. In a series of letters that became known as the Hussein–McMahon correspondence, a deal was worked out: if the Hashemites would lead an Arab Revolt against the Turks, then after the war Britain would see to it that the Sharif would gain the leadership of a sovereign Arab state encompassing not only a wider swath of Arabia—wherein dwelt his fierce enemy, Abdel Aziz ibn Saud[1]—but much of geographical Syria as well. This promise fed Sharif Hussein's ambitions of reuniting the Arabs after the confederal fashion of the Umayyad dynasty into a Greater Syria, with himself, naturally, as King, and his family as hereditary rulers both secular and religious (*caliph*).

Sharif Hussein kept his eldest son, Ali, at home with him in Mecca. After his second eldest son, Abdallah, failed his first test in battle, Hussein assigned his youngest, Faisal, to lead the Great Revolt. To help Faisal, the British sent an agent, T. E. Lawrence. The conjugation was slow getting started, and by itself never penetrated to Syria or Mesopotamia as had been planned and promised, but it was generally successful. In July 1917 Faisal and his legions conquered Aqaba from the Turks, and many Turkish troops were waylaid fighting against the Arab Revolt even where it did not conquer and hold territory. All of this helped General Allenby conquer the area by 1918.

THE IMPERIAL IMPULSE AND THE BIRTH OF TRANSJORDAN

While all this was going on, the British and the French had conspired secretly to carve up the Levant between themselves. In a series of agreements, the most important of which was the Sykes–Picot accord of 1916, France was to get the Syrian area of the Levant, in which it had for many years a special position and interest, and British power was to expand more formally over Mesopotamia and over Palestine.

In other words, during the war, the British had made somewhat ambiguous promises—out of design or haste, depending on the case—to Zionists, Hashemites and Frenchmen concerning roughly the same territory. Or so it seemed when the war was over in 1919. Triangles such as these usually make for interesting diplomatic history, and this was no exception.

As soon as he was able, Faisal established himself in Damascus—having arrived there with the British Middle East Expeditionary Force in October 1918—and proclaimed himself King of Syria in March 1920. His father in Mecca was delighted with this but the French were not. They suspected a British ruse to deprive them of their territory in Syria, and they ousted Faisal from Damascus under force of arms in July 1920.

With this, Abdallah rushed to his brother's aid from Medina, traversing the area from Aqaba to Ma'an by November 11, 1920. From there he headed further north, to the area near Ajlun in modern-day Jordan, to whence his brother had retreated from the French attack. Abdallah attacked French forces effectively at first, seizing the town of Dar'a and holding it for a few days. Now French suspicions of Britain multiplied. Had not Abdallah met with British officials in Palestine? He had. Was not Abdallah Faisal's brother? He was. Had Faisal not come to Damascus in the first place on the back of a British general? He had. British Colonel F. G. Peake, worried about the dangers of an Anglo–French clash in Syria over the antics of the Hashemite brothers, urged the Foreign Office to come up with a solution.

The British eventually solved this myriad of problems in 1921 by creating the Hashemite Emirate of Transjordan east of the Jordan River in territory separated from the Palestine Mandate[2] and they put Faisal's brother Abdallah upon it as ruler. Faisal was set up instead in Baghdad, first as Emir and then as King of Iraq. Palestine west of the river was set aside for Jewish immigration and presumably a thriving Jewish homeland in the course of time, and the French were happy with their portion to the north. For a short time, anyway, there was a modicum of tranquillity in the region.

THE FAISAL–WEIZMANN ACCORD AND THE HASHEMITE MIND

But before all of this was made final in 1922, much of it in the Churchill White Paper, an interesting local peripety had developed. The Emir Faisal had written to Chaim Weizmann to seek his assistance, indeed, to propose an alliance. In late 1918 Faisal, having recently ensconced himself in Damascus, proposed to Weizmann a joint stand *vis-à-vis* France and even, by implication, against Britain, in order that he remain King in Syria. The idea was appropriately conspiratorial in essence. Arab numbers and Jewish money would create an independent power in the east sufficient to oust the hated Europeans, and bring back independence for both peoples. Faisal promised his support for the right of Jews to settle and freely cultivate Palestine so long as the rest of the Arab world was emancipated from colonial rule.

Negotiations ensued, and Weizmann carried out what he later called "a somewhat hazardous journey into the desert" to meet with Faisal, a trip aided by British military authorities. Weizmann and Faisal quickly reached an agreement in principle, a treaty consisting of 9 articles, signed in London on 3 January 1919.[3] It was short of the specifics that Faisal wanted, but it was nonetheless significant to both parties. For the Hashemites, in particular, it seemed to assure them of Jewish support for the Arab position in the upcoming Paris Peace Conference.

On 3 March 1919 Faisal, as a member of the Hejazi delegation to the Paris Peace Conference, expressed the same sentiments to Justice Felix Frankfurter, a member of the US delegation and a prominent American Zionist, that he had expressed to Weizmann. On 5 March, Frankfurter wrote back and thanked Faisal, looking forward to Arabs and Jews helping each other politically, and living side by side in the area that Faisal generically called "Syria."[4] The point of this, it seems clear, was to try to add American support for the Hashemite position, using the US–Zionist connection as a means.

But in the end the Zionists were wary of antagonizing the British or the French, the most powerful states in the world at that time, on behalf of extravagant plans laid by a Hejazi prince far away from home.[5] The Zionist–Hashemite treaty was never disavowed,[6] but when the Hashemites were disappointed at Versailles, and when the French kicked Faisal out of Syria shortly thereafter in 1920, the Zionists did nothing about it, nor made an effort to try. The Zionist movement had gotten the essence of what it was promised in the Balfour Declaration, but the promise to the Hashemites was overtaken by Sykes–Picot and its subsequent amended implementation. In essence, the Hashemites sought in the Zionist movement an ally to oppose the British and the French directly, and because of Zionism's American connection, a way to enlist the United States actively on the side of Arab independence. Alas, the Hashemites ended up with much less than half of the cake they expected, a portion which has been reduced still further over the years.

Still, this episode of Hashemite–Zionist cooperation from 1919 points up some enduring characteristics of Hashemite–Zionist relations. First, the Hashemites, having come from Arabia, had no special ties to Palestine. Of course they saw Palestine as part of the Arab world, and it was included, as far as they were concerned, in the promises made to Sharif Hussein by Henry McMahon.[7] And they almost certainly looked upon the idea of the Jewish presence in Palestine after the manner of the concept of *dhimmi*,[8] which is why when Sharif Hussein first heard of the Balfour Declaration he was not especially angry; he said, in effect: "That is all right; Jews have always been welcome in a Muslim land." It was only after the real meaning of the Declaration was explained to him—that Palestine was not to be a Muslim land but a Jewish one—that he became upset.

But coming from Mecca, Jerusalem meant at least a little less to the Hashemites than it did to local Arabs. This is an important facet of the Hashemite attitude toward Palestine in the early years of the Hashemite–Zionist relationship. There were also many Arab Christians in Palestine (about 10–12 per cent) and that, too, may have made it seem a different and somewhat alien area for many Hashemites who attended Abdallah—although not for Abdallah himself, who spent 16 formative years in cosmopolitan Istanbul.

And as for the Jews, the Hashemite image of them came not from contact and reality, but from the Quran and oral folklore. Thus, the Hashemite image of the Jew was fixed as negative in most ways, admiring in certain others, but manageable just the same. Traditional Arab stereotypes of Jews never contained an image of the Jew as someone feared—these stereotypes more popular today, were imported from Europe—but rather as an underling that one felt superior to. The Emir Abdallah, moreover, seems to have believed that the restoration of the Jews to Palestine was the will of Allah, and that together the Hashemites and the Zionists could restore the land and drive out the West. When his father visited Transjordan in 1922 Abdallah introduced Sharif Hussein to some Jewish farmers. Abdallah said to Moshe Shertok (later Sharett) in 1926 that Arabs and Jews should work on both sides of the river: "We, Jews and Arabs, can converse between ourselves to live a life of peace on the undivided soil. We are poor, you are rich. Please consent to come across the Jordan. I guarantee your safety. Together we shall work for the good of the land."[9]

In sum, for Sharif Hussein and his sons, with their dreams of Greater Syria, Palestine was not a very important place compared to Damascus and Arabia, and they simply could not conceive of the Jews as being able to gain the upper hand. Together this meant that, while the Hashemites were in the

Levant, their backs remained turned away from the Mediterranean world, and their faces were turned toward the Syrian
desert and the mountains of eastern Arabia.

Hashemite images of the world around them changed again
with the displacement of the dynasty from the Hejaz at the
hands of Abdel Aziz ibn Saud in 1924–6. As time passed the
longing for revenge against the Saudis led Faisal and
Abdallah to focus more on inter-Arab politics and rivalries
than on Zionism. This was even true to a considerable degree
in Palestine proper for Abdallah. The rise of radical Palestinian nationalism in the 1920s and 1930s challenged Abdallah's self-assumed position in Palestine. Transjordanian
ambitions to expand the family's purview into western
Palestine was constant throughout the period, but the main
enemy was seen to be Haj Amin al-Husseini and his
supporters, not the Jews.[10] Indeed Abdallah cooperated in
many ways with the Zionists. He had cordial personal
relations with many leading Zionists, whose code name or
nickname for him was "Meir," or "the illuminator." He
accepted gifts and bribes, and he hired a Jewish carpenter
named Mendel Cohen who doubled as a Zionist informer. He
even offered to sell or rent his own land to the Jewish
National Fund, even on the east bank, to augment his British
subsidy during the depression.[11] Only opposition from other
Arabs and from the British foiled that particular scheme.

TRANSJORDAN AND THE "OTHER" ARAB REVOLT

During the Arab Revolt (1936–1939) in Palestine Abdallah
discouraged his fellow east bankers from aiding the Palestinian cause—not entirely unlike what his grandson, King
Hussein, has done with respect to the upheavals of the late
1980s and early 1990s.[12] Consider the following tale told by a
traveller to Amman during the revolt which, though impossible to verify, definitely has a ring of truth about it.

The globe trotting journalist, Ladislas Farago, had an
audience with Abdallah in 1936. Although he was ardently
pro-Zionist, Farago opined before the Emir, just to see what
Abdallah would answer, that an Arab King in Jerusalem

might be the best way out of the Palestine impasse. To this Abdallah said that it was not up to him but the British. Then he asked Farago in a meaningfully lower voice if he had put his opinion before the High Commissioner for Palestine.

A bit later in the conversation, Abdallah openly condemned terrorism and, of the Arab Revolt itself, he expressed pessimism that it would either end soon or accomplish anything positive. He said to Farago:

> Very difficult, a peaceful solution is almost impossible. We are not concerned anymore with organized bands but with certain elements from the lower strata of the population. My opinion is that these have gone mad like a man bitten by a rabid dog. How can you negotiate intelligently with crazy people? I have always had the idea of erecting in Palestine and Transjordan a great Semitic State which Jews and Arabs—both Semites—should help to build in common. The Jews have great advantages, they have European culture and much money. It would be more sensible if they would share these things with us for a common aim, instead of simply excluding the Arabs from the development which they are now making.[13]

Perhaps even more interesting were Abdallah's attitudes toward the east bank's responsibilities in the Revolt. Farago reports that the Emir addressed a large number (200) of sheiks and notables under a tent one day, and said to them:

> We were not disappointed after the war. We enjoy freedom and independence. We have no Jews around our necks. We are freely allowed to carry our weapons. Not the English but I am your lord, and your sheiks are lords of your tribes. What more do you want? But if you now organise an open revolt and participate in the Palestinian conflict, then we shall run the risk of losing all these rights. You are strong and I have confidence in your strength, but you must believe me when I say that the English are still stronger. An open war against them is no Ghazzu [noble fight]. What will you do against aeroplanes?[14]

As Abdallah aged he took advantage of every opportunity to increase his position in Palestine. The Peel Plan of 1937, he

thought, offered a way in to an enlarged Hashemite role west
of the Jordan, and he increased his representation to the
British. He also made friends and acquired allies in Palestine
among those families who resented or feared the Husseini clan
and who, for the most part, were residents of the hill country
of what later became the West Bank. He maintained his
contacts with the Jewish Agency, too, and he occasionally
rode from Amman to visit the King David Hotel in new
Jerusalem, where he met with all sorts of people, Jewish,
British, and Arab.

In the 1940s, as the British Resident in Amman, Sir Alec
Kirkbride, wrote in his autobiography, Abdallah became
obsessed with Greater Syria and he hated the Arabs who
stood in its way, mainly the al-Husseinis in Palestine and the
al-Saud in Arabia. Kirkbride suggested that Abdallah tended
to analyze his political difficulties in tribal terms, and since
neither the British nor the Zionists were easily definable as
tribes, they did not fit quite the same way into his passions.
Kirkbride may have exaggerated somewhat, but perhaps not
much. Abdallah's master plan may well have been to create in
Palestine a nucleus for expansion for, like his brother Faisal in
an earlier decade, he believed that he needed the Jews and
their (vastly exaggerated) stores of money and talent to
finance and give counsel to his ambitions. Then he would,
with the help of the family dynasty's other redoubt in
Baghdad, take Damascus back for the Hashemites. And then
he would return in triumph to Mecca and Medina and thrust
the al-Saud back into Nejd, from whence they had come.[15]
This may have been increasingly a pipedream as the years
passed—certainly it was—but it did not, according to
Kirkbride, stop the Emir from contemplating it.

LIMITED WAR, LIMITED PEACE

In any case, what happened in 1947–48 is not open to doubt,
and this was the case before recent books by Avi Shlaim and
others repeated it with more archival detail and evidence.
Abdallah tried to make a deal with the Zionists, brokered

partly by Ernest Bevin, the British Foreign Minister, under which Transjordan would agree not to try to destroy Israel, and in return Abdallah would take those portions of Palestine set aside for an Arab state by the United Nations Partition Resolution. For Israel this meant one less enemy without, and a less daunting enemy within Western Palestine, and so Ben-Gurion agreed. A "phony" war of sorts was planned.

Abdallah had in fact first broached the idea of a partition of Palestine between the Zionists and himself as early as August 1946 in a conversation with Eliyahu Sasson. The Emir, however, presumed himself the dominant figure, and therefore able to tell the Zionists what areas they would retain and which not. Abdallah had a name for his plan: the Program for Division and Connection. It was then, and not later as is commonly believed, that Abdallah renamed the country Jordan from Transjordan—even though it took some time to show up on official documents and currency. His plan specified a Palestinian state within the Hashemite Kingdom, and even in detail was remarkably similar to the United Kingdom proposal of his grandson, Hussein, in March 1972. Abdallah asked the Jewish Agency for money to bribe Syrian and Palestinian officials, and some money, about £5000, was in fact provided.[16]

In November 1947 another meeting was held, this time at an electricity station near the Jordan River at Naharayim. Along with Sasson came Ezra Danin and Golda Meyerson (later Meir). Abdallah affirmed his view of partition, and the Israelis accepted the plan. Abdallah noted that the partition had to be one that would not shame him, implying again that he was the senior partner in the negotiation. As such, he agreed that the Zionists should draw up a written agreement that might be discussed in the future.

As it happened, boxed in between pressures applied by Britain and the other Arab countries, Abdallah could not, or in any event did not, keep his promise of not making war. One last meeting, on 11 May 1948 in Amman, tried but failed to head off war. Golda Meir came to Amman disguised as an Arab peasant woman, along with the Arabic-speaking Ezra Danin. Abdallah, still believing himself the demandeur before the Jews, warned the Zionists against proclaiming a state. He suggested that the Jews accept autonomy, like *dhimmi*, under his sovereignty. This was totally unacceptable to the Zionists, and as she left, Mrs Meir said to the King: "So, we shall meet after the war."[17]

The war that the Arab Legion fought, especially in Jerusalem, was hardly phony.[18] Many people died. However, the conflict over Jerusalem aside, the Jordanians clearly had very limited objectives, aimed more at preventing an independent Palestinian Arab state than at depriving Israel of territory allocated to it by the United Nations Partition Resolution. Ben-Gurion felt safe during the fighting to leave parts of Israel's narrow geographical waist adjacent to Jordan almost naked because he trusted that Abdallah would not move into the vacuum—and he was correct. By 1950 the final and official Hashemite annexation of what remained of Arab Palestine took place.

Moreover, after the 1948 War, Abdallah rushed to refine, define and consolidate a mutually acceptable arrangement with the Zionists, the better to get on with his inter-Arab ambitions. In 1949, Abdallah and the Zionists worked out an armistice, which was formally sealed on the island of Rhodes on 3 April 1949. The armistice was a by-product of discussions between the sides that, in a way, had never stopped. The armistice was negotiated between Moshe Dayan and General Abdallah al-Tal in Jerusalem from their respective headquarters. It was Dayan who suggested a telephone link between the two in mid-1948, and the Jordanians accepted. Indeed much of the armistice arrangement was worked out over the phone during the next year, although on at least one occasion, to seal the deal and discuss more ambitious matters, an Israeli delegation was driven across Jordanian lines by Colonel al-Tal himself to meet with the King at his winter palace at Shuneh. The participants were fed, entertained with dancing girls, and played chess with the King. It was left to Dayan and a Jordanian official named Jundi to hammer out the details for the armistice, which was accomplished at subsequent meetings in Jerusalem on 1 April 1949.

The telephone in Jerusalem, which had been so useful in working out the early stages of the ceasefire, which in turn prefigured much of the armistice lines, remained in working order for a short time, and proved useful dealing with violations that arose from time to time under United Nations auspices starting in late 1949 and continuing into early 1950. It was discontinued, but later revived in 1954 after the Qibya incident (described below).

During the discussions for the ceasefire and armistice, it was apparent that Abdallah was eager to move on to more consequential dealings. After the armistice was signed, further negotiations were held. The two sides resolved numerous border disputes and irregularities and went so far as to develop a treaty of peace—literally a five year non-aggression pact—which both sides initialled.[19] This effort required a number of meetings, in Europe and at the winter palace in Shuneh, throughout 1950.

Even ironing out border problems was not always easy. As the fighting stopped, lines of demarcation were often irregular and unkempt. Sometimes farmers were separated from their lands. But Abdallah was eager to resolve such matters because he had greater ambitions to pursue, and because Israel was in a superior position to continue the fighting should Abdallah make a fuss. Indeed Abdallah was extraordinarily pliant and generous.[20] He seemed impatient with details, and partly because of this he allowed the land of Palestinian peasants to be permanently divided away from their villages in some cases. This indicated how much of an outsider Abdallah was to the life of the people in Palestine. It also suggests that he was unfortunately casual about an area whose political control was critical to his future ambitions.

Moreover Israeli military power had by then been clearly demonstrated and this also contributed to strong Israeli pressure on Abdallah to yield, which he generally did. This, and Israel's frequent failure to reciprocate border adjustments granted by Transjordan, made it difficult for Abdallah to gather allies—even from among his closest advisors and friends—whom he needed to run his government, in favor of a broader accommodation with Israel. And here we return to the question of the peace treaty.

Negotiating a treaty of non-aggression between Israel and Jordan was something Abdallah was very keen to complete. His prime minister, Samir al-Rifai, and his defence minister,

Tawfik Abu-Huda, were the two men responsible for the details of the negotiation, but the King himself took a very active interest in the proceedings, and toward the end intervened personally to make concessions necessary to complete the deal, overriding the objections of his own negotiators and confidantes. Abdallah then ordered work on a formal peace treaty to proceed. Rifai and Abu-Huda, however, had a better appreciation of the new mood in the country than did the King. As they feared, a treaty was more than the political traffic in Jordan could bear in the aftermath of the creation of the refugee problem. The treaty ran into opposition from Abdallah's own ministers and government, particularly after news of the negotiations were leaked in an Egyptian newspaper by Colonel al-Tal.[21] The negotiations were suspended and never resumed, for Abdallah was assassinated in July 1951 by a hired thug of the Husseini clan.

Although the peace negotiations stalled, other forms of Israeli–Jordanian cooperation continued on. In 1950 and in 1951 the United Nations insisted on discussing the status of Jerusalem, which was supposed to have been internationalized in 1948. Gideon Raphael notes that Israel and Jordan, through Jordanian UN representative Fawzi Mulki, kept in close touch because each had an interest in maintaining the status quo and in opposing UN efforts to reopen the question.[22]

Not all border problems were resolved so simply, cooperatively, or only in Israel's favor. The case of the Latrun no-man's-land is an illustrative case. The road connecting Jerusalem and Tel-Aviv passed then and now near the monastery of Latrun. Latrun, since it commands an approach to Jerusalem, was one of the two places where the Arab Legion put up a serious fight in 1948, and Israel was never able to dislodge the Arab Legion from the area. After the fighting stopped cars again began to use the road although it was in range of Jordanian rifles, and Arab farmers began again to tend their fields, even though they were in range of Israeli rifles. But no one shot at anyone. The road and the fields intertwined so ornately that no line on a map could be drawn. So the whole area was called a no-man's-land, and this was later confirmed through the arrangements of the Mixed Armistice Commission. There was never any explicit formal agreement about the road or about whose land was being farmed, however, and placidity proceeded in the absense of an agreement that was probably not obtainable anyway.

In addition the border to the south of Jerusalem was ill-defined after the war. The village of Beit Safafa was, in effect, divided in half, even though arrangements were developed so that the village got along as close to normally as could be expected under the circumstances. This was an example, one might say, of pragmatic adjustment to a politically distorted situation.

Another pragmatic development, which persisted until 1967, was that Jordan agreed to allow Israelis to come to Mount Scopus, where Hebrew University was located, to keep the library and the physical plant intact, even though it was in Jordanian hands. Not all arrangements around Jerusalem were so pragmatic, however, that city's future being ever a bone of contention between the two sides. Jordan denied access to Israelis to Jewish holy places, and desecrated Jewish cemeteries, using grave markers at times as building stones.

THE PRAGMATIC ENEMIES: THE MIXED ARMISTICE COMMISSION

Besides direct negotiations over borders and a treaty of peace, the Zionist–Hashemite negotiations in 1947–50 also ran along another, institutionalized and parallel communications channel: the United Nations Mixed Armistice Commission. In the early years, the Israeli–Jordanian Mixed Armistice Commission meetings were longer, more involved, and somewhat more cordial than the other meetings.[23] They had more to talk about, and for reasons outlined above, Israeli–Jordanian ties had a longer and deeper background history.

Held near the Mandelbaum Gate, Armistice sessions typically involved ten delegates plus a few United Nations officials and observers. They lasted for three or four hours each, and continued at different frequencies over the years.

Food was not served at these meetings, but tea and coffee was. It was a working atmosphere, designed to deal with what the United Nations was assigned to do: keep the ceasefire.

This was necessary work, because there were raids into Israel, or sometimes no more than mere wanderings into old orange groves by former denizens of the area, and such matters became concerns for the UN. The Israeli government knew that border penetrations from the Jordanian side were generally not the result of Jordanian government policy. Jordan simply could not stop all such penetrations.[24] But Israel insisted that it try hard. The atmosphere at such meetings was not a social one, but it was not so tense that normal social dynamics did not evolve over time. Also, a telephone line linked the two delegations when they were not meeting.[25]

As time passed, however, the Mixed Armistice Commissions became less and less a forum for personal encounters between Israelis and Jordanians, particularly during 1954, a tense year on the border.[26] One reason was Israel's punitive policy of retaliation for cross-border incursions, developed and put into operation after Abdallah's death. The aim of the policy was to force Arab governments to expand their capacity for patrolling their own frontiers. The consequence, more often, was to demonstrate these governments' incapacity to do that, to embroil angry Palestinians against the Jordanian government in the Jordanian case, and to make needless enemies out of Arab civilians on the other side of Israel's border, most of whom were simple farmers who, in time, might well have forgotten about who lived across the hill given half a chance.

Israel's reprisal policy often got it into trouble with the Mixed Armistice Commission, and then, in turn, on a number of occasions Israel boycotted the Commission. The dilemma was simple in a way. Arab penetrations into Israel, which did hurt and even kill civilians, could not be shown to be the fault or intent of Arab governments, and so the UN, given the narrow definition of its task in the region, could not condemn the governments. But Israeli reprisals were clearly ordered and undertaken by the Israeli government, and they were therefore technically violations. The Mixed Armistice Commission had no coercive power on the ground, so it could not stop the infiltrations, and because of its narrowly defined mandate it could not condemn them. From the Israeli point of view, therefore, the Mixed Armistice Commission was bound to be a snare. The subsequent negative Israeli view of all things that emanate from the United Nations was surely colored by this early experience.

In any event, the Israeli reprisal policy embittered relations and contributed to the sterile absolutisms of the Arab–Israeli conflict. It is worth noting, for example, that the Arab countries never declared war on Israel, and it was not until the early 1950s that Arab UN delegates remarked offhandedly about a state of war existing. Palestinians were understandably uncompromising in their attitudes toward Israel, but it did not follow that all the other Arab governments were. Indeed the stridency of the conflict from the Arab side evolved over time, and Israel was not entirely blameless for the development. Instead of expressing frustration at the inability to make formal peace with the Arab countries, and instead of engaging in a reactive paranoia about cross-border raids, it would have probably been in Israel's longer term interest to have accepted tacit arrangements whenever the political landscape allowed, and to have let its military prowess undergird a "good neighbor" approach to border problems—as was later adopted on the Lebanese frontier—instead of a punitive approach. Indeed, the Israeli government argued over these very issues; but those who favored a less confrontational approach simply did not win out.

Another arrangement, far more positive, that arose out of the experience of the Mixed Armistice Commission concerned information cooperation. Israeli and Jordanian security agencies exchanged each others' newspapers at the Mandelbaum Gate in divided Jerusalem, because it was an easier, quicker and cheaper way to get them than to go to Nicosia or Athens or Rome. This arrangement persists today, only it occurs over the Allenby Bridge instead of at the Mandelbaum Gate. At about 6 o'clock every morning Israeli and Jordanian officers meet on the bridge and exchange papers. Only during the June 1967 War was this pattern interrupted, and it was renewed shortly thereafter.[27]

There were also unique incidents in this period, so many of them that they form an unmistakable pattern of basic pragmatism. For example, in 1950, when thousands of Jews were fleeing from Iraq for their lives, Reuven Shiloah of the Israeli Foreign Office came to Abdallah with an emergency request. The airplanes carrying the refugees, he told Abdallah in Jerusalem, could not make it to Israel without refuelling. Could they use the Jordanian landing strip in Mafrak? This would save time, allow more trips to be made faster, and perhaps save lives. Shiloah offered to return a number of trucks and other vehicles that had fallen into Israeli hands with the armistice line adjustments. Abdallah gave permission for the landing and refuelling, and he told Shiloah that he did not need the trucks.[28]

AFTER ABDALLAH

After Abdallah's assassination in 1951, his son Tallal assumed the throne. Tallal had been educated at Harrow, where all sorts of ideas had entered his young and imperfectly balanced mind. For whatever reasons—youth, temperament, notions he heard in Britain—he took a much less pliant and pragmatic attitude toward Zionists. This had led in earlier days to (unfounded) rumors that, during the Arab Revolt, Tallal had been so furious with his father for standing aside from the Palestinian cause that he took a shot at him.[29] This was untrue and, in any case, Tallal lasted only a very short time as King. He suffered from schizophrenia, and abdicated in favor of his son, Sharif Hussein's great-grandson, Hussein, who took the throne in 1953. A regency was established while Hussein did a quick and intensive stint at Sandhurst. At age 18, he returned to Amman to become King.

Hussein's attitude toward Israel became in time very similar to his grandfather's. But times had changed rather drastically. Whereas Abdallah thought he could either ignore or oppose Palestinian nationalism as he chose, Hussein knew he could not, at least not in the same way. The existence of Israel and the presence of so many refugees in Jordan, not to speak of

West Bank Palestinians who had come under Hashemite rule in 1949, made it necessary that Jordan develop a balancing act.

Jordan simply could not ignore Palestinian aspirations and expect to survive. Unlike all other Arab countries that hosted Palestinian refugees, the Hashemites had to bend from their demographic and economic weight lest they break from it. Thus, Hussein identified Jordan with Palestinian aspirations both for internal purposes and for purposes of managing the maelstrom of inter-Arab politics, where Palestine had become the symbolic lightning rod of the new pan-Arab nationalism.[30] In truth Hussein was all the while trying to coopt and control the Palestinians. He gave them citizenship and passports. He tried to get them out of the camps and into the economy, both to build the east bank and to diffuse their rage and give them a stake in a new status quo consistent with long-term Hashemite interests. He built a crack internal security force to make sure that the Palestinians did not drag Jordan into a war with Israel. And he developed a tradition of communicating with Israel first through London, then through Washington, and also directly, whenever problems arose. Hussein became, in short, a pragmatic man in an inflexible situation.

The pragmatic attitude paid off. The internal Jordanianization program was slowly but surely working, and Jordan was becoming a reality in the minds of its citizens. Troubles with Israel were modest, and what troubles there were, like the 1953 and 1954 reprisal raids on the villages of Qibya and Nahalin respectively, were truly not Jordan's fault.[31]

The Qibya episode started typically enough: a Jewish woman and two of her young children were murdered in their home by Palestinian terrorists. The Israeli reprisal killed 66 people, mainly women and children, and flattened the village. Arab Legion soldiers were not there to defend the village; at the time, they were on duty trying their best to prevent more Palestinian infiltrations into Israel. Israeli policy was designed to make it easier for Jordan to justify cracking down harder near the border, but instead, the raid raised local anger against the King for failing to protect them. This first Palestinian rising persuaded the King to assign his uncle,

Sharif Nasser, the task of building a loyal internal security force capable of dealing with future Palestinian distempers. This he did. At the same time the King avoided all Israeli attempts to draw the young monarch into the sort of relationship his grandfather had had with the Zionists. The King was both a sincere and sometimes hot-tempered Arab nationalist, and besides—it was too dangerous.

WATER

It was also during the period between the 1949 armistice and the June 1967 War that water became an important political issue. The year when all of this really started was 1953.

In that year, Israel began construction of its National Water Carrier. Partly as a result of problems that raised, the US Johnston Plan was born. The Johnston Plan was designed first and foremost to settle immediate problems raised by Israel's actions, but it soon took on more ambitious and important objectives, mainly to use the issue of water in order to forge a more stable political arrangement in the region.[32] It was designed to ease Jordan's refugee problem, defuse the Palestinian issue at one level, satisfy the riparian rights question, and bring Jordan and Israel closer together. It was a conscious attempt to put into practice the theory of functionalism.[33] It did not work as planned, but it worked in a way.

Like many things in this part of the world, the story of the Johnston Plan and that of the Israeli National Water Carrier merge together. There is no other way to tell the story.

In September 1953 Israel began to dig a canal in the Israel–Syrian demilitarized zone just south of a well-known bridge, the Bridge of Jacob's Daughters. The idea, Israel explained, was to divert a small amount of Jordan River water to an electricity generating plant on the shores of Lake Tiberias. The Syrians did not care what the digging was for; they started shooting and tensions rose. The United Nations man on the scene, General Vagn Bennike, ordered the Israelis to stop digging because in his view it prejudiced the stability of the ceasefire. At the same time, the US government did a little poking around and discovered that the canal was larger than that which would be needed for generating a little electricity on the shores of Lake Tiberias. The US government agreed with General Bannike, and did something he could not do: it threatened to invoke economic sanctions against Israel if it did not stop digging. Israel stopped.

The American view was that the Israeli project, whether large or small, should not proceed until the issue of riparian rights was settled. To this end the United States government tasked Eric Johnston with the job of solving the problem in 1954 and that is what he tried to do.

Riparian rights to the Jordan River involve three countries, but not equally. Those countries are Israel, Jordan and Syria. The Syrians were bitterly opposed to any cooperative effort that included Israel, and they remain so opposed today. They have unilaterally tried to block Israeli water projects with their own projects upstream on the Yarmouk, and Israel in turn threatened to respond with military force, and actually did so in a limited but effective way in 1966 and 1967. Jordan, on the other hand, which needs the water more than Syria, was not opposed to Mr Johnston's mission, and indeed wished its success.

In 1955 and 1956 Mr Johnston got remarkably close to getting all three countries to agree. He came so close that he resorted to a tactic later adopted on a grander scale by Henry Kissinger: he showed three different parties three different sets of documents, with three different sets of water statistics, in hopes that after agreement in principle, the parties would be so committed to the deal that the details could be ironed out in compromise. In the end Johnston failed for two reasons: Syria simply would not sign, and Israel had plans—discovered by Johnston's men and made public in 1955 by Ben-Gurion—to use Jordan River water to irrigate the Negev and Israel's coastal plain. Such a use would be a violation of one of the key principles of the Johnston Plan, that water from one catchment basin could not be used in another unless or until all needs within the basin were fulfilled. Jordan had no trouble with the plan, and would have signed if the other two parties were willing.

SUEZ AND AFTER

The next major breakwater in Israeli–Jordanian relations was not a literal one, but rather came with the Suez War of 1956. Early in that year the British, who were still very important in Amman, tried to interest the King in some stabilizing arrangements with Israel. The border was tense that year and the British worried that, as treaty partners with Jordan, they might get dragged into defending Hussein if violence escalated. That was the last thing London desired because what Hussein did not know was that Britain and Israel, along with France, were about to collude against Nasser and launch the Suez War.

From the Israeli point of view preparations for Suez evoked a mixed view of the Hashemites and their young King. The ambiguity had been present for a long time, and only grew worse as the King failed to behave as pragmatically as had his grandfather. The stronger Israel got, the less willing many Israelis were to tolerate Jordan's rule west of the river. Even Moshe Sharett, Israel's first foreign minister and generally considered more dovish than Ben-Gurion, was lukewarm about the prospects for a peace treaty with Jordan back in 1949. "We are not interested," he reportedly said, "in officially recognizing the annexation of any part of [Eretz Yisrael] or any part of Jerusalem by Jordan. At this stage, it is desirable to the extent possible to limit ourselves to resolving the urgent problems by widening the ceasefire agreement, or by concluding a series of special practical agreements."[34] In October 1956 Ben-Gurion reportedly entertained aloud, before his French and British colleagues in Sèvres, France, the proposition that Jordan should be effectively partitioned between Israel and Iraq.[35]

After Suez a humiliated Hussein ousted the British presence, broke his treaty with Britain, and allowed a pro-Nasserist tide almost to overthrow his regime. Suleiman an-Nablusi, the opposition leader, became Prime Minister of Jordan. The King acquiesced because he believed he had no choice but to bend toward the Nasserist "progressive" winds blowing in the region. But he almost bent too far. At the last moment in coup-ripe Amman, he fired Nablusi and restored royal authority. Just in time it was, too, because the next year brought civil war in Lebanon and a murderous coup in Iraq that overthrew the Hashemite monarchy there.

In 1958, during the civil war in Lebanon and the revolution in Iraq, Israel allowed British overflights of Israeli territory in order to get protective paratroopers to Jordan in a hurry. It also informed Hussein, through the British, of an Egyptian assassination plot against him. The King knew the source of the information.

Later in 1958, and again in 1959 and 1960, various attempts on the King's life were made from both the Egyptian and Syrian "regions" of the short-lived United Arab Republic. One such attempt killed the Jordanian Prime Minister, Haza al-Majali, although the bomb was meant for Hussein. Ben-Gurion had been forced to change his mind about Jordan: the status quo was better than any imaginable alternative. Now it was Hussein's turn to change his mind about Israel. He was furious with Syria and considered going to war. But first he ordered his military command to gain assurance from Israel of its non-intervention when it redeployed its troops along its border with Syria.[36] To do this Jordan sent a message through the Mixed Armistice Commission that a senior commander in the Jordanian army requested an urgent meeting with his Israeli counterpart. That turned out to be General Haim Herzog. Herzog got permission from Ben-Gurion to proceed, but instead of someone from Jordanian military intelligence, Herzog encountered upon passing through the Mandelbaum gate a lieutenant colonel who was the King's confidant. The Jordanian told Herzog that Jordan was about to invade Syria and wanted a pledge that Israel would not take advantage of Jordan. Herzog drove straight off to Sde Boker to inform Ben-Gurion, and Ben-Gurion agreed to the request.

After this incident, it became clear to Hussein that Israel was one of the only neighbors he had that had not tried to kill him. For their part, the Israelis accepted the status quo in Jordan, and were eager to improve relations if Jordan was willing. The Israeli leadership stepped up efforts to interest Hussein in a face-to-face meeting. Others tried to help arrange a meeting too, including the Shah of Iran in 1962. It did not work, but a meeting finally did take place, in London, in September 1963 between King Hussein and Yaakov Herzog. The meeting, the first of many to come, accomplished rather little of specific value. Hussein wanted Israeli help in cementing US military aid to Jordan, including tanks. The Israelis simply could not agree. Hussein also complained over Israel's water plans, particularly the plan to divert water from the Galilee, and therefore from the Jordan River, to irrigate the Negev. Israel tried to assure the King that no harm would be done to Jordanian interests but the King was not so sure. While they achieved little, a rapport was established and they agreed to meet again soon.

But before they could Nasserism swept again through the Arab world, and Jordan was carried along by it. Water was one of the issues, yet again. The first Arab Summits of 1964 tried to devise plans to stop planned Israeli water projects, or punish Israel if its projects could not be stopped. Since King Hussein had not got any satisfaction from the Israelis face-to-face, he was willing to try his luck at a pan-Arab solution. Moreover it made sense for Hussein to cooperate with the other Arabs because Egypt had just formed the Palestine Liberation Organization in 1964, which Jordan could not mistake for anything other than an existential threat to the monarchy itself. If Jordan was to maintain leverage over such an organization, normal inter-Arab relations were a necessity.

Arab plans to foil Israel's water projects were themselves foiled by the Israeli air force. Israel smashed bulldozers in Syria every time they began work on diverting the Yarmouk out of its banks. Meanwhile, since no formal cooperative agreement over water existed as of 1964, and none appeared possible, Israel proceeded unilaterally by building the National Water Carrier, which first came on line in 1964. Again in late 1966 and early 1967, as Syria moved once more to dam the Yarmouk River, Israel again responded militarily. This, in turn, contributed to the escalation of tensions that led to the June 1967 war.

Rhetorically Jordan supported Syria throughout the period but, in reality, Amman approved of the Johnston Plan and had cooperated quietly with Israel through US mediation after its formal failure. Indeed Jordan's plans to build the

East Ghor Canal, since renamed the King Abdallah Canal, is an excellent example of Israeli–Jordanian cooperation, for if Israel and Jordan had not agreed essentially on water issues, Jordan would never have had the confidence to build the East Ghor project. As evidence, it is worth noting that Jordan also had plans for a West Ghor canal in the West Bank, but Israel was not keen on that idea so plans were stillborn. Finally, in addition, US aid helped Jordan plan uses of its water—part of the US Agency for International Development project in Jordan—in the related Baker–Harza Plan.[37]

Many observers have assumed that the cooperation on the Ghor project was tacit, but this is not so, at least not entirely. A second Jordanian-Israeli private summit was held in Paris in 1965, this one between the King and Foreign Minister Golda Meir. The summit failed to achieve anything ambitious, and again Israel was reluctant to help Jordan acquire US tanks, but progress was made on water issues.

The basic terms of the Johnston Plan concerning how much each party would take from the Yarmouk and Jordan were reaffirmed, and Jordan was promised that Israel would not disrupt construction, completion and use of the Ghor Canal. Again Israel promised that its National Water Carrier would not harm Jordanian interests; this time, the King believed it. Thus, in retrospect, although no one signed the Johnston Plan, it has been more or less adhered to by all parties in the region (even Syria). Whenever disputes have arisen, as will be detailed in chapters 3 and 4, Jordan and Israel typically turn to the United States for mediation, using the principles embodied in the Johnston Plan as precedent. So the plan was hardly a failure.[38] Partly thanks to Johnston's effort, Israel and Jordan can be fairly confident even today that neither side will use the river unilaterally in ways that would harm the other's basic interests. As a result Israel and Jordan share an interest in preventing Syria from disrupting a workable relationship. Thus when Israeli military action stopped Syrian designs in 1966–67, Jordan was not unhappy, for the Syrian dam would have been used, potentially at least, to its disadvantage as well.

Indeed, in recent times, efforts to dam the Yarmouk and more efficiently use its waters have foundered over the

inability of the surrounding states to secure Syrian cooperation. In principle Israel has agreed to a dam on the Yarmouk
since the middle 1950s, provided that it is apportioned a fair
share of the riparian rights. Jordan and Israel do not agree
exactly what those rights amount to, but they both recognize
that both countries will suffer if some compromise is not
reached. As is detailed below in chapter 4, the effort to find
that compromise is still proceeding.

This is not to say that Jordan was or is entirely satisfied
with how much water Israel takes from the river just south of
Galilee, or with how Israel has, since 1967, interfered with the
well water system in the West Bank. But the point is that
Israel is sensitive to Jordan's needs, and that sensitivity is a
function, in part anyway, of the fact that these matters have
been discussed quite directly for a number of years, beginning
in the 1970–71 period. As the Israeli journalist Reuven
Pedatzur rather matter-of-factly put it: "A series of meetings
held with Jordanian government officials in 1976 tackled
common Israeli–Jordanian water problems, among other
things."[39]

As Jordan's and Israel's need for water has grown with
agricultural expansion, the issue has become an ever more
tricky. Sometimes cooperation is the rule. When a proposed
Syrian project in 1986 threatened to divert water away from
both Israel and Jordan, the Jordanians appear to have
secretly investigated the possibility of Israeli military action
to stop it. On the other hand, when a sandbar blocked inlets
to Jordan's East Ghor Canal during a period in 1985–86,
Israel apparently delayed permission to clear the sandbar in
order to pressure Jordan and to let more water flow into its
intake channels farther south.

STORIES: NEW YORK, STANFORD, JERUSALEM, PETRA

The period before the 1967 war is filled with both anecdotes
and more substantial examples of quiet Jordanian–Israeli
communication and cooperation. One story tells that at the
1964 New York World's Fair Israeli and Jordanian officials

met informally to complain about each other's exhibits—the Jordanian pavilion was organized around the refugee issue— and ended up drinking coffee for hours in the evenings as they argued.[40] This was hardly practical coordination of any sort, but it was face-to-face contact that was rare in those days.

In addition Israeli and Jordanian graduate students at American and European universities, many from prominent, well-connected families, were known to meet discreetly and get to know each other. Some of these relationships have endured for decades.

A related incident concerns a group of Jordanian and Israeli engineers who worked together at Stanford University in the 1960s on potential regional water projects. This incident resurfaced when Louise A. Wright wrote to the *New York Times* to vent her *angst* over the Arab–Israeli morass. This is the way she told it:

> For 40 years I have watched the situation in the Middle East with concern. My concern began in 1946, when a member of a delegation of experts attached to the English– American commission of inquiry was a house guest of ours in Paris . . . One non-political project that might achieve a great deal for the region and perhaps even pave the way for peace is not mentioned. The project came to an abrupt halt with the war of 1967. Perhaps now is the time to revitalize it. I have never known whether the project was an official secret. During the early years of the 1960s, when the attention of many Americans was on the war in Vietnam, there was on the Stanford University campus a group of engineers from Israel and Jordan working on a large Jordan River project. They envisioned a project that would make the whole region bloom. I knew about it because I was working with their families. Stanford University has a graduate students housing complex, in which students from foreign countries and their families make up 46 per cent. The children attended the Escondido Elementary School, where I was a volunteer working to help the parents and children become part of the social life of the school . . . When I talked to them in their apartments, they talked freely and with great excitement about what they planned

to do when they returned home. The Jordanians and Israelis planned to make the desert bloom. I looked at the maps with them.[41]

Within the region there are stories, too, of how Arab–Jewish business ventures set up in Jerusalem before 1948 survived the bitterness of the battle for Jerusalem, and persisted into the 1950s and even the 1960s.[42] The peripeties of the profit motive may mean very little politically, but they contribute to a lore of private dealings that at a minimum puts a human face on the conflict.

One such story tells about the last Jewish soldier to survive in the Jewish quarter of Jerusalem in the siege of 1948. According to Yehuda Litani this fellow, now 60 years old, left Israel for Europe 25 years ago and has become very rich. But he made his initial fortune working the black markets in pre-1967 Jerusalem and Amman with an Arab partner who very nearly blew his brains out in 1948. This surviving Jew became a prisoner of the Jordanians for a time, and his Arab counterpart connived to be his guard in return for a promise from the Jew to supply a large bride price so that he could marry the woman he loved. The money was supplied in due course, and from there the relationship bloomed. Before the Jewish soldier was repatriated, a Circassian sergeant was bribed to keep the two men in contact. Then, afterwards, they managed to remain in contact by bribing a series of United Nations officials bivouacked in divided Jerusalem. He told the story to Litani this way:

We became the kings of the black market in Jerusalem and Amman. Abed became an officer and almost every week he used to send me things to be sold on the black market in Israel. It was the period of austerity, the beginning of the 50s—I sold the stuff in Israel for at least 10 times its value. We shared the profits 50–50. As a result we both became very wealthy. Abed made his way, slowly but steadily, to the top. He became a brigadier-general in the Jordanian army . . . After leaving Israel 25 years ago, I used to see him every now and then. Our business relations continued for a long time, and even became more extensive. I believe he has given up business and now has a high position in the Jordanian government . . . Money has no borders, and trade has no limits.[43]

Finally it is known that King Hussein gave personal permission to an eccentric Israeli archaeologist to investigate ancient sites in the Jordanian desert.[44] Before that time many Israelis, out of curiosity and claustrophobia, had been attracted to the Nabatean ruins of Petra, a mere 12 miles from the border, from which some did not return. An Israeli song of old, long banned from the radio, called *Ha-selah Ha-adom* (The Red Rock), referred to this mysterious and alluring adventure.[45] It seems that all Hussein was waiting for was to be politely asked.

MORE BORDER TROUBLE

The final topic of the 1965 Israeli–Jordanian Paris Summit concerned trouble on the border. Jordan proved unable to stop all raids into Israel undertaken by Syria's Palestinian proxies from Yasir Arafat's young Fatah organization. But Jordan asked Israel to show restraint and to avoid reprisals, for these would only weaken Jordan and cause trouble, just as had the Israeli raid on Qibya eleven years earlier. A third summit meeting in mid-1966 between King Hussein and Yaakov Herzog discussed this and only this issue.

Israel showed much restraint as a result, at least until 11 November 1966, when three Israeli soldiers were killed by a mine near Arad. On 14 November Israeli commandos, led by one Ariel Sharon, destroyed the West Bank village of as-Samu and killed nearly two dozen Jordanian soldiers when they tried to defend the town. The response, as Hussein had predicted, was much the same as after the Qibya raid. The Palestinians revolted, the PLO called for a Palestinian Republic to be formed in Jordan, and Palestinians aimed their barbs against the King. To restore order martial law had to be proclaimed. The disturbance of Jordan's internal peace was one factor that contributed to Hussein's throwing in his lot with Nasser in those heady days of May 1967, just before the war. Had he not done so, with a restive population and foreign armor (Syrian and Iraqi) on his soil, the alternative was even worse.

AN AUSPICIOUS BEGINNING

These incidents and anecdotes illustrate well enough the flavor of the pre-1967 state of play between Israel and Jordan. More could be described, but the points are presumably taken that:

- The Hashemite attitude toward Zionism and Israel has been characterized by a pragmatism born mainly of weakness but also with a measure of ambition toward other Arab states and groups, including Palestinians. Jordan accommodates Israel in part because Israel is stronger, and in part because Jordan's agenda in the Arab world requires a predictable relationship with Israel.
- The momentum of day-to-day contact between Arab and Jew before 1948, however meagre and however hostile at times, made it impossible for many Arabs and many Jews to believe in exaggerated stereotypes of the other, unlike the case in Syria, Iraq, Saudi Arabia and even Egypt.
- Therefore, Israel has for the most part reciprocated with a realistic pragmatism of its own toward Jordan, certainly true for the period before 1967, even before 1977, and even still today, although that understanding has become a potential victim of Israeli political evolution.

Generally, Israeli statesmen have seen Jordan as having many common interests with Israel. Both are targets of radical Palestinian nationalism, both benefit from the moderation of the conflict and both suffer from its radicalization. Neither side wants or benefits from war. This is a relationship whose origins go back at least a half century, and whose dynamics are not easily changed. Newspaper headlines come and go; tactical feints do, too. Regional dynamics shift and the balance of risks shifts with them. But the basic architecture of mutual interest has endured fairly well.[46]

Nowadays, much of the texture of Jordanian–Israeli relations dates from the aftermath of the 1967 war, when Israel came to occupy the West Bank and that part of its Arab population that remained, which was most of it. Much changed, but the essential relationship described above did not; it simply acquired a new layer, much the way that civilization in the Middle East typically has, as a visit to any advanced archaeological dig will illustrate. It is to the period between 1967 and 1984 that we now turn in chapter 2.

Notes

1. Britain did not promise the domains of the al-Saud to Sharif Hussein, and indeed, London had a deal with Abdel Aziz as well, but Hussein had his own calculations of what he could make of British support and a wider power in geographical Syria. For some entertaining background on British–Saudi discussions of the period, see Robert Lacey, *The Kingdom* (New York: Harcourt Brace Jovanovich, 1982) pp. 124–133.
2. I am aware of the fact that technically the east bank remained part of the mandate for Palestine, at least in the eyes of the League of Nations. Only one visa was required for both banks; documents pertaining to both were filed in Geneva in the same "drawer," and only one British governor at a time was assigned to oversee the two. There was a British economic-administrative arrangement linking Palestine and Transjordan too. Still, the separation was politically real, and was meant to be seen that way. To cite an almost random example, Isaiah Bowman's popular text, *The New World: Problems in Political Geography*, Fourth Edition (Yonkers-on-Hudson, New York: World Book Company, 1928) has this to say on the matter: "Transjordan came into existence as a separate political unit in 1921 with Abdullah of the Hejaz as Amir, supported by an annual grant from Great Britain. [T]he country was shortly to be separated from Palestine and have independent relations under the British. These became official in 1923 when Abdallah was given a recognized status . . ." (p. 536).
3. See Appendix A for the text.

4. For the texts, see John Norton Moore (ed.), *The Arab–Israeli Conflict: Volume III, Documents* (Princeton: Princeton University Press, 1974), pp. 43–44.
5. This story has been told many times, but never better or in more detail than by Neil Caplan, *Futile Diplomacy: Early Arab–Zionist Negotiation Attempts, 1913–1931*, Vol. 1 (London: Frank Cass, 1983).
6. Weizmann later referred, on 18 October 1947, in testimony before the United Nations Special Committee on Palestine, to the "Treaty" he had signed with the Emir Faisal.
7. See Moore, *The Arab–Israeli Conflict*, pp. 6–23. McMahon himself later expressed the opinion that Palestine was *not* included in the British promise to Hussein. See his letter in *The Times*, 23 July 1937. But this was a very complex matter. See Ronald Sanders, *The High Walls of Jerusalem* (New York: Holt, Rinehart, and Winston, 1983) chapter 16, pp. 229–255. In his notes, on page 690, Sanders notes that other authors, consulting the same documents and archives as he did, nevertheless reach different conclusions. It seems this will never really be settled.
8. Here see Bat Ye'or, *The Dhimmi: Jews and Christians Under Islam* (Rutherford, New Jersey: Fairleigh Dickinson University Press, 1985), especially chapters 1 and 2.
9. Quoted in Yossi Melman and Dan Raviv, *Behind the Uprising* (Westport, Conn.: Greenwood Press, 1989) p. 33.
10. Abdallah's dislike for the Mufti was deep and in one instance, at least, it was directly relevant to events of great import. Abdallah sent a military unit to Safad in 1948 in preparation for the fracas that would attend the end of the Mandate, and to make sure that forces already there would not get tangled up with the Arab Legion as it came rolling through. But Abdallah heard a rumor that the Mufti was about to declare a provisional government in western Galilee, and he was not about to help him. So he ordered the commander of this force to leave for Damascus and he did so on 9 May 1948. The Palmach attack that took Safad happened on the very next day. See Benny Morris, *The Origins of the Palestinian Refugee Problem* (New York: Cambridge University Press, 1988) p. 103.
11. See Kenneth W. Stein, *The Land Question In Palestine* (Chapel Hill: University of North Carolina Press, 1986), pp. 192–99, for a discussion centered on the land itself. For a detailed account of a meeting held at the King David Hotel on 8 April

1933 to discuss this and other matters, see Aharon Cohen, *Israel and the Arab World* (New York: Funk and Wagnalls, 1970), pp. 252–255.

12. See Geraldine Brooks, "Jordan's King Deflects Unrest at Border," *Wall Street Journal*, 10 May 1988, p. 35. See also my "Getting It Right?: US Mideast Policy in the Bush Administration," *The Jerusalem Quarterly*, No. 52 (Fall 1989) especially p. 62 where the point is made that Jordan's disengagement deliberately undercut the *intifada* financially. For more detail, see David Rosenberg, "Jordan Cuts Farm Import Quota from West Bank," *The Jerusalem Post*, 19 January 1989, p. 8. For further comparisons between the Arab revolt of the late 1930s and the *intifada* see Kenneth W. Stein, "The Intifadah and the 1936–1939 Uprising: A Comparison of the Palestinian Arab Communities," The Carter Center of Emory University, *Occasional Paper Series*, Volume I, Number 1 (March 1990).

13. Ladislas Farago, *Palestine on the Eve* (London: Putnam, 1936) pp. 266–7.

14. Ibid., p. 269.

15. Sir Alec Kirkbride, *A Crackle of Thorns* (London: J. Murray, 1956), pp. 181–3, 200.

16. Melman and Raviv, *Behind the Uprising*, p. 35.

17. Quoted in ibid., p. 37.

18. This is the main problem with Shlaim's historical recapitulation. He does distinguish between what was planned and the messier reality that occurred, but not sufficiently. Moreover his accusation of collusion does not fit his own facts, and Shlaim himself backs away in his narrative from asserting a collusive Hashemite–Zionist alliance, calling it instead tacit alliance or adversary partnership. Even some of Shlaim's better reviewers missed the mismatch between the book's thesis and its own evidence, like Fouad Ajami's otherwise masterful essay, "The King Of Realism," *The New Republic*, 10 April 1989, pp. 23–33. For an insightful critical review, see Bruce Maddy-Weitzman in *Middle Eastern Studies*, 26; 2 (April 1990), pp. 261–264.

19. See Avraham Sela, "From Contacts to Negotiations: The Jewish Agency's and the Israeli State's Relationship with King Abdallah, 1946–1950," *Dayan Center Occasional Paper*, Tel-Aviv University, December 1985 (in Hebrew); H. Gelber, "The Negotiations Between the Jewish Agency and Transjordan, 1946–1948," *Studies in Zionism*, 6;1 (1985); and see also

Kirkbride's dispatches back to the Foreign Office, most notably British diplomatic archives, drawer EE 1015/77, 3 July 1950, and EE 1015/79, 29 July 1950. Both of these are cited in Mordechai Gazit, "B'diduto shel ha-melekh Abdallah b'hatirato l'hesder im yisrael, 1949–1951," *Gesher*, 2/113, Winter 5846 (1985). Finally, see Amin Abdullah Mahmoud, "King Abdallah and Palestine: An Historical Study of His Role in the Palestine Problem from the Creation of Transjordan to the Annexation of the West Bank, 1921–1950," unpublished Ph.D. dissertation, Georgetown University, 1972, cited in Aharon Klieman, *Statecraft in the Dark: Israel's Practice of Quiet Diplomacy* (Tel-Aviv: Jaffee Center, 1988), p. 153.

20. Interviews, Aryeh Shalev, Tel-Aviv, December 1986.

21. For archival details here, see Bruce Maddy-Weitzmann, *The Crystallization of the Arab State System: Inter-Arab Politics, 1945–1954* (Syracuse: Syracuse University Press, forthcoming 1991), chapter 3.

22. Gideon Raphael, *Destination Peace* (London: Weidenfeld & Nicolson, 1981) pp. 74–5.

23. Interview, Aryeh Shalev. Besides Shalev, some of the Israelis who remember this and later periods on the armistice commission include Shaul Ramati, Touvia Navot, Avraham Biran, and Aryeh Doron, who sat on the commission between 1954 and 1956. On the Jordanian side was Ahmad Abd al-Fattah Toukan and a General Mohammed Daoud, who became Prime Minister for a brief time in September 1970 when King Hussein set out to destroy the PLO state-within-a-state in Jordan. There was probably no connection between his prior experience with Israel and his sudden elevation; he was a useful Palestinian figurehead for the military government, however. I am grateful to Asher Susser for corroboration on this matter concerning Daoud.

24. Here see the letter of Sir Patrick Coghill, who was head of the criminal investigation department of the Jordan Police at the time, to *The Times* of London on 13 October 1956, quoted in E. L. M. Burns, *Between Arab and Israeli* (Beirut: Institute for Palestine Studies, 1969), pp. 49–50. Burns, a Canadian national, was Chief of Staff of the United Nations Truce Supervision Organization from August 1954 to November 1956.

25. Interviews, Aryeh Shalev.

26. See Burns, *Between Arab and Israeli*, chapter 3.

27. Interview, Yaacov Heichal, Philadelphia, May 1985.

28. Interview, Moshe Zak, Tel-Aviv, December 1986.
29. Farago, *Palestine on the Eve*, pp. 267–8.
30. For background see Shaul Mishal, *West Bank/East Bank* (New Haven: Yale University Press, 1978); and Clinton Bailey, *Jordan's Palestinian Challenge, 1948–83* (Boulder: Westview, 1984).
31. For some details about this period in Israeli–Jordanian ties, see Burns, *Between Arab and Israeli*, especially chapters 3, 4 and 9.
32. Georgiana Stevens, *Jordan River Partition* (Stanford: Hoover Institution, 1965).
33. See Miriam Lowi, *The Politics of Water: The Jordan River and the Riparian States* (Montreal: Center for Developing Area Studies, McGill University, 1984), especially pp. 11–29.
34. Sharett quoted by Yuram Nimrod in *al-Hamishmar*, 16 April 1984, as in turn quoted in Shibley Telhami, "Israeli Foreign Policy: A Static Stragegy in a Changing World," *Middle East Journal*, 44:3 (Summer 1990), pp. 400–01.
35. Melman and Raviv, *Behind the Uprising*, p. 53.
36. Noted in Klieman, *Statecraft in the Dark*, p. 98. Klieman cites two columns by Chaim Herzog in *Ma'ariv* from 1980 for this information.
37. Harza refers to a hydraulics engineering firm, based in Chicago, active in Middle Eastern water plans since 1953.
38. For background, see Moshe Inbar and Jacob O. Maos, "Water Resource Management in the Northern Jordan Valley," *Kidma*, 1983, pp. 20–25.
39. Reuven Pedatzur, "Water from the Rock of Contention," *Ha'aretz*, 25 April 1989, p. B1; also in FBIS-NE, 28 April 1989, p. 32.
40. Interviews.
41. "Jordan River Project Could Help Peace Bloom," *New York Times*, 26 April 1988.
42. See Yehuda Litani, "Money has no borders," *The Jerusalem Post*, 25 April 1987.
43. Ibid.
44. See Yaakov Salomon, *In My Own Way* (Haifa: The Gillie Salomon Foundation, 1982).
45. Charles E. Rittenband, "Israel and Jordan: Peaceful Coexistence," *Swiss Review of World Affairs*, August 1984, p. 20.
46. I elaborate these themes in "The Importance of Being Hussein," in Robert O. Freedman (ed.), *The Middle East From the Iran–Contra Affair to the Intifada* (Syracuse: Syracuse University Press, 1990).

2 The June War and the New Reality

"Nature abhors a vacuum."—Baruch de Spinoza

The June 1967 War had a paradoxical effect on Israeli–Jordanian relations. Naturally, the occupation upset the very basis of Israeli–Jordanian coexistence, overturning the arrangement established in 1947–48 and deepened for 18 years thereafter. This naturally worked against enhanced cordiality. On the other hand, each country's need for the other, and the range of contacts and problems that arose, grew apace. Thus, after 1967, what modest comity there was in the private relationship was reduced at least for a while, even as the level of exchange and intercourse at nearly every functional level was increased.

To understand fully the changes wrought by the June War in Israeli–Jordanian ties, the origins of the war must be dealt with, for this influenced subsequent mutual perceptions in important ways.

THE ACCIDENTAL WAR

The June War was something of an accident. After the February 1966 Ba'athi coup in Syria, the Arab Cold War rose to new levels of vitriol and cant.[1] Syria, with its Palestinian client, al-Fatah, and Egypt, with its Palestinian sheath, the Palestine Liberation Organization, vied for the leadership of the Arab world by competing to see whose Palestinians could cause more trouble for Israel. Terrorism increased, as did the level of Arab invective against Israel from Syria and Egypt. As noted above trouble over Syrian designs on the Yarmouk River added to the brew.[2] Jordan, having been abused by both countries in the past, sought as low a profile as domestic politics permitted, but this turned

51

out to be not low enough. Nasser's charms infected the West Bank in particular, and as 1967 began Jordan was forced to resort to draconian security measures to keep the West Bank from exploding.

The war hysteria that developed among the Arabs, together with the treacherous machinations of inter-Arab political maneuvering, also led by 1967 to the placement of both Iraqi and Syrian armor inside of Jordan, awaiting the great battle with Israel. When, in May 1967, these developments led to fever-pitched expectations of war, Jordan was forced to choose between joining the doomed Arab war coalition against Israel, or risking civil war abetted by foreign intervention. At the last minute, King Hussein chose the former, preferring to lose territory than to lose all.

Nasser almost certainly did not want war; he merely wanted to reverse what was left of the Israeli victory in 1956 by closing the Red Sea to Israeli maritime traffic coming to Elat, and by so doing to win the latest round of the Arab Cold War with Syria. He hoped that Israel would relent. But Egypt was not the only country capable of taking risks; Israel did not relent and the Arabs lost the war.

JORDAN'S PREDICAMENT

In the process the Egyptian commander (Abd al-Munim Riyad) who had been set in charge of Jordanian forces foolishly provoked Israel, and Jordan lost the West Bank.[3] Israel had communicated that if Jordan refrained from firing the first shot, Israel would refrain too. Jordanian officials sometimes claim that Israel fired the first shot in June 1967, but those who matter know better. Except for Jerusalem, where the Jordanians fought very hard, their performance was spotty.[4] Indeed, according to Jordanian sources, some crack troops were withdrawn to protect Nadwa Palace, which is interesting evidence of King Hussein's real interests, fears, and intentions in that war.[5]

Many Israelis in government understood this, and did not think so badly of the King,[6] even though the common knowledge began to develop elsewhere that Hussein was just as impetuous, foolish and bloodthirsty as the rest of the Arab leaders. In Amman things looked bad, but mixed.

At first the King deeply resented Israel's having taken such complete advantage of his peril, and he understood that one price of the unification of Israel's Labor parties into one bloc was to bring into the government factions led by Yigal Allon and Moshe Dayan that were not inclined to give the West Bank back to Jordan. But, on the other hand, he was buoyed by private messages sent almost immediately after the war that Israel had no intention of keeping the territories, only of trading them for peace which, given the right circumstances and the right company on the Arab side, would have suited Hussein just fine.[7] In addition, Hussein met with Yaakov Herzog again in early July 1967 and heard the same message.

In a way, losing the war and the West Bank might have been seen as a blessing in disguise in the palace; that is, as a way to move the conflict off-center in order to reestablish the territorial status quo ante, but this time in a firmer and more stable political fashion. But this did not happen. The other Arab combatants uttered the four "no's" at the August 1967 Khartoum Summit, and acted as though time were on their side. Jordan was too weak to do anything about it, and that is why it was so pleased at the passage of United Nation Security Council Resolution 242 in November 1967. Jordan acceded happily to UNSCR 242, which literally contradicted the Khartoum Summit, and was so seen by Israel and the United States. Looking forward to the possible return of the territories when diplomacy finally got on track, the Jordanians were willing and eager to engage in limited negotiations with Israel to build an interim regime that would protect their interests until that happened.

Israeli–Jordanian talks in the wake of the June War included a great many topics. Some were advanced by novel problems on the ground, some involved low-level contact, and some involved more Israeli–Jordanian secret summitry. The two most important of these summits took place on 3 May 1968 in London at the home of King Hussein's private physician, Dr Emanuel Herbert, and again in London around the end of September.

Foreign Minister Abba Eban led the Israeli delegation to both of these summits, Prime Minister Zaid al-Rifai joined the King on the Jordanian side. At the second meeting, Yigal Allon joined the group. Both meetings were about the terms of Israeli withdrawal from occupied territories, and at the latter meeting Allon presented his famous plan, complete with maps and pointers, to Hussein and Rifai. To Israel's proposal to make major changes in the border, the Jordanians gave a swift and contemptuous rejection. Some changes were possible, said the King, but only on the basis of reciprosity, even imbalanced reciprosity. The Israeli government was divided on what it wished to do, and Hussein could not offer enough concessions even to tempt the Israelis to agree among themselves. No progress was made.

At the same time Israel's preparations for these meetings foreshadowed the evolution of the Israeli–Jordanian relationship in the years ahead. Yaakov Herzog's memorandum to Prime Minister Meir stressed not only high political factors, but introduced practical, functional issues too. Here is a paraphrasing of Herzog's 10-point memo according to Melman and Raviv. The summits aim to:

- assess the possibility of coexisting with Jordan using the existing ceasefire agreement as the basis for an open and separate peace;
- establish whether Hussein is willing and able to conduct separate negotiations with Israel, and whether he would sign a peace treaty even without the support of the other Arab states;
- clarify whether the king would agree to the demilitarization of the West Bank;
- see whether Hussein would agree to minor border rectifications;
- test the king's attitude toward Jerusalem remaining united and under Israeli sovereignty;
- explore ways of housing the Palestinian refugees through cooperation among Israel, Jordan, and international bodies;
- begin setting up, even before a formal peace treaty, temporary systems for preventing terrorism, quick com-

munications in case of border tensions, and economic cooperation;
• agree that Israel, with Hussein's agreement, would not change the status quo of the West Bank's residents;
• help improve the international and regional standing of the king; and
• encourage the Palestinians to work for an agreement between Israel and Jordan.[8]

Clearly items six, seven and eight fall squarely under the domain of functional cooperation. As it turned out, by the end of the September 1968 summit, both Israel and especially Jordan despaired of finding a comprehensive solution to their problem. Jordan doubted that Israel was sincere about returning the West Bank, and Israel was uncertain that Hussein could go public with a peace treaty, no matter what Israel offered. At the end of the September summit, indeed, Hussein and Rifai tried to explain to the Israelis that Jordan could not make such dramatic public concessions to Israel so long as stronger Arab countries remained at war. Hussein suggested to Eban and Allon that they try to make a deal with Egypt first; thereafter, Jordan might have more elbow room for compromise. It took ten years, but that is more or less what Israel did.

Since a major political deal was out of reach, what was left were functional matters to manage. Some of these percolated up from below, others were the subject of future summits. Most, in time, ended up being combinations of the two.

ADMINISTRATION AND EDUCATION

Most basic of all in the aftermath of the war, Israel had no desire to administer the West Bank at the level of day-to-day affairs. Jordan did have such a desire, and it was therefore remarkable how little changed within the territories despite the disruption and change of effective political sovereignty from Jordan to Israel. Jordan continued to pay most of the salaries to the civil servants that worked in the West Bank, and Israel began to pay many of them, too, hoping to build up a dependent, if not friendly, cluster of local people. This basic relationship persisted until the summer of 1988. It did not necessarily entail direct coordination, merely a willingness to let parallel courses run their way. Education is a case in point.

Jordanian teachers, curriculum and textbooks remained standard fare in West Bank schools, although Israel was prepared to censor anti-Israel and anti-Jewish bias and did alter a few texts. As a result the Jordanians themselves made an effort to change some of their texts to remove some of the more vociferously anti-Israel passages. Moreover, in at least one Jordanian high school text on Arab society introduced after 1967, the work of two Israeli scholars (Gabriel Baer and Raphael Patai) is cited.[9] Needless to say that other Arab texts do not do this.

There were no universities in the West Bank in 1967. West Bankers who wished to go to universities in the east bank or elsewhere had to take matriculation examinations to qualify. Israel allowed these examinations to take place without fail until the *intifada*. By then, however, universities were established, with Israeli assistance, in the West Bank proper, and these were not under the same degree of Jordanian influence and control. It is not so surprising, therefore, that these institutions became centers of pro-PLO, anti-Hashemite feelings, and their faculties and administration became spearheads of the *intifada*.

Israel's shutting-down of schools during the *intifada* of course interrupted the examination and university matriculation process. During a slight easing in the violence in early 1990, Israel allowed schools to be reopened and university examinations to take place. But widespread cheating on the exams, quite open, occurred. Students and many faculty pointed out that because the schools were closed for so long, West Bank students did not have a fair chance to pass, thus the cheating was justified.[10] But many teachers and education ministry administrators in Jordan did not agree, and the spectacle of such cheating was disheartening, indeed. As of this writing, there has been no final resolution to this problem.

THE NEW IMPERATIVE: OPEN BRIDGES

Before the end of 1967 Israel and Jordan had tried to work out specific arrangements with respect to agriculture, banking and currency control, passport control, tourism, intelligence, land registry, hospital and court operations, electricity gridding in Jerusalem, and the operation of the bridges across the Jordan. Most of these efforts met with at least partial success; others, like banking for example, proved insoluble for the time being.

Part of this effort was directed from above from the capitals, part was generated from below from the crush of practical questions. Part was due to the fact that Jordan was economically destitute, part was a kind of patronage, the royal court asking the Israeli authorities to do or not do certain things in order to protect the property and investments of such and such notable or relative of so and so. It was a decidedly mixed bag, and some illustrations should bring this to life.

Agriculture became an immediate problem, for the June War took place right in the middle of the agricultural season. It was also a time when it does not rain in the Middle East, so the Jordan River was low. The bridges at the time were not open, pending a relaxation of hostilities so that they could be rebuilt. Israeli occupation authorities watched in late June 1967 as Arab trucks forded the Jordan in order to get their produce to market on the east bank.

After a few incidents in which Israeli soldiers stopped the trucks, the most notable at a place called Umm Suff, Moshe Dayan, the Israeli commander of the occupied area, decided to let the trucks proceed across the bridges. If produce had rotted for not having been delivered to market, West Bank farmers would have been destitute, and it seemed a good idea, in the interest of security and comity with the occupied people of the West Bank, not to start off the new relationship with a food and financial crisis. This was how the Open Bridges policy began, not, as is almost universally thought, as a far-sighted vision of a new relationship, but as an *ad hoc* response to a potential local crisis.[11]

In time, of course, the Open Bridges policy acquired a vision, that of Moshe Dayan and also others. It now epitomizes the evolution of Israeli policy toward the territories which, while never completely fixed, has changed dramatically over the past twenty years. The essence of the vision that developed was to use the bridges to transform the kind of pragmatism that existed at the upper levels of the Israeli–Jordanian relationship to the lower levels. As David Grossman has put it, the policy was designed "to break down psychological barriers, create the possibility for Jews and Arabs to become acquainted with each other, and create tight economic dependence and a de facto coexistence. The open-bridges policy," Grossman adds,

> was also meant to demonstrate that Israel allows freedom of access to holy sites in Jerusalem and freedom of worship to all religions. Another goal which guided Dayan, also very important, was to turn the open bridges into a safety valve for releasing the excess tension that he expected would build up among the West Bankers as a result of the occupation. The knowledge that it is possible 'to go out and get some air,' to enter, for a time, the Arab world, to study there, to do business there, to visit relatives, has a huge influence on the people of the West Bank and Gaza Strip.[12]

On the other hand, as Sholomo Gazit has noted, the policy worked so well, and the occupation became so easy to bear for so long, that the need to solve the problems lost any sense of urgency.[13] However, over time generational changes occurred and other kinds of pressures arose. This is what led to the *intifada* more than twenty years later.

Short-term agricultural market fixes aside, other problems with agriculture soon arose after the 1967 war. Israeli drip irrigation technology had made its way to the east bank in the years before 1967 on a small scale. For example, a Belgian and an American company seem to have served as convenient conduits for the materials from Israel to Jordan, re-exported so that the country of origin was expunged from all the records. The Belgian company was owned by Jews, and the

Jordanians who purchased the materials, with government approval of course, seemed not to mind this in the slightest. Nevertheless this technology was applied only by gentlemen farmers with money and connections, and did not change the fact that most Jordanian agriculture remained rather primitive. It seems, too, that these gentlemen farmers operated largely in the East Ghor project area, and this requires a bit more explanation.

THE GHOR CANAL

As noted in chapter 1, in the early 1950s as a part, or rather an offshoot of, the studies done under the Johnston Plan, the United States sought to enlarge the area of agricultural viability in Jordan through a foreign aid program in the Jordan Valley. It began in 1953. The idea was to create a good place to boost agriculture, thus to help settle the refugees and give them a better life. The project was also seen as a boost to the weak Jordanian economy and agricultural sector. But US aid ambitions, motivated by a strange amalgam of technological optimism and missionary zeal, ran afoul of cultural realities, as did so many other programs of that era. The Jordan Valley was not a very popular spot, and unlike many other river valleys, it was sparsely populated. This was partly because the Ghor had a reputation of being a malarial swamp.[14] Idrisi, the great Arab historian, noted long ago that the few original residents of the valley had very dark skin, implying that they were runaway black slaves who fled to the Ghor in the hopes that their former masters would not dare follow. But the US technocrats who designed the Ghor project had little knowledge of this cultural history, and they went ahead. This was yet another functional approach to a political problem, and as with the Johnston Plan itself, the Arabs rejected it. Political matters aside, few Palestinians, who knew the history of the Ghor quite well, were about to go down there. Most Palestinian refugees refused to settle there and no one could make them, it seems, or did not wish to spend the political capital to do so.[15]

So a few wealthy Jordanian businessmen arranged to make use of the opportunity, and they are the ones who indirectly imported Israeli technologies. One of them, Zaid al-Rifai, made a fortune in the Ghor, especially after the Jordan Valley Authority was established in 1977 and the increased water from the Canal enabled a substantial agricultural expansion. Of course he was the son of a Prime Minister, a former Prime Minister himself, and Prime Minister again until April 1989, when riots touched off by price increases forced the King to ask for his resignation. Prime Minister or not, Rifai still benefits hugely from what amount to the subsidies provided by the US Agency for International Development, and he hires Egyptian peasant labor to work the fields. These *fellahin* work for very little. The produce—vegetables usually—is sold in Amman and also exported to the Gulf, where it fetches a handsome price by local standards.

Some of the Jordanian élite resent al-Rifai for this, but, since he is a boyhood friend of King Hussein, there is not very much that they can do about it.[16] Still, in the April 1989 riots, it was not only bedouin from Maan that complained about Rifai's corruption and high living, but also professional associations which, in lieu of political parties, were then a significant channel of political pressure in Jordan. The riots were their chance to let Rifai know what they thought of him, and the Ghor business lay behind their resentment.

AGRICULTURAL GROWTH, QUOTAS AND COMMITTEE WORK

More about the Ghor project follows below, but to return to the point, most of Jordanian agriculture was fairly primitive as of 1967, at least compared to Western and Israeli agriculture. On the West Bank a number of farmers discreetly approached Israeli occupation officials and inquired about technological help. Others skipped that step and, with Israeli associates acting as middlemen, began to purchase new equipment and modernize their farms. Also, since some farmers left during and just after the war, some land was

for sale, enabling those who stayed to enlarge their holdings
and thus more easily apply newer technologies. Due to the
Open Bridges policy, by the summer of 1968, produce from
the West Bank began to flood the eastern markets, threaten-
ing to drive east bank agriculture out of business. This the
King was not ready to countenance. Through the residue of
Jordanian administration in the West Bank, which was very
substantial, meetings were arranged with the Israeli Ministry
of Agriculture to discuss the problem.

The Israelis were thus forced to decide whether to promote
the modernization of West Bank agriculture or to retard it. If
they helped West Bank farmers, they would be helping
themselves and making friends among the residents. They
would also be giving them more money with which to buy
Israeli products. But Israel refused to allow West Bank
produce to compete with kibbutz produce in Israel proper,
for West Bankers were prepared to settle for very low prices
and would thus undercut Israeli agriculture.

This meant that larger crops had to be directed across the
river, but there they would make similar problems for
Hussein; this, it was felt, should be avoided if possible. A
compromise solution of sorts was worked out. Israel would go
slow in its efforts to modernize West Bank agriculture, letting
the marketplace and the availability of credit take over. Such
credits were available really only from Jordan and, as one can
easily surmise, they were extremely difficult to get. Israel
would not object to, and would in fact facilitate, the limited
export of agricultural technology into the east bank, using
West Bank Arab companies as go-betweens. Israel and
Jordan together would establish quotas on how much
produce would be allowed across the river, and Israel would
administer these in direct coordination with Jordanian
agriculture ministry officials in the West Bank.

This system worked tolerably well but not as well as it
might have. In 1971–73, before the October War, Haim Givati
and other senior officials were brought into the secret
diplomacy by Prime Minister Meir, and ever since the system
has run much more smoothly—at least until the *intifada* came
along. The committee has met regularly, sometimes as
frequently as twice a month, year in and year out, usually

in a small villa near Jericho. Sometimes disputes arise as economic balances and political problems change. But at the very least there is always a vehicle to work out the trouble; there is a phone number to call.

How much produce is involved? Firm figures are hard to find, but Avraham Katz-Oz, Israeli Minister of Agriculture said in April 1989 that between 1984 and 1987 the total value of West Bank and Gazan agricultural exports into Jordan equalled about $1 billion. In 1988, however, due to the *intifada*, the figure was far below the yearly average. Katz-Oz provided a list: 15 000 tons of tomatoes, 5 000 tons of olive oil, and 60 000 tons of citrus and vegetables.[17] The disruptions of the uprising accounted for much of the decline, but measures associated with the Jordanian "disengagement" of 31 July 1988, and the manipulation of bridge traffic and export quotas by Jordanian authorities, had more still to do with it.

Over time one can see the results of Israeli–Jordanian agricultural cooperation, particularly on the Jordanian side. The Jordan Valley today is much greener than it has ever been, and that is partly because Israel has helped in both direct and indirect ways. It did this not through altruism alone, but because it wanted to ensure that Jordan would have something important to lose in a new war. Now it does. Aside from helping to facilitate the export of agricultural technologies, Israel works by example. Palestinians on the West Bank who use Israeli agricultural technology are the most natural conduit for the spread of these techniques to the east bank, but there is some evidence that these matters—such as the introduction of new crops and seed varieties—are discussed directly between Agriculture Ministry representatives.

And then there is the question of status. Some years ago, a story goes, some West German experts came to Jordan at the request of the government to investigate the possibilities of expanding the valley's electrical power supply. It seems that on the Israeli side the kibbutzim had expanded their fields and facilities down to the water's edge, and at night, the lights, music and social noises from the Israeli side were audible on the Jordanian one. The Germans concluded that the Jordanians had all they needed by way of electrical supply—but

The June War and the New Reality 63

what they wanted was more than they needed. One fellow said
to the Germans at dusk, when the Israeli side began to light
up: "Why shouldn't something like that happen here?"[18]

An additional area of technical cooperation concerning
agriculture has to do with the modern craft of rainmaking.
Israel's water authority, *Mekorot*, has a subsidiary called
Electrical and Mechanical Services (EMS) which has developed an effective means of seeding clouds with silver iodide.
As much as 15 per cent of Israel's average rainfall is
"artificial" these days. As news of EMS's capabilities
spread, *Mekorot* signed a contract for EMS's services with
Italy, and engaged in negotiations with Australia, South
Africa and a number of other states as well. When asked if
any Arab states had asked to avail themselves of EMS's
services, director Dan Brown declined to comment.[19] But it is
almost certain that Israel and Jordan have discussed this
technical program, and it is possible that through Jordan the
Saudis have been interested, too. A third Arab country
possibly involved in sharing this technology is Morocco.[20]

In addition to regulating commerce, the agriculture committee has also been responsible for coordinating emergency
responses to plagues of locusts and even mosquitoes along the
Jordan river and farther south along the Arava.[21] Indeed, in
1971, when mosquitoes were about as bad as anyone could
remember, I myself witnessed Israeli and Jordanian technicians working near each other spraying infested areas and
breeding pools not far from Beit Sha'an.

It is worth pointing out a peripheral effect of the basic
process in the agricultural sector, replicated in other sectors as
well. Jordan paid all West Bank civil servants until August
1988. Israel paid them, too. This meant that the basic public
service infrastructure of the West Bank was a condominium
of interests. It also meant that in order to solve problems,
West Bank officials have had the option of going to Jordan or
Israel for help, or both. Over time the demands of their jobs
have had the effect of building an intricate network of
interdependence between Israeli and Jordanian administration in the West Bank. This is why it is not easy to
disentangle, even when the links between the two banks are
theoretically severed. The Jordanians know this; clearly for

the PLO to have taken over these functions after the July 1988 disengagement would have required more than money. It would have required knowledge, experience, and personal networking that has developed over many years. It would also have required, in many if not most cases, at least tacit Israeli approval, which Israel was not about to give. For all these reasons high Jordanian officials could not have been very worried that their challenge to the PLO after mid-1988 would be successfully executed.[22]

COMMERCE, TOURISM, BANKING

Agriculture is not the only area in which cooperation has been explicit, direct and protracted since 1967. Another is commerce. With the Open Bridges policy goods and services flow across the Jordan River at some speed, as they have since 1967. This has led, among other things, to a number of joint ventures wherein Jewish Israeli businessmen team up with West Bank Arabs to export various items throughout the Arab world. Some of these ventures represent mutations of commerce, as with the irrigation pipes in Belgium, that pre-date the war. Most are new. Israeli-made *ouds*, a popular musical instrument in the Arab world, are the most popular model in Saudi Arabia, although the Saudis do not know that a company of Moroccan Jews located near Hadera makes them. They bear Jordanian export tags instead.[23] On the other hand, Israeli Arabs and some Oriental Jews developed a taste for an Iraqi confection called *manna* during certain festive times of the year, and they get it—from Iraq through Jordan and the West Bank.

Of course there are restrictions on trade, some legal and some actual. Officially all Israeli products are banned from Jordan, as well as all other Arab countries except Egypt. But such a ban is impossible to enforce, and often very profitable to skirt. In addition the special position of the West Bank allows the fudging to be much greater than it otherwise would be. Officially Jordan allows only those companies in existence before 1967 on the West Bank to export merchandise to

Jordan. Also, any raw materials used in manufactured goods must be from Jordan or transhipped through Jordan. But any resourceful or well-connected businessman can get around such strictures, and they do. Even security restrictions have been soft in many cases. For example, the Silvana Sweets Company, located in Ramallah, has imported its raw sugar from Jordan, but it was inspected not on arrival, but rather in its melted down state at the factory.[24]

In truth the main restrictions on trade stem from Amman's efforts to protect east bank businesses that are not as efficient as businesses engaged in manufacturing on the West Bank and in Israel. Jordanian policy has been restrictive, and in a way continued the anti-West Bank discrimination of the pre-1967 period. Jordan has favored those few industries established before 1967 whose owners still have economic ties to Jordan, and has discriminated against new efforts. Thus Jordan takes chocolate, liquid margarine and some plastics from older establishments, but only 12 of 201 plants in the West Bank—most of them new since 1967—exported anything to Jordan in 1983.[25] This means, in turn, that is has become more lucrative for some West Bank entrepreneurs to tranship disguised Israeli products, filling gaps in Jordan that neither West Bank nor Jordanian industry can fill.

Therefore the total yearly volume of this trade, licit and not, is probably larger than figures show or that one might suspect.[26] Exports from the West Bank alone to Jordan have run to as much as $100 million yearly. One estimate put the flow between 1968 and 1976 at $316 million, but that seems an understatement if all factors are counted in.[27] Before the *intifada*, at 1988 prices, exports from Israel to the Arab world, and less impressive, Arab imports into Israel—through Jordan, the bridges and the West Bank—were probably closer to a half billion dollars yearly.[28] And the trends, in both directions, were upward bound before the end of 1987.

Tourism and commerce are of course related, and here a number of developments are worth noting. Because of security considerations not just any automobile or bus can cross the bridges over the river; only those approved can do so. Tourist buses are included. The bus system that transports tourists across the river—a brisk business, particularly when it involves large numbers of Christian pilgrims around Christmas and Easter—is owned by a single family and is run as a special concession. The family involved is close to the royal court in Amman, and has family branches in the West Bank. Israel is happy to let the family make money; the family polices its own staff and sees to the security situation on its end. Everyone is satisfied with the arrangement.

And on the bridges themselves, Israeli and Jordanian border guards fraternize regularly. They cadge cigarettes from each other and drink copious amounts of coffee. They know each others' first names; Israel goes out of its way to station Arabic-speaking guards at the bridges. This does not mean that the crossing process is efficient, or even pleasant as Westerners understand that word. There are delays, searches, intimidations, and from the Arab point of view there is no question that the entire process is humiliating. But the difficulties of the crossing are probably not much worse— and sometimes even better—than similar border ordeals between Arab countries.

This much trade and tourism begs other questions— currency exchange, for example. In the West Bank both Israeli and Jordanian currency is legal tender and has been since the early weeks of occupation. Inside Israel only Israeli currency means much (and dollars, of course) and inside Jordan only Jordanian currency means much (and dollars, of course). Therefore a good deal of the transhipping involves US dollars, since they work everywhere. Dollars are more liquid and less prone to inflationary erosion than either shekels or dinars. This, in turn, leads to a higher demand for dollars, and a market in currency speculation in the West Bank. If an Arab merchant in Amman gets dollars for dinars, he can take those dollars and sell them to someone else for more dinars than he paid, because that person wants to use the dollars to finance an import into the West Bank either from Israel or from Jordan. This can happen when the relative exchange rates for dollars in relation to dinars and shekels is uneven.[29] Hence a complex triangular currency speculation market has arisen, and those with the electronic facilities or a fast car can make a lot of money without much effort. Especially at times of high inflation in Israel, the business of exploiting the uneven demand for dollars became very lucrative indeed. But it also has facilitated trade, so it is not properly thought of as an exclusively parasitic endeavor.

If one travels outside of Jerusalem headed down the road toward Jericho, one can see on the side of the hill Arab villas whose luxury is not outmatched by the best homes at Malibu. The right informant can tell whose homes they are and how they got so rich, for example, merchant in the Old City, old money, land, currency speculation, stone mason, and so forth. More than a few of the newer villas are owned by people whose primary or secondary trade involves currency speculation.

Then there is banking. The money that Jordan formerly used (and, in some cases, still uses) to pay civil servants in the West Bank rests in Jordanian banks on the east bank. To pay the money to West Bankers, the funds must get to the other side of the river one way or another. This has not been easy to do.

As early as August 1967 an attempt at a banking agreement was made between Israel and Jordan under the auspices of the International Monetary Fund but the problems were severe. Israeli authorities were reluctant to allow banks to reopen because that would have caused immediate bankruptcy for most, their funds having been withdrawn to the east during the war. Since the funds were not flowing back, Israel asked the banks to sever contact between the branches and the head office, hoping that sound reconstitution of the banks in the West Bank alone might be possible. The banks refused, suspecting ulterior motives. After protracted negotiation, no solution could be achieved.[30] Not until 1986, with the help of the United States, was this problem finally solved.

Once made solvent, Israel in fact would have been happy to allow the old standing arrangements to continue, so long as reports to the Israeli instead of Jordanian authorities about the flow of transactions were forthcoming. Israel sought the lightest possible hand in day-to-day administration; in the post office, for example, Israeli stamps and rates were put into use, but only six Israelis worked in the service—all other employees were Arabs, the great majority of whom had held the same jobs under the Jordanians.[31]

Additionally Israel resisted the use of any currency besides the Jordanian dinar in the territories until the use of Israeli currency became so widespread that its use was formally allowed. This, in turn, required decisions on the relationship between the value of the dinar and the Israeli pound, and the dinar was effectively devalued.

The result of all this was that financial conditions generally were quite poor in the territories. Instead of the old Jordanian banks, Israeli banks opened. They were more efficient in many ways than the old banks but their interest rates, pegged to the Israeli economy, were higher and credit was expensive. And for almost twenty years Jordanian-paid officials on the West Bank had considerable difficulty collecting their pay, for only on the east bank could Jordanian salaries be drawn from a bank. Occupation authorities, too, had only vague notions about the total amount of dinars flowing into the West Bank across the bridges.

Like all such data in the Middle East, the numbers were soft. But they came to mean more when the PLO began competing with Jordan for fealty, using mainly Saudi and Kuwaiti money as a means, especially after the 1976 municipal elections. Later, in 1986, when Jordan's campaign to raise the level of its patronage system was undertaken, the banking system was judged grossly inadequate for the new development program through which substantial US funds would now flow (roughly $30 million per year, as was estimated at the time).[32] As discussed below in chapter 3, this is what fuelled the effort to reopen the old banks.

THE PERSONAL DIMENSION OF OPEN BRIDGES

The Open Bridges, by allowing people to go back and forth fairly easily, has also led to other interesting interactions between Israelis and Jordanians.[33] For example, a gentleman who had worked in the Jordanian Ministry of Information, and who had been the Jordanian information-point man in Washington for six years told me that he had personally visited Israel. He told me of a poignant episode that took place years ago when he went to Jaffa, to the house in which he was born, to see what it looked like. There he found an Arab family, rather well-to-do, who had purchased the house, the owner said, from a Jewish owner (who had never lived in the house) more than a dozen years before. The Jewish owner, in turn, had reportedly purchased it in 1950 from an Arab who was living in the house but either had no deed, or did not have a legal deed. This Jordanian official and the current "owner" had tea, talked, and they took a walk up the road into modern Tel-Aviv. I asked this official, rather naively: "How did you get in to the country?" "I walked," he said. He travelled across the Allenby Bridge with his cousin's papers. No one checked; no one cared. "Many Jordanian officials have visited Israel as private citizens," he added. "It is a very interesting country but we have mixed feelings about it, you know."[34]

How many Jordanians have visited Israel, and what they do and whom they talk to when they are there, are statistics that have never been compiled and probably cannot be compiled.[35] But the numbers are probably not insignificant. Moreover, by the same general methods, visitors from many other parts of the Arab world have visited Israel. When Israeli authorities for various reasons wish to encourage this sort of intercourse, particularly in the summer, they reduce the price of the permit that has to be paid to enter the country.[36]

The bridge crossings have also led to wealthy Arabs using Israeli medical facilities. Israeli hospitals are among the best in the world. On a number of occasions prominent Arabs in the West Bank have gone to Hadassah and other hospitals for treatment. More remarkable, however, is that prominent Arabs in Jordan have made use of the hospitals too. Many seem to have a belief in the near infallibility of Jewish doctors. For this reason Jordan allows West Bank doctors to train in Israel and issues them Jordanian licenses for having done so; and it has not objected to Israeli medical teachers working in Ramallah.[37] For this reason, too, perhaps, *Kol Yisrael* has developed an ingenious radio program in its Arabic service that features Jewish doctors giving medical advice. Arab listeners can write to a European post office box with their questions, and then a select number of them are answered on the air by Israeli doctors, in Arabic translation. It is one of the most popular weekly radio shows in the Arab Levant.[38]

As a case in point, in 1986, Tahir al-Masri's father was at Shaare Tzedek Hospital. Al-Masri, at the time, was Foreign Minister of Jordan. Unfortunately, after a period of recuperation that lasted a few weeks, the elder Masri passed away. It is not so odd that important people go to Jewish hospitals from the West Bank, and the elder Masri was from Nablus. But what was unusual in this case was that his son came secretly to Jerusalem to visit him on at least two occasions, and that word leaked out about it.[39]

INTELLIGENCE AND TERRORISM

Another area of direct communication that developed after the 1967 war had to do with intelligence about terrorism and border security. Between 1968 and 1970 Palestinian fedayeen in Jordan created a state-within-a-state and for a time used it to open a Jordanian front in the War of Attrition. This provoked harsh Israeli retaliation, whose impact transcended the border itself. In October 1968 in London the Israeli and Jordanian Chiefs-of-Staff met directly, over Havana cigars, to discuss the problem. Amar Khammash and Haim Bar-Lev, along with Zaid al-Rifai and Yaakov Herzog, tried to reassure each other that all that could be done was being done.[40] The meeting was amicable, but Jordanian authority was eroding and the Israelis knew it.

After Israel's partial bombing of the East Ghor canal in June of 1969, the pace of private exchanges quickened, many of them funnelled through Dr Herbert in London. Israel was again trying to force Hussein to police his own border, as it had done in 1954 and 1966, but the Jordanians, through the United States, West Bank channels, and directly, claimed that they simply could not do so. Indeed this was the case, and it was not until after the Civil War of 1970–71 that the Jordanian military was able to reassert control over its frontier. In the meantime another high level secret summit occurred at sea, in the Gulf of Aqaba, in March 1970. In these talks Israel agreed to withdraw forces it had sent temporarily to two Jordanian villages near the Dead Sea—Al-Safi and Fifi. Otherwise, with the conversation dominated by Moshe Dayan and Zaid bin Shaker, the Jordanian Chief-of-Staff and a blood relative of the King, the meeting focused on military problems created by the War of Attrition and the PLO's rising power within Jordan. Still another meeting followed at Jezirat Faron in the Gulf of Elat. Mrs Meir herself attended this meeting. The King wanted assurances that if he moved against the PLO, or had to fight Syria, Israel would not take advantage. He got those assurances, and clearly, to the extent that he had any confidence during the Jordan Crisis in September, they were based in part on Mrs Meir's promises.

In the period following these two summits at sea, Israeli intelligence provided Jordanian intelligence with information about individuals and groups operating inside Jordan. This may have had something to do with the re-accession to the premiership of Abd al-Munim Rifai on 27 June 1970, who may have been the earlier liaison for the Israeli information.[41]

Much of this information came from inside Israel, from Israeli operatives in the West Bank. But some of it seems to have come from Israeli electronic eavesdropping and even a few Israeli agents in the east bank. Although impossible to document, it has been suggested by more than one person in a position to know that King Hussein even requested Israeli agents for use in Jordan proper for fear that his own *mukhabarat* was not dealing adequately with the problem.

THE JORDAN CRISIS AND ITS AFTERMATH

The Jordanian civil war of 1970–71 was occasion for a very dramatic sort of cooperation between Israel and Jordan, aided by the United States. However the cooperation was at the highest political (and military) level; little of it had to do directly with functional matters.[42] Still, the extensive, understood coordination between Israel and Jordan during the crisis led to new levels of cooperation on the intelligence and border security fronts, on functional matters, and it led to another effort, more or less abandoned in 1968, to try again for peace.

The United States helped, too, in nearly every aspect of the new relationship. The United States was instrumental, for example, in upgrading the level of direct communication between Israel and Jordan. In what was known as Operation Lift, telex and secure phone lines were established between Amman and Tel-Aviv, enabling almost instantaneous communication between the two sides.[43] Access to this Middle Eastern version of the Hot Line was restricted on both sides, particularly the Jordanian side, where as few as five individuals knew of its existence.

This Hot Line was used to set up the heavy schedule of Israeli–Jordanian summit diplomacy in the 1971–73 period. The main aim of the summitry was peace, and the main figures were King Hussein and Prime Minister Meir, who came to have a close, trusting personal relationship over this period.

The first secret summit of the post-civil war period took place in November 1970, this time in the Arava, a desert area south of the Dead Sea. Yigal Allon represented Israel. The second was held in 1971, this one held for the first time in the Foreign Ministry's guest house near Tel-Aviv. The King and Premier Rifai landed their helicopter near Masada, made rendezvous with the Israelis, and then flew to Tel-Aviv via Jerusalem at dusk at the King's special request. He wanted an aerial look.[44]

At this meeting Mrs Meir proposed the outlines of permanent settlement to the King, hoping that his victory over the PLO and distance from other Arab states might drive him toward a closer, more open relationship with Israel. Israel offered Jordan the administration of most of the West Bank and the right to oversee Muslim shrines in Jerusalem and Hebron. Israel also offered the King a deep-water port in Gaza, the right to station Jordanian police and administrators in Gaza, and promised to make Gazans citizens of Jordan. In addition Mrs Meir said that all Jordanian citizens would have the right to buy property and reside in Israel. And Mrs Meir proposed expanded economic cooperation, including the joint construction and ownership of a railroad from the Dead Sea area to the Elat/Aqaba terminus on the Red Sea.

In return, Israel asked Jordan to sign a peace treaty and establish diplomatic relations with Israel. Israel demanded border changes and the right of Israel to station troops in the West Bank within certain specified areas. Israel would retain sovereignty over an undivided Jerusalem. Israel also proposed that its settlements would be left intact, and that more could be built so long as no Arab property rights were violated.

The King said no. Border rectifications could only be minor and reciprocal. East Jerusalem had to be Jordanian in terms of formal sovereignty. Israel could not have extraterritorial security rights in the West Bank, although he was willing to consider other ways to assure security. Israel, Hussein argued, was giving too little and asking for too much. The talks failed, but they did not end. Israeli concessions were many and far-reaching, and Hussein knew it. He stuck to the belief, however, that these terms became the minimum that Israel would always be prepared to offer. His weakness was so acute that he both needed more, and believed that he might in fact get more from the Israelis. It was in preparation for the "next" Israeli proposal that, in March 1972, the King's United Kingdom proposal was prepared. This proposal was designed for protection within the country and among the Arabs, and it contained an outline of the sort of settlement Hussein hoped he might reach with Mrs Meir. Alas, the King misestimated how much more the Israelis could or would give. He expected more but he got instead the October War of 1973 and the Arab Summit of 1974, both events profound setbacks from the Jordanian point of view.

The period between the Jordanian civil war and the October War was in many ways a watershed in Jordanian–Israeli cooperation. The two sides came about as close to reaching agreement on peace as they have ever come, or perhaps as they are ever likely to come. These were relatively innocent times. The PLO had not yet been crowned by the Arab League to represent the Palestinians, and the Israeli Labor Party had not yet lost its political crown to Likud. The level of functional cooperation also increased vastly, notwithstanding the failure of the political process to fully succeed. It was during this period that cooperative functional contacts that had been allowed to develop from below, or that had arisen because of the 1967 war and its aftermath, took on the firmer hand of government officials on both sides, who looked not merely to control the negative, but to advance the positive aspects of the functional relationship.

AGRICULTURE AGAIN

While the issue of a full settlement was by far the central item on the agenda at the 1970 and 1971 summits, much of the conversation centered on water, agriculture and economic development. At both these meetings functional as well as high political matters were discussed, and this set the stage in a way for the concerted effort of the 1984–86 period to use functional ties for diplomatic purposes. At the latter meeting the King and Mrs Meir worked out a series of agreements that facilitated the resettlement and agricultural expansion of both sides of the Jordan valley. At both meetings, too, terrorism and how to respond to it was an issue of immediate and intense concern and the two matters were in a way connected. Both sides recognized that the more people and activity there were on the Jordanian side of the river, the harder it would be for terrorists to infiltrate into Israel. Where to plant crops and where to put fences, roads and security devices was a matter that had to be worked out together. It was, and both sides' security forces have very specific knowledge of the military topography of the other side. It is often said that good fences make good neighbors; it is hard to think of a better example of the truth of this statement than the Israeli–Jordanian example. As a result, the valley, which had been desolate and barren, became within a few years, as described above, verdant and prosperous.

After the 1970–71 period, as Palestinian terrorism became a growing problem, Israeli intelligence also provided information to Jordan about planned terrorist attacks on Jordanian facilities in Europe. Remember: Jordan was the foremost target of Palestinian terrorism after the Jordanian civil war; even its Prime Minister, Wasfi al-Tal, was assassinated by

Palestinian gunmen in Cairo. And after the war in Lebanon Israel turned over a great many dossiers on guerrillas captured in Lebanon who were Jordanian citizens. Indeed, it has been suggested that the intelligence haul made available to Jordan by Israel from Lebanon partly provided the confidence that the King needed to resume his tête-à-tête with Yasir Arafat.

In any case, so long as the King remained firmly in control the border was generally quiet—on both sides.[45] In one incident in early 1984, Syrian-trained infiltrators tried to move into Israel through Jordan. According to an unconfirmed, and probably unconfirmable, report, things went like this: the Jordanians spotted the guerrillas first, but too late to apprehend or stop them. They radioed the Israeli patrol on the other side, gave coordinates, and the terrorists were stopped.[46] This sounds very adventuresome, and it is not impossible. But it does seem improbable that it occurred; few Israelis who are familiar with border patrolling believe this story.

The United States has been involved as well. One thing it did after 1970 was to ensure that Israeli and Jordanian border patrols carried walkie-talkies whose range frequencies were compatible.[47] Of course this does not mean much unless one side wishes to talk to the other. There is no hard evidence that this equipment has ever been so used, but it may have been, and it still might be in the future.

AIR TRAFFIC CONTROL

Similarly, although less significantly, there has been direct coordination over air corridors, commercial and otherwise, especially since 1970. The eastern Mediterranean is one of the most heavily trafficked air corridors in the world. There is much military and commercial traffic, and it is difficult to keep up with it all. Planes get off course, and emergencies arise. Quite a number of stories have been generated from this mixture, all united by the fact that Israeli and Jordanian air traffic controllers talk with one another and over the years have developed a tolerable rapport.

Although less systematic, air traffic incidents have been the occasion for other Israeli–Arab contacts. In June 1987 an El Al captain helped a thoroughly lost Saudi airliner that was straying over Israeli airspace. Having lost communication with its flight tower in Nicosia, the Saudi plane was instructed back to its flight path by El Al captain Eitan Arev. At first the Saudis may not have known the source of their help. But afterwards they did; their parting words were: "Thank you, El Al."[48]

The most interesting aspect of this, however, concerns not commercial but military matters. After the Israeli withdrawal from Sinai in April 1982, Israel had to find a new way to test fly its fighter aircraft. Using bases in the Negev, a Phantom jet or an F-16 gets moving so fast that to terminate the training flight within Israeli airspace becomes difficult or impossible. Headed south at high speed, the only way to avoid entering Egyptian or Saudi airspace is to turn over southern Jordan. Headed north, there are two choices: to turn into the commercial corridor, or to turn over Jordan. At least before June 1981, when Israel violated Jordan's air space for the purpose of bombing the Osirak reactor in Iraq, the Jordanians seemed not to mind very much. It helped Jordanian radar men get some practice.

Communications in the skies also work in Jordan's favor. In unconfirmed reports it is said that when Jordan and Syria were at the brink of war in December 1980 and May of 1981, Israeli intelligence from its airborne Hawkeyes told Jordanian officials where Syrian Migs were when Jordanian commercial flights from Europe passed over Lebanon to land in Amman. Also, Jordanian training flights abut on Israeli airspace near Galilee, too. In one incident in 1986 two Jordanian planes flew across the border and the incursion became known. Defense Minister Yitzhak Rabin took some heat for the slow reaction of the Israeli Air Force. But in point of fact Rabin knew more than he dared say. He told a reporter, in what was probably a slip, that because of how the plane was armed, Israel knew that it had no ill intent—suggesting experience and prior arrangement and understanding on such matters.[49]

AQABA/ELAT

Yet another example of direct communication concerns navigation and cooperation at Aqaba and Elat. As noted above, air traffic control is one thing that Israel and Jordan have cooperated on for many years. The airports both countries built near the Red Sea are quite close to one another, leaving little choice but to talk directly. This became unusually public knowledge during the Kuwait crisis of 1990. *Haaretz* reported that Israel had been monitoring more closely than usual the air traffic in the region, and relayed relevant selected information about commercial air traffic directly to the Jordanian tower in response to Jordanian requests. According to the report, "the level of understanding and communication between the Jordanian and Israeli air control towers was excellent."[50]

Yet, as in other areas of Israeli–Jordanian functional cooperation, not all is roses. There are frictions. But these frictions are worked out like countries that know and acknowledge each others' interests. That is why a veteran Israeli diplomat can say, quite rightly:

> The de facto peace between Jordan and Israel these last 16 years does not rest on so much as a single signed document. But more traffic, tourism, and trade have passed over the 'open bridges' with Jordan than over the border with Egypt, with which all these matters were laboriously negotiated and formally agreed on.[51]

In a sense, Aqaba/Elat provides the longest-standing and most interesting group of examples. A little history is useful here.

Before 1956 there were few problems at the northern tip of the Strait of Tiran because there was very little traffic, and very little going on down there. But as both Jordan and Israel developed their southern ports, traffic occasionally became congested. Israeli and Jordanian workers developed a way to insure that ships avoid hitting each other en route to their respective ports. This cooperation became quite extensive at times. As both countries built airstrips on their sides of the border, the air traffic dimension was added on. And in 1967, despite the fact that the two countries were briefly in a shooting war, not a single shot was fired at or from Aqaba, and it was no accident.

After 1968, when terrorism became a greater problem, the Jordanians took special care to make sure that swimmers could not make it across to Elat carrying explosives meant for Israeli ships. The coordination there has been nearly perfect; with a single exception, *fedayeen* have never been successful in their attempts to cause trouble near Elat.

Noise has been a problem, also, for the King, who has a villa in Aqaba where Israeli visitors can—and have—come and gone. A story has it that on one occasion the Israeli Navy was using the Red Sea opposite Hussein's vacation house as a target-practice area. Supposedly Hussein got on his 20-foot skiff and motored over to the Israelis, where he asked them if they would cut it out, please. The Israeli commander, with a shocked look on his face, agreed.[52]

More recently Israel and Jordan appeared to agree to crossing points at Aqaba and Elat to allow tourists from third countries to pass more easily between the two. A Jordanian tourist ministry official denied the report, issued by an Israeli tourist ministry official, but given the nature of contacts and the history of cooperation at Aqaba, the story was not far-fetched.[53] The issue, however, has not been settled. In July 1990, according to the Egyptian newspaper *Al-Wafd*, about 5 000 Egyptian pilgrims returning home from Saudi Arabia were stranded at Aqaba when a ferry service between Egypt and Jordan failed to work properly. They rioted, and Jordanian police attacked them with tear gas. Israel offered to let the stranded Egyptians pass into Israel and then, by bus or taxi, get home by way of the Sinai. Israel even offered to send 12 buses into Jordan to pick up the Egyptians. The Jordanians refused.[54]

Usually, however, the degree of normalcy and quiet at Elat is so striking that it was featured in a glossy 1988 pamphlet issued by the Israeli Ministry of Foreign Affairs. On the last page of the 15-page effort is a striking sepia photograph of the border between Elat and Aqaba taken from the Israeli side. The photo illustrates how slim the undeveloped strip that marks the border is, and shows the extensive development on both sides. The caption above the photograph reads: "Eilat and Akaba—neighbours today, friends tomorrow." Also inset on the page is a remark by Shimon Peres from 1987: "The goal is peace. Direct negotiations are the way to get there."[55]

But there are problems at Aqaba too, increasingly so as time passes. The reason is that the two countries have taken different approaches as to how to use their respective ports. The Israelis have increasingly devoted Elat to recreation and tourism. The Jordanians have increasingly sought to develop the area for industry. This industry is connected integrally to Jordan's potash and phosphate works, which is integrally connected to the Dead Sea and the lower Arava. While it is hard to see through the salt haze from the Israeli side, on the Jordanian side one can witness the beginnings of an industrial sprawl starting at the Dead Sea and heading toward Aqaba. Between 1981 and 1987 this sprawl was joined by a number of barbed wire enclosures behind which "hundreds of East German-made military trucks and army jeeps bake in the hot sun; a steady stream of heavy trucks with bright yellow Iraqi license plates moves clumsily northward over the desert road, bringing supplies, cannon fodder for the Gulf War."[56]

All this industrial and once-removed military activity on the Jordanian side created troubles. Garbage and industrial pollution have begun to change the environment, fouling beaches and endangering some of the most beautiful coral reefs outside the South Pacific. A Jordanian water treatment plant, activated in 1983, was the occasion for serious dispute. Built with US help, the plant has a full operational capacity of treating more than 9000 cubic meters of water each day. Given the climate and the prevailing winds, Israelis feared, rightly it turned out, that not only would Elat look worse, but that it would smell worse, too. Since almost $1.5 billion had been invested in Elat's tourist infrastructure in recent years, this was really bad news for the locals.

Since the Likud had limited direct functional contact with the Jordanians, the only resort was to go to the United States to complain. And that is what the Israeli government did, noting that the plant—and the problems it caused—was financed by the Agency for International Development. In

July 1984 the director general of Israel's interior ministry, Charles Kuberski, sent a sharply worded protest to Washington. In return Washington sent out an Environmental Protection Agency (EPA) team to examine the evidence. They found that Israel was right, and scrubbers were added to the plant, and Jordanians were trained to use them.[57] The solution, however, was only partial, and in the future things are liable to get even worse. Indeed, such troubles at Aqaba became an item on a broadening array of Israeli–Jordanian discussions in 1985–86.

Mention of Aqaba and the Dead Sea immediately brings to mind two other celebrated issues: the proposed Mediterranean–Dead Sea Canal (Med–Dead for short) and the proposed Iraqi oil pipeline. Neither one of these projects has proceeded very far, the former for lack of money,[58] the latter mainly for lack of a reason since the end of the Gulf War. But the pattern of Israeli–Jordanian conduct in both areas has been interesting.

THE MED–DEAD CANAL AND THE PIPELINE EPISODE

In the Med–Dead Canal case Israeli aims were primarily economic and ecological, not military/strategic or political. And Jordan was considered. The idea goes back to the 1950s, and rose again briefly in the 1960s. But only in the 1970s was the notion given serious practical consideration. Studies were done in 1978–79 about the environmental effects on the Dead Sea levels, and what a canal would do to the potash industry in both countries. Ironically, Israeli studies were at first more alarmist than private studies undertaken by Jordan. Israeli studies feared a reduction of the salinity of the Dead Sea to the point that it would reduce industrial salts by 15 per cent. But Jordanian studies, later backed by US government ones, showed that adding more water in the Dead Sea would only require technicians to lower the brine-intake valves in the respective plants a few feet, and that the effects on salinity were therefore less than estimated by the Israelis. This is because the inflowing water would be lighter, and form a separate layer in the Sea.[59]

In public the Jordanians yelled and screamed about the proposal, claiming it was a violation of international law, that Israeli aims were security related *vis-à-vis* Egypt, and that there was deliberate Israeli sabotage of Jordanian industry.[60] (That is the way things are.) Actually the Jordanians had been considering their own canal—from Aqaba—and together, if both had been built, the water might well have swamped the Dead Sea and hurt mining operations. Initially that is what the Jordanians were afraid of. But the Jordanians were never too serious about their own project, largely because of the enormous estimated cost (over a billion dollars at 1980 prices). Once Amman was assured that the Israeli canal would probably be good for the area, it too became a minor part of broad technical discussions in later years concerning not just the Dead Sea, but the Arava, and even the use of Haifa as a Jordanian port facility. Much later on, again based on these studies and subsequent others, the Jordanian government much accelerated its Dead Sea development plans.[61]

As for the pipeline business, it is better known in the United States because of its peripheral connection to the Iran–Contra scandal, the inner machinations of the Israeli Labor party, and the seamier side of Israeli domestic politics. The events took place in 1985, in the heat of a number of Israeli–Jordanian exchanges; the scandal only surfaced in February 1988. To sum up, Israel was ready to guarantee the pipeline's security both to Jordan and to Iraq in return for an honorarium for the Labor Party's war chest. But the Iraqis and Jordanians could not find anyone to insure the pipeline. So the United States arranged to get the Overseas Private Investment Corporation (OPIC) to underwrite the project, and to use laundered Pentagon money to pay off the Israelis "for good behavior" to the tune of about $65–70 million a year for ten years. The National Security Council staff, Robert "Bud" McFarlane, Ed Meese, Eli Wallach, and a Swiss Jewish friend of Prime Minister Peres, named Bruce Rappoport, were all deemed to have played various major and minor roles in the scheme.[62] Naturally Shimon Peres denied the latter part of this deal, but whosoever believes that denial is capable of believing nearly anything.[63]

Not every area where one might expect some kind of cooperation produces it. In the Dead Sea both Israel and Jordan mine potash and phosphates. The Kaiser Aluminium Company tried in 1968 to work out a joint venture. It did not succeed. But that was not the last attempt.

Not every Israeli–Jordanian summit has been at the highest level. In the spate of secret summitry in the 1971–73 period, the discussion of functional matters became more important. Israel's Ambassador to the United States at the time, Yitzhak Rabin, advanced the process in Washington in 1971 when he met and spoke with Crown Prince Hassan.[64] They discussed the disastrous state of the Jordanian economy, and how Israel might help with water, housing and the like. Later on the subject matter turned to industry, and this thread in Israeli–Jordanian discussions continued for some years.

In May 1973 the two sides met in the Foreign Ministry's guest house just outside Tel-Aviv, where the King had been some months earlier. Crown Prince Hassan led the Jordanian team; Mordechai Gazit, long of the Israeli Foreign Ministry, led the Israeli one. Hassan told Gazit and Haim Givati about Jordan's plan to expand its Dead Sea works for the manufacture of potash. He did more than talk; he brought plans to show the Israelis. The Israelis were impressed. Hassan asked if Israel would like to join in and help, knowing that Israel's extraction technology was the best in the world, and that Israel had greater access to reliable financing for the project. The Israelis agreed that it was an interesting possibility, and suggested that the way to do it was to charter a company somewhere in Europe, with the real owners being half Jordanian and half Israeli.

The Jordanians, especially Zaid al-Rifai, were enthusiastic, and another meeting was scheduled after a number of technical details were worked out. The date chosen was Sunday, 7 October 1973, at the same location.[65] Unfortunately, on October 6, the October War broke out, and close cooperation became impossible for many months. No deal was made. Jordan proceeded with its plant alone; it is less than one third as efficient as Israel's operations. If the level of the lake continues to go down, or the level of political cooperation goes up, cooperation in and near the Dead Sea is likely to be a primary area of mutual interest. Indeed it already has been. *Haaretz* reported in 1986 that Israel and Jordan agreed to cooperate on a project in which Israel taught Jordanian engineers how to process shale oil deposits as a source of fossil fuel to provide electricity to desert regions.[66] In return, Israel was to receive some shale or some electricity. And Israeli engineers have also helped teach their Jordanian counterparts a new and less expensive way of extracting potassium from the Dead Sea area;[67] this takes place in Jordan, where Israelis have made use of a special road across the border, the entrance to which—near a hotel featuring hot springs for tired muscles and bones—is separated from the road by much fencing and some barbed wire.[68]

MEDIA RELATIONS

It would not be accurate to conclude from any of these examples or from all of them taken together that Israel and Jordan have good relations. Even Yitzhak Shamir has spoken of Israeli–Jordanian relations as a condition of *de facto* peace. But things are not quite that stable. There are real conflicts of interest, and they are serious ones. Also worth noting is that while the Hashemite hierarchy operates in a normal, civilized and pragmatic manner toward its neighbors, including Israel, the attitudes of the population of Jordan do not exactly follow suit. Rather, there is a kind of inverse proportionality at work; thus, while a Saudi Little League baseball team was willing to play an Israeli team at a tournament held at a US air force base in West Germany, the Jordanian team was not.[69] The reasons for this inverse proportionality are interesting.

Most original resident east bankers, especially, it seems, the younger generation, resent the Palestinians in their midst. After all these years, they are still referred to as a group as aliens, at least in private, honest conversations. And east bankers are aware that they have to deal with these aliens because of Israel. So when east bankers swear up and down that they support the right of Palestinians to return to their land, by which they mean the area west of the Jordan River, they are sincere if only because they would like to rid themselves of Palestinians east of the river. So they hate Israel not because it is a Jewish state so much as because Israel has been the cause of the cluttering up of their traditional and formerly quaint east bank Arab state.

And then there are the Palestinians themselves, more than half of Jordan's population on the east bank. They hate Israel, liken Zionism to Nazism, and are almost never heard to contemplate recognition or peace. One reason for the level of their hatred is that it is a compensation for not living under occupation, and for having made, most of them, a kind of peace with the Jordanian status quo. They feel a kind of guilt, and they compensate for their detachment by being "more Catholic than the Pope." This is not an unusual phenomenon; Americans of Irish, Italian and Jewish origins are often more thoughtlessly, radically and romantically patriotic about Ireland, Italy and Israel respectively than are the Irish, Italians and Israelis themselves.

Another factor is that, precisely because Jordanian government attitudes are so pragmatic and contacts with Israel so extensive, the Jordanian media is allowed to bend over backwards to give the opposite impression as a kind of cover for the government's real deeds. As one Israeli put it, exaggerating a bit,

> It may sound surprising, but . . . the most venomous propaganda against Israel does not emanate from Damascus or even from Riyadh; it comes from Amman. The Jordanians want to demonstrate to the Palestinians in the territories that they do not fall short of Arafat or Syria, and they may also want to cover up secret contacts with Israel. That is why Jordan never says "the prime minister of Israel," which even Syria says, but "the prime minister of the Zionist enemy," or "the Zionist war minister."[70]

It is simply not true that the Jordanian media does not talk about Israel or use the word as such. But the gist of the remark is well taken. During the high emotions of the *intifada* was been more true than ever. To take one good example, the

Jordanian daily *al-Dustur* ran an article by a Palestinian historian on 26 September 1988 one Nimr Sirhan, who titled his article: "Yes, We Will Recognize Israel in Return for an Independent Palestinian State." That, too, was the essence of his essay, in which he implored his readers to recognize reality, and not to repeat the mistakes of 1947 by rejecting the partition boundaries and resolution. "Let us be realistic," he said. But there was more to it than that. Consider this passage:

> I would say that under the present international balance of powers and in the era of the uprising, the establishment of a Palestinian state is impossible without the recognition of Israel. But I would also say that those demanding the liberation of Palestine from the river to the Mediterranean Sea do indeed represent our people's conscience and strategy, but we would be satisfied now with the partition lines . . . Let us learn a lesson from what Saladin did during the era of the Crusades, when he accepted a liberated part of Palestine and recognized a crusader state on another part of Palestine, until a century later when al-Ashraf Khalil and Al-Ashraf Qalawun unleashed their swords and wiped out the crusader invasion, as Rajih al-Salfiti, the voice of the uprising, says . . . We should benefit from the role of the uprising to press our demands, improve our image and gain recognition for the first time . . . I tell those demanding liberation from the river to the sea that the moment when their dictum will be achieved will come later.[71]

What is remarkable about this article is that, in the Jordanian domestic context, this statement was the most moderate statement about Israel that one could find. And it went no further than the letter and the spirit of the PLO's 1974 phased program, which envisioned the destruction of Israel in stages, as opposed to all at once. And note, the boundaries of the compromise state are not to be the pre-1967 boundaries—those are unattainable for all practical pur- poses—but the 1947 partition resolution boundaries that never came into *de facto* existence. Nevertheless the publica- tion of Sirhan's essay was a major media event, even though it was probably published solely to allow the spleen-spilling repudiation that followed it for days. One example of that repudiation should suffice to give a sense of the "normal" press attitude toward Israel. Badr abd al-Haq answered that Palestine is from the river to the sea and "should accommodate either us, the Arabs, or them, the Jews. There could be no compromises. I would go even further," he continued,

> and say that I would like to throw the Jews into the sea, to be devoured by hungry Mediterranean fish, exactly as expounded by the late Ahmad Said . . . The idea of recognizing Israel has come out of the Arab impotency of which the Palestinian impotency is but a part . . . [W]hat is required is to end this state of impotency and reject all formulas that lead to recognizing Israel . . .[72]

And while all this sort of thing is going on everybody in the country, in their private honesty, knows that Palestinians by the hundreds and thousands work in the Jordanian government and even in the Palace, at high positions, and that they do not really believe any of this jabbering. Nevertheless, the fact that the attitudes of most Jordanians toward Israel are so unrelenting does put limits on what King Hussein can do with Israel, certainly in public. How much of a constraint they really are at the limit were, for example, the King to enter direct negotiations with Israel, is hard to say. Even the King cannot know for sure.

Despite this considerable obstacle, Israel and Jordan do have good self-interested relations. Given the constraints imposed by popular attitudes, the achievement is rather remarkable. These relations are not always deliberate, or at least do not start out as being deliberate. The examples noted above are all characterized by explicit connections of one kind or another—real people being together, talking, exchanging money, or whatever. Some of these arrangements are blessed from above, some are not. But another area of connection involves only tacit cooperation or acquiescence. Television and radio transmissions are a case in point.

Israel and Jordan are both small countries and they are very close to each other. Radio and television waves are notoriously cavalier about not respecting political borders. Anyone with the right technology in Jordan or Israel—

namely an antenna—can pick up the other country's radio and television shows. Israeli and Jordanian ham radio operators, too, can easily tune one another in. Even King Hussein, who is a ham radio buff, has participated.[73] Over the years the Israeli side has developed its Arabic television and radio programming, not just for Israeli Arabs, but also for Jordan and other nearby Arab countries. Israeli radio is popular throughout the area, including in Jordan; the Hebrew language programs that play rock-and-roll and more modern musical forms are listened to quite widely. Israeli television is popular too. There are the Arabic-language variety shows, and the old American shows, but Arab viewers also tune in *Rehōv Soomsoom* (Israel's version of *Seseme Street*) and an Austrian-made animated show dubbed in Hebrew called *Aliza Ba'Eretz Haplaot* (*Alice in Wonderland*). Here is how Charles Ritterband described his experience in Jordan:

> In the coffee houses of Aqaba the Arabs sit puffing at their waterpipes, their eyes glued to the screen across which flickers some banal American love story of the 1960s; they are undismayed at the fact that they are watching Israeli TV. And the two girls from Jordan's upper class, sporting at the swimming pool of the "Intercontinental" in Amman, have their transistor radio unabashedly—and loudly—tuned to *Galei Zahal*, the station of the Israeli army. 'A very good station, excellent music,' they remark, surprised at my surprise, no thought of politics anywhere in their mind.[74]

Also, more lately, Jordanian television has begun broadcasting the news in Hebrew. Both sides broadcast in English. Jordanian broadcasts, until the summer of 1988, always gave the weather in the West Bank and Gaza as a matter of course—as a service to listeners and as a reminder that Jordan still had claims to the area, notwithstanding the Rabat Summit and Yasir Arafat's pretensions. (They still give the weather for the West Bank, now called Western Heights; Gaza has been dropped.)

In recent years the television and radio stations have been both a source of friction and a source of calm. Israeli television showed the rioting and rock throwing of the *intifada*, and all of Jordan was able to see it too.[75] The extensive and continuing coverage worried the Jordanian government, which feared that Palestinians on the east bank might wish to imitate the West Bank–Gaza proceedings they saw on Israeli television.[76] On the other hand Shimon Peres used the power of *Kol Yisrael* and international telephone connections to host a call-in show, where he talked with people from all over the Arab world, some of whom were cut off by their governments, mainly Syria and Saudi Arabia, in mid-sentence, but most of whom were not.[77]

In a less dramatic fashion, Israeli and Jordanian TV officials have worked out a way to show *Dallas*, which both stations buy, in the proper sequence so that episodes are not shown out of turn. There is no hard evidence that Jordanians and Israelis regularly speak to each other about this, but then again, they do not need to speak in order to make it work tolerably well. Still, some Israeli newspapers list Jordanian television offerings and they always seem to get them just right, even when changes in the Jordanian sequence of shows occur.

Moreover, with respect to the electronic media, it is clear that each side listens closely to what the other side says about it. On occasion a form of dialogue takes place, with one country "talking" to the other through the radio or television. One example, ideal in the ambiguous between-the-lines impression it conveys to the careful listener, goes like this:

> The Israeli radio announced in its 10:30 newscast today, 27 September 1988, that the Jordanian and Israeli foreign ministers shook hands during a reception President Reagan hosted in New York after he introducing [*sic*] them to each other. The official Jordanian spokesman would like to stress that this report is absolutely baseless and that it is part of the series of falsehoods broadcast by the Israeli news media every now and then.[78]

Note that this news item does not deny the reception, or that the foreign ministers met and talked with each other. Only the handshake is denied; this is a sort of reverse "have you stopped beating your wife" approach to admitting that contact does take place. Note, too, that it implies a close attention to the Israeli media, which lies only "every now and then."

A more recent example dates from May 1989. Akiva Eldar reported in *Haaretz* on 5 May that when King Hussein was in Washington in April he proposed to US officials that Jordan and Israel work out a secret defense pact to protect the region from an irredentist Palestinian state. The *very same day* Radio Amman denied the story, proving, incidentally, how well the newspaper exchange works.[79] It remains to be seen whether *Haaretz* or Radio Amman was correct on the substance of the matter; the story lacked a certain sense of reality, but *Haaretz* is Israel's most reputable and professional newspaper and rarely if ever runs pure speculation, something that *Al-Hamishmar* and other papers are less reluctant to do. Finally, American Jews with dual citizenship in Israel have long been welcome in Amman as long as they use their American passport, and Abie Nathan and other Israeli doves have visited Jordan without a great deal of muss and fuss. American Jews and Israelis have even been invited to appear on Jordanian television, even though the show with Israelis was taped in Europe (at Jordanian expense).[80]

ANOTHER TRY AT DIPLOMACY

By October 1973 what may be called the density of the Israeli–Jordanian functional relationship was so considerable that it had accumulated a virtually irreversible quality. Despite the October War and the Rabat Declarations, low-level contacts and functional cooperation proceeded along quite smoothly. After the war the King met Dayan in London in December 1973 to coordinate Israeli and Jordanian positions should an international conference become a serious on-going diplomatic forum. It did not; it met once for a short period and proceeded to become completely irrelevant.

The King again came to Mrs Meir in secret in March 1974 in the Arava. By then Mrs Meir and General Dayan were in political trouble at home; they were blamed for Israel's lack of preparedness on October 6, and there was a good chance that they would pay politically for the public's wrath. The only way they could fend off being thrown out of office was to process a dramatic breakthrough on the Jordanian front. This summit, of all the summits over the years, was one in which the King held the political leverage, and the Israeli participants were more the supplicants. The King was also cheered by the nature of US shuttle diplomacy, which aimed at disengaging the protagonists of the October War, an endeavor in which Secretary of State Henry Kissinger had made much progress. By March 1974 one agreement had been worked out between Israel and Egypt, another was imminent between Israel and Syria. Hussein, even though he had not gone to war in 1973, could not have been faulted for supposing that his turn was next, and that the United States would take his side.

At the Arava meeting, Rifai laid out Jordan's proposal for a separation of forces; it became known as the Jericho Plan.[81]

The plan, which had been suggested to the Jordanians in the first place by Dr Kissinger, called for Israel to back up five miles all along the river and for a Jordanian civil administration to take over. Jordanian military forces would stay five miles to the east of the river. The two sides would recognize Jordan as the negotiator for the Palestinians in any future talks. Mrs Meir's response offended the King; she said that she did not understand why a disengagement was necessary since Israel and Jordan had not just fought a war. To this the King responded: "Do I have to attack you to get the same treatment as Egypt and Syria?"[82] No agreement was reached, and two weeks later Mrs Meir and General Dayan were out of office.

Mrs Meir's replacement, Yitzhak Rabin, had had long experience with secret diplomacy with Jordan, and wasted little time in resuming it. Rabin met with Hussein and Rifai on 29 August 1974. Five more summits between them followed over the next three years. No progress could be made on the central issues, but a new wrinkle was introduced in time by Shimon Peres, who, with Rabin, attended every meeting. Peres talked of federal or confederal arrangements; the State Department, which called the proposal "balloons and sausage" after aspects of Peres's semi-territorial scheme, was interested too.[83] At first the Jordanians were contemptuous, but in time they began to see possibilities for themselves in such arrangements in the context of other changes—especially after Rabat and the 1976 municipal elections put them on the defensive against the PLO in the territories.

Also important as this period progressed was the chance that the momentum of Israeli–Egyptian diplomacy could offer a wider security net for anything that Jordan might do. Israel had the same idea. Just a week before the Rabat Summit, on 19 October 1974, another Israeli–Jordanian summit discussed how to proceed after Rabat renewed with urgency the Jordanian role in the peace process. The Jordanians were full of confidence that this would be the case; they had President Sadat's promise of support.

The result of Rabat was quite different. Egypt changed its position, the Jordanians were dumped by the Arabs, and the PLO enthroned. Hussein was angry and depressed. He blamed everybody, but he was especially angry at the Israelis who, he believed, should have accepted the Jericho Plan. Had they done so, the King thought, none of this would have happened. Rabin requested more meetings; the King refused until the negotiations that led to Sinai II between Israel and Egypt in September 1975 raised again the prospect of major diplomatic movement. Hussein did not want to be left out, so another summit was held on 28 May 1975. Hussein's aim was to head off a separate Israeli–Egyptian peace that would leave Jordanian interests hung out to dry. Hussein warned the Israelis about Sadat's perfidy and untrustworthiness.

Rabin responded with a new version of Mrs Meir's 1971 offer to Hussein. Again the King rejected it.

The only major functional progress that developed during this epoch of secret summitry concerned intelligence and terrorism. Before 1975 the Israeli and Jordanian intelligence services were in direct contact only episodically. But now that terrorism, incubating dangerously in Lebanon and elsewhere, was becoming such an enormous problem, the two sides decided to create a Hot Line between the Mossad and the Jordanian *mukhbarat*. Direct telex and telephone lines were installed and Israeli intelligence personnel visited Jordan from time to time to talk and exchange ideas.[84] On 5 July 1976, the day after Israel's raid on Entebbe, this Hot Line was used by the Jordanians to congratulate Israel on striking a hard blow against international terrorism.

Otherwise, more progress was made on ecological matters at Aqaba, water, aviation, sailing rights, and even a minor border marking in the Arava area. Jordan had hired Chinese to build a road, and the Chinese could not find the border. It turned out that the border was marked wrongly, so Israel withdrew its posts a few hundred yards so that the Jordanian road could be built. It was.[85]

Of course Israel and Egypt, aided by the United States, proceeded ultimately to Camp David in 1978 and to peace in 1979. Unfortunately for Jordan, by May 1977 the Israeli government was no longer in the hands of those inclined to make a deal. It is quite likely that had Labor remained in power during the key period of Israeli–Egyptian diplomacy between November 1977 and March 1979, Jordan would have joined the public diplomacy. There was one summit—between Dayan and Hussein in London on 22 August 1977—but all it proved was that the chance of an agreement was farther away than it had ever been since July 1967. After Camp David Hussein cut off all personal contact with Israel until 1984. This proved that Hussein's confidence that Israel's 1971 offer was a minimum that he could always avail himself of was seriously in error.

Hussein was not always wrong, however; sometimes the Israelis were. In 1976, for example, Hussein warned Rabin that holding municipal elections in the territories would be disastrous for both Israeli and Jordanian interests, and help only the PLO and their sponsors. The Israelis thought otherwise; they were wrong.

THE NEW REALITY

Between 1967 and 1985—nearly a twenty-year period—Israel and Jordan, and especially the residents of the West Bank, proved once again that it is impossible, even amid largely frozen politics, to freeze social relations. Adam Ulam once said that in international politics, nothing endures like the provisional and the realities of the Middle East have proved him right once again. Necessities forced new patterns on people and institutions over these twenty years, even as larger political patterns changed in different ways. As the occupation took on a more permanent aspect, as a new generation came to take for granted the jerryrigged arrangements of 1967–68, things changed. So too, did the changing politics within Israel—the coming to power in May 1977 of the Likud bloc—and the enhanced challenge on the local level mounted by the PLO.

Clearly, then, both before 1967 and especially after it, the broader political context has influenced day-to-day arrangements in the territories and between Israel and Jordan. And the apparent calm between Israel and Jordan, buttressed by these private relationships, has also been at least a modest factor in determining larger issues. In the next chapter we take up these broader themes, and their movement after the war in Lebanon, and especially between 1984 and 1987. The latter period witnessed a remarkable attempt to put diplomatic and political flesh on the bones of these functional realities.

Notes

1. The best general account is still that of the late Malcolm Kerr, *The Arab Cold War*, 3rd edition (New York: Harper & Row, 1971).

2. Good background to this can be found in John K. Cooley, "The War Over Water," *Foreign Policy*, No. 54 (Spring 1984), pp. 3–4. Cooley, however, exaggerates the role of water in the origins of the 1967 war.

3. Here see Samir A. Mutawi, *Jordan in the 1967 War* (New York: Cambridge University Press, 1987).

4. On a historical point that one would think is settled by now, there are differences. Some Israelis claim that in the northern section of the West Bank, the Jordanians were tough customers. Others typify their effort as half-hearted with the single exception of Jerusalem.

5. Interview, Musa al-Kailani.
6. Interviews, Gideon Raphael, Mordechai Gazit.
7. See Gideon Raphael, *Destination Peace* (London: Weidenfeld & Nicolson, 1981), p. 43.
8. Yossi Melman and Dan Raviv, *Behind the Uprising* (Westport, Conn.: Greenwood Press, 1989) pp. 87–88.
9. Husni 'Ayish and 'Isa Abu Shaykha, *Al Mujtama' al-'Arabi: li's-suff ath-Thani ath-Thanawi* (al-Matba'a al-Markatiya, adopted 1987–88).
10. "Massive cheating mars most Arab matric exams," *The Jerusalem Post*, 11 August 1990, p. 3.
11. Interview, Tzvi Elpeleg.
12. David Grossman, *The Yellow Wind* (New York: Farrar, Straus & Giroux, 1988), pp. 162–63.
13. Sholomo Gazit, *The Carrot and the Stick*, cited in Grossman, *The Yellow Wind*, p. 163.
14. This reputation has persisted. See, for example, Rami G. Khouri, *The Jordan Valley* (London: Longman, 1981), pp. 55, 67, 216.
15. Some Palestinians did go to the Ghor. See Avi Plascov, *The Palestinian Refugees in Jordan* (London: Frank Cass, 1981), pp. 69, 185.
16. Interviews.
17. "Katz-Oz Denies Exports," *The Jerusalem Post*, 4 April 1989, p. 8.
18. Ritterband, Israel and Jordan: Peace for coexistence," *Swiss Review of World Affairs*, August 1984, p. 21.
19. Judy Siegal, "'The world's best rainmaker'," *The Jerusalem Post*, 8 April 1989, p. 4.
20. See also Meir Merhav (ed.) *Economic Cooperation and Middle East Peace* (London: Weidenfeld & Nicolson, 1989), p. 71.
21. Interviews.
22. For a remarkably blunt statement of this view by the Jordanian Minister of the Interior, Raja'i al-Dajani, see "Interior Minister on West Bank, Passports," *Al-Ra'y*, September 10, pp. 14, 15, also in Foreign Broadcast Information Service, Daily Report, Near East & South Asia (hereafter, FBIS-NE) 14 September 1988, p. 30. See also, in the same vein, Ibrahim Abu Nab, "Dialogue is Better than Sleep," *Al-Ra'y*, October 2, 1988 in FBIS-NE, 6 October 1988, p. 39.
23. Interviews.
24. See, for example, "Jordan: West Bank and Gaza Trade," *MidEast Markets*, 10, 8 August 1983, pp. 15–16.

25. Meron Benvenisti, *The West Bank Data Project* (Washington: American Enterprise Institute, 1984), p. 14.

26. Early data, of uncertain accuracy, is available in *Statistical Abstract of Israel 1971* (Central Bureau of Statistics, September 1971), pp. 629–32; and in Brian van Arkadie, *Benefits and Burdens* (New York: Carnegie Endowment, 1971).

27. Ian Lustick, *Israel and Jordan: The Implications of an Adversarial Partnership* (Berkeley: Institute of International Affairs, 1978), p. 10.

28. For a more pessimistic view, see Benvenisti, *The West Bank Data Project, inter alia.*

29. This was most certainly the case after the Jordanian economy hit bottom in late 1988, and the dinar was left to "float" for the first time ever. Its value fell fast, but not equally in the West Bank and in Jordan: it fell farther in the West Bank. Thus smugglers could take dollars and buy "cheap" dinars on the West Bank, and then take the dinars to the east bank, buy dollars with them, and have more dollars than when they started out. Also, the decline in the dinar resulted in the dumping of dinars in the West Bank stock exchange, weakening the dinar against the Israeli shekel. See Radio Jerusalem in Arabic, 19 January 1989, in FBIS–NE, 19 January 1989, p. 36.

30. For details, see Ann Mosely Lesch *Israel's Occupation of the West Bank: The First Two Years*, (Santa Monica, Ca.: The RAND Corporation) Rand RM–6296–ARPA, August 1970, pp. 23–26.

31. Ibid., p. 9.

32. Interview, Frank John Kerber, Department of State, 3 May 1986.

33. Melman and Raviv, p. 190.

34. Private conversation, April 1981.

35. See *Yediot Aharonot*, 30 April 1987 for some details and anecdotes.

36. See "More Visitors Encouraged in Territories," Jerusalem Domestic Service, FBIS–NE, 2 May 1986, p. I2.

37. Daniel Pipes, "The Unacknowledged Partnership," *The National Interest*, No. 10 (Winter 1987/88,) p. 97.

38. Interviews.

39. Interviews.

40. See Melman and Raviv, *Behind the Uprising*, pp. 97–101.

41. Rifai became Prime Minister on 26 March 1969 and stayed in office until 12 August. He was reappointed on 27 June 1970,

and remained until 15 September when the military government of M. Daoud was formed with the onset of the Civil
War.

42. I have covered this subject in detail. See my "U.S. Decision-
    making in the Jordan Crisis of 1970: Correcting the Record,"
    Political Science Quarterly, Spring 1985.
43. Melman and Raviv, *Behind the Uprising*, pp. 104–05.
44. Ibid., p. 115.
45. See the long article, filled with anecdotes, "Along the Jordan
    border," in *The Jerusalem Post*, 27 August 1988, pp. 9–10.
46. See Ritterband, "Israel and Jordan," p. 20.
47. Interviews.
48. Jonathan Karp, "Saudis Send Thanks," *The Jerusalem Post*,
    13 June 1987, p. 7.
49. "Two Jordanian Planes Stray into Israeli Airspace," Jerusalem
    Domestic Service, FBIS–NE, 30 October 1985, p. 13.
50. Zohar Blumenkrantz "Cooperation with Jordan on Monitor-
    ing Air Traffic," *Haaretz*, 25 September 1990, p. 42.
51. See Shaul Ramati, "Hussein's Plan," *The Jerusalem Post*, 10
    January 1987.
52. Interviews. This story sounds too wild to be true. I report it as
    heard.
53. "Contacts on Al-'Aqabah Crossing Point Denied," Paris
    Radio Monte Carlo, 22 February 1989, in FBIS–NE, 23
    February 1989, p. 32.
54. Sayid 'Abd-al-'Ati, "5000 Egyptians Protest Ferry Delay in
    Al-'Aqabah," *Al-Wafd*, 5 July 1990, pp. 1, 4, in FBIS–NE, 9
    July 1990, p. 26.
55. *Peace: Israel's 40 Year Quest*, Israeli Ministry of Foreign
    Affairs, Information Division, Jerusalem 1988, p. 15.
56. Ritterband, "Israel and Jordan," p. 21.
57. Melman and Raviv, *Behind the Uprising*, p. 183.
58. See "Energy Minister Orders Halt to Canal Project," Jerusa-
    lem Domestic Service, FBIS–NE, 13 June 1985, p. I2.
59. Here see "Livening Up the Dead Sea," *MidEast Markets*, 19, 8
    September 1980, pp. 15–6.
60. A thinly veiled academic example of this hysteria is Abdullah
    Hamadneh, "Aims and Dimensions of the Israeli Mediterra-
    nean–Dead Sea Canal Project," in Abdel Majid Farid and
    Hussein Sirriyeh (eds.) *Israel and Arab Water: An International
    Symposium* (Ithaca, New York: Ithaca Press, 1985).
61. See "Chemical Complex Planned for Dead Sea," *Jordan
    Times*, 12 September 1989, p. 6.

62. See Stephen Engelberg, "Insurance Plan for Pipeline Involved Israeli Aid Pledge," *New York Times*, 26 February 1988.
63. "Peres Says Suggestion of Bribe Offer to Party is 'Nonsense'," *New York Times*, 24 February 1988.
64. Melman and Raviv, *Behind the Uprising*, p. 179.
65. Ibid., p. 182.
66. *Haaretz*, 16 November 1986, cited in Aaron Klieman, *Statecraft in the Dark: Israel's Practice of Quiet Diplomacy* (Tel-Aviv: Jaffee Center, 1988), p. 155.
67. Pipes, "The Unacknowledged Partnership," p. 96.
68. Personal observation, December 1986.
69. See Danny Ben-Tal, "Baseball little leaguers play Saudis," *Jerusalem Post* (International Edition) 5 August 1989, p. 8. The Saudi team won the game 30–0; perhaps their superior skill was a factor in the decision to play.
70. Shaul Menashe, quoted in Pipes, "The Unacknowledged Partnership," p. 97.
71. "Historian Writes on 'Future Palestinian State'," *Al-Dustur*, 1 October 1988, in FBIS–NE, 5 October 1988, p. 33.
72. "Writer Defends PLO, Palestinian Positions," *Al-Dustur*, 1 October 1988, in FBIS–NE, 5 October 1988, pp. 33–34.
73. Interviews.
74. Ritterband, "Israel and Jordan," p. 20
75. In truth the Jordanian government showed it too, a little, at the start, but they showed it very carefully. I am grateful to Asher Susser for this piece of information.
76. See Ihsan Hijazi, "23 Palestinians Seized by Jordan; Plot to Subvert Regime is Charged," *New York Times*, 25 January 1988. The PFLP claimed in January 1989 that Jordan was holding 56 PFLP members, and that it was treating them "inhumanly." See "PFLP Accuses Jordan of 'Inhuman Measures'," Paris AFP in English, 28 January 1989, in FBIS–NE, 30 January 1989, p.10. Of course, paraphasing Jody Powell on Lester Maddox, to be accused of inhumanity by the PFLP is a little like being called ugly by a frog.
77. Thomas L. Friedman, "A Radio Call-In Show Brings Peres and Arabs a Bit Closer," *New York Times*, 27 March 1987.
78. "Spokesman Denies Handshake with Israeli Minister," Amman Domestic Service, in FBIS–NE, 28 September 1988, p. 32.
79. See Akiva Eldar, "Jordan's Hussein Urged Secret Security Pact," *Haaretz*, 5 May 1989, p. A1, and "Official Denies 'Haaretz' Treaty 'Allegations'," Amman Domestic Service, 5 May 1989, in FBIS–NE, 5 May 1989, p. 32. This was not the

only attempt to "report" what the King and President Bush said to one another in April in Washington. Perhaps in response to the Israeli press report, *Sawt al-Sha'b* on 18 June 1989 purported to carry an unattributed report of the "minutes" of the talks, followed by a commentary praising the King for his steadfastness, written by the editor-in-chief. *Sawt al-Sha'b* is majority-owned by the Jordanian government. For both items, see FBIS–NE, 19 June 1989, pp. 30–31. If the report in *Haaretz* lacked a sense of reality, the material in *Sawt as-Sha'b* was positively silly.

80.   Avi Bettelheim, "Jordanian Television Invites Israelis to Appear," *Ma'ariv*, 29 April 1986, p. 6.
81.   Melman and Raviv, *Behind the Uprising*, p. 125.
82.   Ibid., p. 126.
83.   Ibid., p. 130.
84.   Ibid., p. 134.
85.   Interviews.

3   These Bones Shall Live

"They say ya can't do it, but sometimes that ain't always true."—*Casey Stengel*

In the book of Ezekiel is the famous story about the valley of the dry bones. In the story God tells the Prophet to speak to the bones, that they should come together, bear flesh, and breathe alive. Of course, they do so. The story is a parable about the children of Israel returning from exile to rebuild their country. On a far more mundane level, however, the metaphor works as a way to describe what Israeli Prime Minister Shimon Peres and Jordan's King Hussein connived to do between roughly 1984 and 1987. Functional ties between them were the bones, peace was to be the result, and diplomacy, secret and otherwise, was to play the role of the Prophet. In a nutshell, Peres and Hussein secretly agreed to expand greatly the range of existing Israeli–Jordanian ties in conjunction with a new agenda for the high diplomacy of the Arab–Israeli conflict. They hoped and believed that each track would work to support the other, and to protect the process as a whole from its natural enemies: the PLO, Syria, and the Likud bloc—the other half of the Israeli government. To future generations, if not also to present ones, this may sound improbable. But it is so improbable that no one would think to make it up.

The United States was a party to this process to a considerable degree, and before long set about to promote, aid, finance and coordinate it, largely through the work of Ambassador Wat Cluverius, appointed as a special assistant to Assistant Secretary of State Richard Murphy in 1986. The US Ambassador in Israel, Thomas Pickering, also played an extremely important role.

The Soviet Union, although it was really not involved in any significant way, understood the new tack. This understanding may have contributed to the evolution of Soviet thinking about the Arab–Israeli conflict in recent years.[1] Well before November 1988 Moscow had stopped insisting on an independent Palestinian state as a solution to the Palestine problem, and professed not to see it as the most desirable outcome of the political processes at work. It improved relations with Jordan at a time when many Western observers erroneously concluded that Jordan had become superfluous to the peace process. Insofar as the Soviet government today retains any energy to devote to thinking about Arab–Israeli matters, Moscow still sees a process wherein the West Bank becomes an independent entity "even if only for five minutes" that then proceeds to confederate itself with Jordan.[2]

The two tracks of Israeli–Jordanian diplomacy in these years were tightly intertwined, far more so than in the only other comparable period—1971–73—when the two strands of Israeli–Jordanian interests comingled closely. In order to appreciate how this worked, the background to the high diplomatic aspect requires a brief, and admittedly not inclusive, review.

HIGH DIPLOMACY

As discussed above in chapter 2, in 1967 and 1968, just after the June War, Israeli–Jordanian contacts were premised on the likelihood of a political settlement that would re-establish the territorial status quo ante or something very close to it. In Israel there were always groups opposed to returning the West Bank to Jordan, and in time these groups began to have more influence. A policy that was developed at first in order to make any return of the West Bank to Jordan unproblematic turned into a policy with different aims as time passed and perceptions changed. One of the initial reasons that Moshe Dayan outlawed any regional political organizing in the West Bank was out of fear that it would reduce Jordanian leverage and complicate a settlement. Later, fear of the PLO filling the vacuum, as it virtually did in 1976 municipal elections, became the more immediate reason. After the Likud came to power in May 1977 the aim of policy as it evolved was to feed a graduated *de facto* annexation that had earlier grown not out of design but the habits of power.

Nevertheless, the Likud revolution changed less on the ground than might be thought. Many low-level private channels with Jordan were maintained, although high-level summitry was abandoned.[3] But during this time, for example, small border disputes in the Arava area south of the Dead Sea, and in an area south of Galilee where the Israeli, Syrian and Jordanian frontiers meet, were settled by discreet, direct negotiations, even though formally these disputes remain unsolved.[4] On the other hand, when Ariel Sharon, as Minister of Defence, was responsible for the occupied territories, his ultimate motive was to depopulate them of Arabs and by so doing topple Hashemite Jordan.[5] But the level of emigration from the West Bank under his tenure did not much change.[6] Hussein invited Shamir to meet with him in 1984 at Aqaba, but Shamir refused; then Shamir called on Hussein to meet with him in 1987 but Hussein refused.[7] Eventually they did meet secretly, on the last weekend of September 1987 in London.[8] But the meeting was not particularly friendly or useful, and there seemed to be little enthusiasm on either side to meet again. While during Labor's tenure the occupation of the West Bank was undertaken with ambivalence and shifting aims, the Likud attitude was always quite clear: the territories were not to be given up, either to Jordan or to anyone else.

What this shows, once again, is that Israeli–Jordanian ties are predicated partly on the realities of living in close quarters, and partly on political volition. During Likud tenures, the former has remained even if the latter has ebbed. Indeed, throughout many profound changes since 1982 the underlying Jordanian–Israeli relationship has endured through bad and not-so-bad times. As time has progressed, however, it is fair to say that the regional context in which Jordan must work has become more constrictive and dangerous.

In general Egypt's having made peace with Israel in 1979 without including other states made it impossible for the rest of the Arabs either to make war or peace except in close concert with each other. And since Syrian politics led

Damascus away from cooperation with Jordan and Egypt instead of toward it, this was virtually impossible too. What this meant from the Jordanian point of view was that the slowly evolving status quo with Israel, within the Arab world and within the territories, was all there was likely to be in the foreseeable future: no breakthroughs, no new Camp David accords, no exit from the basic conundrum. So instead of being a temporary condition, the Israeli occupation and its thin connective tissues to Jordanian interests became more a fixed one.

This meant, in turn, that Jordan's competition with the PLO had entered a new stage, the PLO's weakness after the Lebanon war furnishing opportunities for Jordan to demonstrate to those in the territories that if they wanted the Israeli occupation to end, they had better understand the utility and necessity of the Jordanian role. Jordan's relations with Israel then became more than just protection and a means to a predictable *modus operandi* in lieu of a formal settlement; they became an *asset* in the competition with the PLO. For although the Hashemites were consorting with the enemy, they were also delivering services and patronage to the social strata in the territories that had always been of greatest political importance. Besides, West Bankers knew that their future included a connection to Israel; even the Palestine Communist Party was for open economic borders with Israel after a settlement was reached. Jordan's pragmatism, therefore, was cautiously displayed as a harbinger of the inevitable future, and as time passed between 1982 and December 1987 the grudging logic of it began to impress increasing numbers of West Bankers. They did not like it, but they understood it.

AFTER THE LEBANON WAR

After the War in Lebanon, the PLO–Jordanian struggle accelerated. The Lebanese War reshaped the local constellation of power in the Arab world. Israeli leaders had so intended it; their aim was to destroy the PLO in Beirut, the better to work their will in the West Bank. Ariel Sharon, in particular, sought a pliant Christian Lebanon, a Jewish

Greater Israel and, most portentous of all, a "Palestinian" Jordan. The scheme was misconceived and failed grandly. The ultimate irony, perhaps, is that the war did evoke moderation in the West Bank, not for Israel's version of autonomy, but for a renewed Jordanian role, precisely the sort of moderation Likud leaders most feared and Jordan most sought.

The Lebanon War frightened West Bankers. With the final Israeli withdrawal from Sinai in April 1982, many of them vaguely expected some progress toward peace. Instead they bore witness to war in Lebanon, a concerted Israeli effort to crack down on political activity in the territories by creating a civil administration and experimenting with the Village Leagues scheme, then the Sabra and Shatilla massacres in Lebanon. Fear gathered into local pleadings to the PLO to allow King Hussein to take the lead in ending the occupation before it was too late. The September 1982 US Reagan Plan, which highlighted anew the Jordanian role, provided the framework of hope at the time. With the loss of Lebanon as a base of operations, and mindful of these pleadings, Yasir Arafat endeavored to test the King's willingness to readmit the PLO to Jordan. Jordan's price was clear and it was steep: it wanted Arafat's support for a Jordanian role and his submission to Hashemite desiderata when it came to security and foreign policy.

The war in Lebanon aided Jordan in the regional competition over the Palestinian movement in many ways. First, it dispersed the PLO away from areas in Lebanon controlled by Syria, and it weakened Syria itself. Second, the war did not radicalize the Palestinians or the Arab states as some had predicted, but brought forth a moderation demonstrated in particular by the Fez Plan of early September 1982. Seeing these developments, Egypt pursued its reintegration into the Arab world, and its first point of contact was Jordan. Finally, American policy, as noted, was re-energized, and US energies have always tended to elevate the Jordanian role both on account of the inertia of diplomatic formulas and geopolitical logic.

Jordan promoted these developments. The King encouraged the United States, professed to see compatibilities between the Reagan and Fez plans (although there were few), talked explicitly about Israel's right to exist, and tried to entice the PLO toward him. The King also asked his patrons on the West Bank to put pressure on the PLO, although they needed little encouragement.

Arafat saw the writing on the wall after his first eviction from Beirut; he started a quiet dialogue with King Hussein, pursuing the possibility of basing al-Fatah in Jordan. Arafat met in Amman with the King from 8 to 12 October 1982, and said nice things about the Reagan Plan. At the same time, however, Arafat tried to re-establish himself in Lebanon.

Syria, though bloodied, was determined not to bow to either Israeli, PLO or American desiderata. Arafat thus had less room to maneuver than he thought. Syria began mustering its Palestinian allies to ensure that Arafat would not dominate the next Palestine National Council (PNC) meeting, and it succeeded. Fatah started splitting under Syrian pressure, and in this environment the price for a firm Jordanian ticket to a US-brokered settlement was too much for too little as far as Arafat was concerned. But for lack of a choice, Arafat continued to test the King, trying to secure both an operational base and a route into Washington as near to his own terms as possible.

Arafat wanted to hold the Palestine National Congress in Amman, and he visited the King in Amman in November and again in December 1982 to discuss that and other matters. PLO radicals wanted to meet instead in Damascus. Arafat countered with Tunis. It ended up, in February 1983, in Algiers. In the meantime, based on his conversations with Arafat, the King came to Washington in December 1982 with hopeful things to say, and he persuaded the Reagan Administration that there was a chance that he could finally land Arafat, now in his most desperate condition ever, over UNSCR 242. But Syria increased its pressure on the PLO, on Jordan, and on American "peacekeeping" forces in Lebanon. The PNC meeting undercut Arafat, Jordanian diplomats suddenly began getting shot in Europe and India, and the US Marines in Lebanon found themselves targets of Syria's Lebanese proxies.

Arafat sent mixed signals to the King: he wanted to continue the dialogue, but he stayed away from Amman lest he stir the wrath of his enemies. Finally he showed up on 31 March 1983 and began a week of "brutal talks" with the King. Hussein demanded a serious commitment to the peace process, which meant UNSCR 242 and essentially the subsuming of Palestinian interests beneath Jordanian ones. Hussein promised a base in Amman in return, but little else. Arafat came close to agreeing but, in the end, he did not. On 10 April 1983, the Jordanian regime lost patience and ended the matter. But Arafat came close enough to convince the Syrians to up the pressure still further. Now that Arafat had alienated Jordan, who would oppose them?

Arafat smelled the political wind; on 4 May he turned up in Damascus for the first time in eight months. His meeting with Assad supposedly "turned a new page in Syrian–PLO relations," but all it really did was express joint opposition to US efforts in Lebanon. Arafat did have another motive; much as he distrusted the Syrians, he still needed a base next to Israel. He had failed to get one from Hussein, and hoped to secure Syrian acquiescence to his carving out a new one in Lebanon. In mid-May Arafat reorganized his remaining forces in Lebanon, and began wheeling and dealing again amid Lebanon's many factions. This abraded against Syrian interests in Lebanon and it was then, with Syrian knowledge and aid, and taking full measure of Arafat's weakness, that the al-Fatah mutiny began.[9]

Between June and September 1983 the PLO was one of many factions in Lebanon. But when Israel vacated the Shouf area in September 1983 and the PLO tried to fill part of the vacuum, the mutiny took a decidedly military turn. Arafat and his minions soon found themselves besieged in Tripoli by rival PLO factions and the Syrian army. On 20 December 1983, Arafat's second expulsion from Lebanon landed him in Tunis, this time for an extended stay. On the way Arafat stopped off in Cairo, partly to explore what possible support he might obtain from Egypt in order to put him in a better position to face down the coming pressure from Amman.

In the meantime Jordan ingratiated itself further with the Palestinians of the West Bank, taking advantage of the new consciousness in the territories after the Lebanon war and the PLO's plight. Jordan sought to demonstrate authority over the territories, such as when, in March 1983, a military court sentenced a number of West Bankers to prison terms for cooperating with the Israeli Village League scheme. Above all Jordan sought to persuade West Bankers of the community of interests they shared with Jordan in opposing the Israeli occupation and stemming the demographic erosion of the area. Jordan also gave wide publicity to any positive statements made by prominent West Bankers about the Jordanian role. And the government spread rumors in the wake of the breakdown of Jordanian–PLO negotiations in April that it was considering the constitutional reformulation of Jordan solely on the East Bank, leaving West Bankers either to defend their own interests alone against Israel or depend on the PLO.[10] This was done partly to remind West Bankers of practical constraints and interests and it had the desired effect on the West Bank. But it had a predictable effect in Damascus too; even as the Syrians were attacking Arafat in Lebanon, they were shooting Jordanian diplomats and setting off bombs in Amman on a regular basis. On 5 November as the battle of Tripoli raged, the King accused Syria of trying to subvert and terrorize his country.

The weakness of the PLO, promoted at the hand of Syria, nevertheless whetted Hussein's appetite despite Syrian pressures on Jordan. The King had failed to bind Arafat to him as a minor partner, in 1983, but he had denied him shelter and forced the PLO back to Lebanon, there to be despoiled and massacred by Syria's Palestinian and Lebanese allies. The mutiny failed to displace Arafat, but it now drove him toward Hussein, and the PLO was not long in coming around. Almost as soon as Arafat arrived in Tunis, he recommenced contact with Hussein. The mutiny had hurt him, he more than ever needed a base close to Israel, and he feared the progress that Jordan was making in the territories at PLO expense. The King knew that Arafat was farther than ever from being able to deliver the PLO as a whole to some version of a Jordanian solution, but Arafat could deliver himself *qua* symbol and that would have been victory enough. And so the deadly game began again, with Arafat and Hussein needing each other for different, antithetical purposes, each one betting that in the end he would prevail. Arafat refused to capitulate to the

King's demands, but he wobbled. On 2 January 1984, from Tunis, Arafat managed to call simultaneously for the rejection of the Reagan Plan and for PLO–Jordanian cooperation over the West Bank.

The Jordanians kept up the pressure. After Rabat constitutional life was suspended in Jordan lest the structure of parliament represent an overt Hashemite claim over the West Bank. But Jordan never altered its constitutional arrangement either; any such alteration would have signified an end to its West Bank claim. Thus, on 16 January 1984, the King renewed parliament in its original form, a signal of renewed interest in the West Bank and claims to it. At the opening meeting of the parliament, Hussein called on the PLO to adopt a "practical framework" for peace, that is, a Jordanian framework. A few days later, seven new West Bank delegate seats were filled—all by Hashemite Palestinian patrons.

The early months of 1984 represent the most concerted Jordanian effort before 1991 to seize Arafat and bring him into a negotiation with Israel under American auspices. The King and his court put on a full press. While maintaining the formal sanctity of the Rabat Declaration, the Jordanians did almost everything in their power to undermine it in practice. Pilgrimages of prominent Palestinians from the West Bank arrived in Amman to plead the King's case with visiting Arafat, all arranged by the royal palace. Jordanian statements now referred to the PLO as the "legitimate representative of the Palestinian people," conspicuously dropping the key word "sole." The press stressed the West Bankers as the silent majority, the people who mattered most. The revival of parliament was discussed as a solely internal matter with an insistence so artificial as to convey the opposite impression. Jordanians recalled aloud their doubts about Rabat, noting repeatedly that Rabat had failed to produce any positive result. They explained that for practical purposes they could not abandon the West Bank, lest Israel be unopposed in all its designs. Jordanian officials said that the 1950 "free will" declaration of unity still pertained legally "until the liberation," and that there was no contradiction between the 1950 unity agreement on the one hand and an "independent" PLO role on the other. Finally the King spoke broadly of history, destiny, Arabdom, and the graves of his ancestors in Jerusalem and Gaza.[11] Jordan also began activating an Egyptian dimension to its strategy. All of this activity got the PLO's attention. Khalil al-Wazir was dispatched to Jordan in late January to arrange the resumption of the Jordanian–PLO dialogue and, on 26 February, Arafat showed up again in Amman.

For much of March Arafat and Hussein continued to circumnavigate one another. Arafat resisted the King and the talks again failed to settle on the details of what a Jordanian–Palestinian delegation would look like and how it would operate. In the King's calculation, the weight of the argument might now be settled by the United States; perhaps what Washington could give or threaten to take away from the PLO would finally do the trick. But Washington soon proved to be a major source of disappointment to Jordan.

THE US CONNECTION

Jordan had long sought to make the Reagan Administration understand that establishing American credibility within a negotiation was crucial to the negotiations ever starting. Hussein's litmus test was the US ability to get the Israelis to stop building and expanding settlements in the territories. If he could not do that, then his own credibility as protector of the West Bank would be undermined. If he could not get that, then he could not promise Arafat anything at the end of a negotiating process because he could not be sure there would be anything to give. As the King saw it, the United States was obligated to reward Jordan for its pragmatism, its opposition to violence, and its deliberately limited contact with the Soviet Union, and to help it establish credibility in the West Bank and the resultant power it would bring over Arafat. Jordan's very weakness obligated Washington to speak its case if it really wanted peace. During his meeting with President Reagan in Washington on 13 February Hussein thought he had extracted firm promises directly from the President over a number of issues, but within a month Jordanian expectations were shattered.

First, despite direct promises to the contrary, the United States withdrew from Lebanon under Syrian and Iranian pressure. If the United States would not stick it out for Lebanon, what might Hussein expect Washington to do for Jordan?[12] Besides, the US presence in Lebanon guaranteed poor US–Syrian relations, and that enhanced the prospect that if the Syrians caused real trouble for Jordan, Washington would help the King to deal with it.

Second, an arms deal for Jordan, though proposed by the Administration, quickly evoked Congressional opposition. The President then made his appeal on Jordan's behalf to a Jewish audience, urging American Jews who wanted peace to support the arms deal. From an American perspective, this was a logical tack but from Jordan's perspective it was a humiliation.

Third, Hussein had promised Arafat that he could get the United States to bring pressure on Israel to allow West Bank delegates to travel to the next Palestine National Council meeting. Only with those delegates would Arafat have a chance to win permission for a formal nexus with Jordan. Hussein thought he had a direct promise on this matter. But Washington brought no pressure, and a private letter in early March iterated that it would bring none, forcing Hussein to admit to Arafat that he could not deliver the Israelis even on this point.

Fourth, and more damaging, a second letter from the White House contained a polite but firm refusal to support, or even not to veto, the King's own UN draft resolution condemning Israel's West Bank settlements as illegal. (In fact, some weeks later the United States vetoed the resolution.) As one Jordanian official put it: "While Washington was demanding on the one hand that Jordan participate in the peace process, on the other hand the administration refused to help Hussein re-establish his authority with the Palestinians."[13] It was actually worse than that: to put it bluntly, the King did not trust the administration's basic competence. The Jordanians could see that high officials in Washington had not a clue as to the particulars of Jordan's tactics *vis-à-vis* Arafat and the

West Bank, and that the President's word was subject to rapid and complete reversal. Hussein did not have to tax his imagination to understand what such a condition would mean in the middle of a difficult, detailed negotiation with Israel. So on 14 March the King bitterly denounced the United States, refusing to join direct negotiations under American auspices. The peace process ground to clattering halt as the last Marines left Lebanon.

HUSSEIN TRIES AGAIN

Arafat and Hussein met again in Amman on 3 May 1984 and discussed plans to hold the next PNC in Amman in November. In the meantime Arafat strove to mend fences with other PLO factions to insure that there would *be* a PNC meeting with almost everyone in attendance. To prepare this, Arafat was willing to make marginal and cosmetic concessions to his peers. The Jordanians understood.

The next major development in Jordanian–PLO relations represented more of the same tactics that both parties had pursued in 1983 and early 1984. The Jordanian desire to hold the PNC meeting in Amman in November 1984 was designed to advance the King's strategy of partly coopting, partly displacing the PLO. With no hope of good relations with Syria and physically out of Lebanon, Arafat had little choice but to accept the King's offer.

King Hussein's subsequent performance at the PNC was meant to make life as uncomfortable as possible for Arafat and his deputies, not just for the sake of it, but to drive Arafat away from the radicals and toward a Palestinian constituency more amenable to compromise with Israel in a way that would strengthen Jordan's general position. As Arafat and his colleagues squirmed in their seats while Hussein spoke of UNSCR 242 and peace, Jordanian television beamed the scene into the occupied territories and, for that matter, into Israel proper. The aim, clearly, was to suggest that Arafat was with the King, that PLO views were moderating, and that Jordan was a partner in the process.

THE PERES FACTOR

Changes in Jordanian–PLO relations that seemed to favor Jordan were of great interest to the new Prime Minister in Israel. Shimon Peres took a direct interest in all things Jordanian. That soon had the effect of widening King Hussein's range of tools for use in bringing Yasir Arafat under *de facto* Jordanian influence once and for all.

The essence of Israeli policy between September 1984 and 1987 was that by helping Hussein improve his position on the ground in the territories, Israel was, in effect, voting for the Jordanian option. It must be remembered that Shimon Peres only became Prime Minister on 14 September 1984; before that time, since May 1977, all chances of real progress in the peace process had been stymied by Likud's unwillingness to consider territorial compromise, or compromise of any other sort, for that matter. Peres sincerely desired a settlement with Jordan and knew that Israel would have to make sacrifices to get it. In his view, and in that of Labor's youthful brain trust—an ad hoc assembly of Israel's one hundred best and brightest intellectuals and academics—continuing the occupation was bad for Israel in many ways. It was not that any of them believed that by trading territory for peace, or by reinforcing or substituting for such arrangements with functional compromises, that the Arab–Israeli conflict would be ended. They understood well the intractable nature of the conflict on account of the depth of Arab hostility. The question was: would Israel's position in what was probably a protracted life-and-death struggle be enhanced or worsened by continued occupation of the West Bank and Gaza? Their answer was that it would be worsened.

Peres's campaign to re-engage the King started even before the 1984 Israeli election. In the spring of 1984 Peres sent feelers to King Hussein to express his potential interest in a new working relationship should Peres become Prime Minister. These messages were delivered both by the State Department and by the British Foreign Ministry in what could be seen as a breech of diplomatic conduct.[14] Also, Peres entrusted Yossi Beilin, one of his young aides, to assemble a team of academics—called the 100-Day Team—to study the possibilities.[15]

One of the first things Peres did upon becoming Prime Minister was to call upon King Hussein to negotiate peace with Israel. Another aide, Nimrod Novik, spoke to friends in Washington about Peres's ideas. Novik had worked at the Foreign Policy Research Institute during his days as a graduate student at the University of Pennsylvania. Alexander M. Haig, Jr, between returning from being Supreme Allied Commander of NATO forces in Europe and moving on to be President of United Technologies and then Secretary of State, also alighted at the Foreign Policy Research Institute. When Haig became Secretary of State he took with him the associate director of the Institute, Dr Harvey Sicherman. Novik and Sicherman were friends, and when the time came to test the waters in Washington, Novik knew who to ask.[16]

Thereafter, as soon as the pieces were in place, a series of Israeli initiatives toward the King began again the interrupted process of indirect, and sometimes direct, negotiations. Peres and his group understood, however, as did the King, who is an expert in Israeli domestic politics, that as long as Likud remained a part of the Israeli government, dramatic breakthroughs were possible only in potential. The idea was to build up functional ties and a series of interim measures or changes that implied change in the Israeli occupation of the West Bank and Gaza. These changes would create a certain trajectory that ultimately would force the divided Israeli government to break up. Peres's hope, and no doubt Hussein's too, was that by the time the domestic political crunch came, enough hopefulness would have been created in Israel and in the United States to tip the scales toward Labor.

Going slow initially was also important for Peres in 1984 because the national unity government had prior problems to solve, and they were of the type that a national unity government could solve best—economic crisis and the withdrawal of Israeli forces from Lebanon. While it took a national unity government to solve these problems, it did not follow that equal credit would go to the two halves of the government. Peres hoped that if progress in these areas could be turned to Labor's credit, then it would become additional political capital for use in forging a political solution with Jordan.

Jordanian motives in cooperating with Israel, to the extent that it did before the *intifada*, included the possibility of the Jordanian option, but there were other, more proximate reasons for the cooperation, too. First, keeping channels with Israel open gave the King a friend of last resort in case his Arab neighbors again became violent and predatory. The dialogue with Israel also served as a kind of immunization for the relatively new Jordanian claim to Gaza against that of the PLO. The dialogue encouraged internal Israeli elements to oppose the "Jordan is Palestine" platform of the Israeli right wing. Most of all, the Israeli dialogue in effect helped the King to slow the slippage toward the PLO on the Israeli left for, ironically, Israel was the main barrier to anti-Hashemite forces in the region.[17]

But Jordan's interests and Israel's were not the same, nor were perceptions of the dangers posed by the PLO the same either. This lack of overlap is largely what foiled the process in the end.[18] For Peres and the Labor Party, the higher the profile of the PLO in any negotiation, the harder to create a political majority for the process in Israel. For Hussein and the Hashemites, the higher the profile of the PLO the fewer the risks in any negotiation, both in the regional and in the Jordanian domestic framework. Hussein felt he could not proceed without the PLO; Peres could not proceed with it.

In the end this underlying difference is what prevented the cooperation from growing, but this is not to say that the effort was without benefit. It was during this period that the Israeli (Labor) side began to develop its view that a negotiation with Jordan might involve Palestinians connected to the PLO. But as long as Jordan provided the protective shield to any agreement, the real dangers of such an arrangement were manageable. This view has become increasingly important with the passage of time, and is seen by many observers as the best way to finesse the issue of PLO participation in a settlement process in its early stages.

The US government, although it tried mightily, could not bridge the Israeli–Jordanian gap. On the functional level, however, it did what it could to help Jordan reassert its influence in the territories by agreeing, after the usual bureaucratic constipation, to funnel a portion of its development funds for the West Bank through Jordan.[19] More important, as a clear sign of a new level of cooperation between the Israeli Labor Party, Jordan and the United States, the then US Ambassador to Israel, Thomas Pickering, brokered the opening of new branches of the Cairo–Amman Bank in Nablus and elsewhere, thus expanding the financial network to keep pace with and better that of the PLO.

With US aid, Israel thus allowed Jordan a considerable advantage in the late 1980s when the Cairo–Amman Bank was reopened. PLO patronage money had literally to be carried into the country across the bridges. The Jordanians could instead use the wire service to existing banking facilities. Throughout the *intifada*, as the PLO tried to replace Jordan's role in the West Bank, the presence of Jordanian banking facilities aided the King. There was no other easy way for PLO funds to enter the West Bank—aside from literally carrying bills across the bridges or carrying them into Ben-Gurion airport in suitcases—except through banks centered in Amman. Thus in October 1988, as the PLO sent funds into the West Bank to replace Jordanian salaries that had been suspended in August, they used the Arab Bank in Amman which, of course, was subject to Jordanian supervision and law.[20]

In all, US motives were harmonious enough with those in Amman and Jerusalem, and were encouraged, too, by the fact that no successful public diplomacy seemed possible given the constrictions of regional and local domestic politics.[21]

ISRAELI–JORDANIAN STRATEGIES AND THE PLO

The full court press against the PLO that began in the fall of 1984 was coordinated between Jordan and Israel in a way more extensive than anything that had gone on before. This coordination was hardly complete or fine-tuned. Still, the effort involved everything from the broadening of old arrangements to the contemplation of new ones.

It turned out that the motives of the two sides in this scheme were not quite close enough for it to lead to a dramatic breakthrough on the political level, but no one knew that at the time, and a functionally based plan also seemed preferable to doing nothing, which was the only other alternative. Also important was that while the Israeli–Jordanian campaign did not lead to a diplomatic breakthrough, it almost certainly had an important influence on Jordanian–PLO relations in this period. Arafat must have known something about what the Jordanians and Israelis were up to, and he was forced to decide whether getting closer to Hussein would be better protection for PLO interests in the territories or not. Of course getting closer to Hussein had its dangers as well, for the King was trying to force decisions upon him that he did not wish to make. Thus, simply put, Israel's cooperation with Hussein had the effect of adding a sharp new arrow to the King's quiver, at least to the extent that the cooperation allowed the King to claim credibly that, because of Jordan, the daily lives of Palestinians under occupation improved. Between February 1985 and February 1986, that is, during the tenure of the Jordanian–PLO accord, Jordanian–Israeli cooperation took many forms.

First, an effort was made to reduce independent PLO power in the territories by punishing those individual West Bankers close to the PLO and rewarding those close to, or willing to do business with, Amman. Israel and Jordan were involved in this together; there were simply too many "coincidences" to believe otherwise. Jordan invited certain notables to come to Amman; Israel lifted travel restrictions in order to make it possible.[22] Of special significance in the initial stage were the visits of such local notables as Mohammed Rashad al-Jaabari of Hebron, Khalil Musa Khalil of Ramallah, and Walid Mustafa Hamad of el-Bireh.

Second, new functional arrangements were developed and old ones expanded with respect to electricity and the power grid, and these were public knowledge. Israel agreed to let Jordan provide some electricity to the West Bank from the Tallal Dam on the Zarka River, and there were reports of

Jordanian–Israeli talks about connecting the Israeli electricity grid to the Jordanian one in the West Bank in the Nablus region.[23] The Jerusalem Electric Company, long in arrears to Israel for electricity it had purchased but never paid for, was suddenly bailed out by Jordan after dozens of refusals from Amman on that score.[24]

Third, this cooperation was in turn quickened by mutual fears of new Syrian water projects that threatened both Israeli and Jordanian interests.[25] Jordan and Israel established an ad hoc working group to deal with the Syrian matter; Jordan, remembering 1966–67, reportedly queried Israel on the possibility of its using force to stop Syria. Israel demurred. Also, whereas before the concerted effort Israel was reluctant to help Jordan clear a sandbar from its intake channel on the Yarmouk that feeds the East Ghor Canal—as had regularly taken place for a number of years—in November 1985 the Israeli press reported that Jordanian and Israeli tractors together cleared the way.[26]

All of this chummy activity had a predictable effect on Syria, and drew a predictable response; after all, Hussein was not the only head of state with designs on Arafat's head. As part of the Syrian campaign of terror and intimidation that ensued, a Palestinian inclined to cooperate with the King's endeavor, and well placed to do so—Fahd Kawasmeh, the former mayor of Hebron—was assassinated in Amman by Syrian agents. Arafat then began frequent public recitation of his rejection of UNSCR 242 and Hussein, unable to work his way against Syria and unable to interest the United States in helping him with the Palestinians, threw up his hands in despair.

The PNC meeting and the King's failure to secure US support had made two things clear. First, Syrian pressures on Arafat were working. The split in Fatah seemed institutionalized and it appeared that Assad might carry some heavy leverage not only within the PLO umbrella, but also within Fatah itself. This was not necessarily bad news for Hussein, for to the extent that Arafat concluded that his problem with Syria was not tactical and temporary but unconditional and permanent, the more appealing a nexus with Jordan would appear, notwithstanding the price. Hussein explained to

Arafat that Jordan could get him half a loaf, some independence, and let him live; but Syria could get him nothing,
offered him no real independence, and was not beyond taking
his life. And the King pressed Arafat by saying that his refusal
to heed the needs and the views of Palestinians in the
territories was tantamount to delegitimating the PLO's right
to speak for the Palestinian cause. The King intimated, not
for the first time, that he might consider entering into
negotiations with Israel without the PLO, which would then
find itself in the dustbin of history. Whereas before such
threats had been rare and had little power, with Peres in
Jerusalem such threats took on a very different meaning.

To make this threat credible, however, Hussein needed
more than Peres's willingness to play along. He also needed
active US attention paid to the conflict again; to force
matters, there had to be a prospect of a negotiation to
enter. That required more than Jordanian will; it required
Washington. But it was clear that until Israel had extricated
itself from Lebanon neither Israel nor the United States
would have the time or energy to tackle the Palestinian
problem. So, when Israel announced its intention to withdraw unilaterally from Lebanon in January of 1985, Hussein
quickly set up his tactics for the next round.

Intensive private negotiations between the King and Arafat
resumed. Then on 11 February 1985, after more than two
years of negotiation, the King announced a PLO–Jordanian
accord based on UNSCR 242 and 338, and aimed the
breakthrough squarely at the White House. The King
implied that Arafat accepted these resolutions, renounced
terrorism, and would strive for a political solution if only
the United States would help out by talking with the PLO.
King Fahd, keeper of the PLO bankroll, happened to be in
Washington at the time—a neat little piece of political
theater—and President Reagan, loving a good show, pronounced himself delighted with the accord. But the State
Department, having seen no document and having heard
nothing from Arafat, wisely awaited "clarifications." In the
meantime, on 20 February Prime Minister Peres pronounced
himself delighted, too, and offered to go to Amman to talk
directly with the King.

Then on 23 February, King Hussein, without first notifying Arafat, published the text of the PLO–Jordanian accord, presumably to force the issue one way or the other in the PLO. The text, which talked of "land for peace" and confederation with Jordan, showed that Arafat had allowed himself to be reeled in far enough to get himself into deep trouble with his own Fatah lieutenants. But it was still not far enough in for the United States to pronounce the PLO fit for negotiations. In truth, the 11 February agreement was merely a shift in the pattern of Jordanian–PLO competition, for although there was an "accord," there was no agreement on precisely what it meant.

Thanks in part to a stir caused by a botched Egyptian initiative, the State Department thought nevertheless that a new possibility had opened up to make some progress in the peace process. The United States tried to arrange direct negotiations between a Jordanian–Palestinian delegation and Israel. The American tack was to accept a US meeting with a Jordanian-Palestinian delegation if it led to direct negotiations and was not meant to substitute for them. If they led to direct negotiations, the United States suggested that it might be prepared to press Israel on who would be allowed to represent the Palestinians—if not, then it would not. Israel watched and worried. The Jordanians were agreeable to the trade: semi-official US recognition of the PLO in return for direct negotiations in which the PLO role would be subsumed *de facto* beneath the Jordanian one.

But the King raised another requirement: an international conference attended by the five permanent members of the Security Council. This requirement, although formerly in the air, had been absent from the previous round of diplomatic maneuvering. Its return can be accounted for partly because of the Syrian factor. Ideally the King would enter a negotiation with Arafat on one arm and Assad on the other. If he could not have Assad, and by 1985 it was clear that he could not, then he could perhaps have some degree of protection against Assad by having the Soviet Union which, for its own purposes, was amenable to the notion. At first Israel and the United States were opposed but, soon facing a stalemate, both Peres and Secretary Shultz decided to explore the proposal, albeit in a new and secret context of Israeli–Jordanian negotiation described immediately below. The condition, however, was the same: that an international conference not be a substitute for direct negotiations but a prelude to them.

This was just what the King hoped for. Hussein proceeded to press Arafat, this time on explicit endorsement of UNSCR 242 and the question of direct negotiations. He hoped that Arafat's lack of a Syrian option, ironically for Damascus, would finally break Arafat's will. But Arafat resisted: he did not say no and he did not say yes. Instead Arafat told the King, and the King told the United States, that Arafat would accept UNSCR 242 only in return for US recognition of the Palestinian right to self-determination. Jordan must have had mixed feelings about pressing this point in Washington because the emphasis on self-determination could be read as implying Jordanian support for an independent Palestinian state. If so, then the "acceptance" of UNSCR 242 in this form would have meant, in effect, its nullification. On the other hand, if Palestinian confederation with Jordan were a foregone conclusion, and if this were understood in Washington, then Arafat's acceptance of UNSCR 242 was precisely what Hussein was after. In a sense it all came down to the King's level of confidence that he could, after all, control the PLO–Hashemite struggle in the ensuing, post-UNSCR 242, stages, a risky but unavoidable business.

There were other items on the table, too. When the King visited President Reagan in Washington in May, a major US arms replenishment for Jordan was long overdue. But the King was told that unless he subscribed explicitly to the principle of direct negotiations, any major arms deal was doomed in Congress. Hussein told the President that, at this stage in the process, while he was still trying to solidify his new relationship with Arafat, he could not do that. The President chose to press for an arms deal anyway, which ran into predictable trouble in Congress. In the summer Assistant Secretary of State Richard Murphy was dispatched to the region, in part to tell the King that things were not going well on Capitol Hill, and in part to try again to extract Jordanian motion toward direct talks.

The King tried to set the stage. In mid-July he reached agreement with Arafat on a list of seven Palestinians who might form the Palestinian part of a unified delegation. Hussein sent the list to Washington and Washington sent it to Jerusalem where, in the end, two of the seven names were accepted (Hanna Siniora and Fayez Abu Rahme) after a few weeks of dithering and arguing within Israel.[27] Meanwhile Arafat worried that some of the names would leak out, and that his Palestinian adversaries would try to murder the list. His fears were well founded, as Fahd Qawasmeh's murder a few weeks thereafter seemed to show—even though Qawasmeh was not "accepted" in the delegation. The development and vetting of the list of seven represented a *de facto*, albeit once-removed, Israeli–PLO negotiation, a "shape of the table" stage of negotiation—seemingly trivial and idiotic at first glance, but essential all the same.

No final agreement between Jordan and the PLO on a joint delegation could be reached, so Richard Murphy decided to come to Jerusalem to see if he could push the process to completion. He could not. Israel pulled Hussein in one direction, and Arafat's opposition within the PLO pulled him in another. The United States stood ready to meet with a united delegation if it ever formed—this despite lingering Israeli apprehensions about the entire process. But it never did finally form, and Murphy was ordered by Secretary of State George Shultz not to meet with a rump delegation in Jerusalem lest it strengthen the PLO hand and weaken the King's. Besides, there was no sense in alienating Israel in order to talk to a delegation whose construction was unfinished and whose longevity would be uncertain even if it did form.

Arafat thought hard about all this slow "progress" and apparently concluded that he had to maintain a safe distance from the Jordanian gambit in case it failed. But he did not want to be too far away, in case it succeeded. Arafat remained engaged in the process, but continued to insist that UNSCR 242 was unacceptable by itself, since it did not mention Palestinian rights to self-determination. The more significant reason Arafat needed to avoid 242 was that it only concerned the occupied territories and its adoption, it was believed, would end the PLO's right to struggle for all of Palestine; if he forsook that, he himself might very well be forsaken. The Jordanians were hard bargainers throughout, leaving no space between a fully independent and likely irredentist Palestinian state, which they vowed to prevent, and a "federation" in which the PLO would be the junior partner. But since Arafat lacked the option of renewing relations with Syria, he coveted the rocky relationship with Jordan just the same, particularly since it enabled Fatah to work more effectively in the occupied territories. Arafat waited and hoped for someone else to mess up the "progress" and it did not take long; the August 1985 Casablanca Summit failed to endorse Hussein's strategy.

Israel, for its part, also resolved to push Arafat off the fence, although not for the same purposes. Jordan wanted to coopt Arafat; Israel wanted to emasculate him. After the murder of three Israelis in Cyprus in September, Israeli planes flew 1500 kilometers on 1 October to raid PLO headquarters outside of Tunis. Then one of Arafat's PLO allies from the Palestine Liberation Front (PLF), a small PLO affiliate, organized the (botched) *Achille Lauro* incident of October 1985. Designed to embarrass Arafat, it worked. As far as Hussein and Hosni Mubarak were concerned, the incident was either an act of bad faith or an admission that Arafat did not control his own organization. In the same month the divided PLO played against itself again, sabotaging a London meeting arranged by the King that was designed to extract PLO recognition from Britain in return for PLO accession to UNSCR 242. Hussein was very angry; he summoned Arafat to the palace on 28 October and told him that if he did not stop the duplicity, Jordan would pursue a negotiated settlement without the PLO.

In fact, Jordan had been playing its own double game, negotiating in private with Israel over West Bank arrangements and more portentous matters besides. Indeed, on 5 October 1985 Hussein and Peres had met in London just three days after the Tunis raid. They assembled at the King's own house near Palace Green, just doors away from the Israeli embassy. They worked hard, and so did the technical teams that accompanied them and that kept in touch thereafter, on the Israeli side under the direction of Avraham Tamir, the Director-General of the Prime Minister's office.[28] They produced a major breakthrough. In effect, they agreed tentatively on a plan for joint rule of the West Bank.[29] The United States was well aware of all this. The liaison for the United States was Ambassador Wat Cluverius, who had been US Consul-General in East Jerusalem and was now, to repeat, Assistant Secretary of State Richard Murphy's special assistant.

It is worth describing in some detail the Fall 1985 negotiations between Israel and Jordan and what they accomplished, if only because they represent a precedent for the future. More important, the terms of the agreement show specifically what aspects of functional cooperation were being collected to produce, in turn, a diplomatic breakthrough. They also explain the great attention paid to an international conference at that time, and especially the change in the Israeli and US attitudes toward such a conference from negative to conditionally positive. This is because Israel's agreeing to an international conference was part of the quid pro quo that produced the October 1985 agreement.

Point one of the plan specified joint Jordanian–Israeli rule over the West Bank, but the parties could not agree on how long the joint rule would last. Jordan suggested three years, Israel five years. The two sides disagreed most about the question of ultimate sovereignty, but agreed not to let this disagreement stand in the way of further discussion. Point two was about Jerusalem. There was an agreement to keep the question of Jerusalem open, for no agreement could be reached. But Israel did agree to a Jordanian presence on the Temple Mount and to the hoisting of the Jordanian flag there.[30] Point three, supposedly, was an agreement at Israeli insistence that after the period of joint rule, the West Bank would be "secured" from without by Israel but "policed" from within by Jordan. Point four was that a Jewish police force would operate in Jewish settlements, a Jordanian force in Arab ones. Point five specified agreement on joint administration of the bridges on the West Bank; on the east bank there would be only Jordanians. Point six agreed that Jordanian citizens would vote for the Jordanian parliament:

Israeli citizens—Arab and Jew, theoretically anyway—would vote for the Israeli parliament. Point seven was that no more Israeli settlements would be established in the West Bank, and that existing settlements would not be expanded. Point eight was that Israel and Jordan would share land admin- istration: Point nine was that they would share water administration. Point ten was that there was agreement that there should be an international conference, including one with Soviet participation, and that the international confer- ence was a necessary ingredient, together with Great Power understandings and guarantees, for all the other points to be put into operation. Israel agreed to the conference in principle, but rejected Soviet participation until Moscow re- established diplomatic relations with Israel. Point eleven, finally, specified agreement on Syrian inclusion in the conference, but disagreed rather heatedly about separate PLO inclusion.

Israel for its part—or at least the Israeli Labor Party—was eager to promote the condominium notion, and this meant helping Jordan in the territories. For some insiders condo- minium represented a way to reinforce the potential for conciliation and lead to a territorial compromise. This was so important to Peres that he appointed a special advisor, Amnon Neubach, to coordinate functional matters. But for others, who believed that territorial compromise was an idea that had been overtaken by events, condominium was meant to substitute for a conventional territorial settlement.

Either way, the most important initial public symbol of this approach was the naming on 26 November of Zafir al-Masri, a prominent pro-Jordanian Palestinian from a prominent Jordanian political family, to be mayor of Nablus. Jordan clearly knew and at least tacitly approved Masri's selection, but Masri made positive noises about the PLO and sought to secure—successfully—Yasir Arafat's approval as well. Mas- ri's elevation was a perfect example of Israeli–Jordanian cooperation that Jordan tried to use to pressure the PLO toward a *modus vivendi* with Israel on Jordanian terms.

Not everything Israel did helped Jordan, however. Some- times functional questions drive matters in two directions at once. In order to improve Israel's bargaining power with the

EEC over a new economic arrangement, for example, Israel agreed to let Palestinian goods from the West Bank and Gaza be exported "directly" to Western Europe. This led to acrimonious dispute between the Palestinians, who wanted to label their products as being from Palestine or the West Bank and Gaza, and the Israeli authorities, who insisted that they be labled locally (e.g., made in Jericho).[31] There were disputes about other matters, such as purity standards for some prepared products, and in virtually all of these the EEC took the Palestinians' side—not surprising considering the general tilt of European attitudes since 1974.[32] As far as Jordan was concerned, direct Palestinian economic links to Europe were not unwelcome as long as Israel could be counted upon to limit their scope and symbolic mantle, which Israel did. Besides, in late 1985, King Hussein had more important problems to worry about.

In order to make sure that Arafat lacked the option of returning to the Syrian fold, King Hussein also commenced an effort to improve Jordanian–Syrian relations. The aim was not only to isolate Arafat, the better to coopt him, but to moderate Syrian support for Iran in the Gulf War. Amman must also have hoped to persuade the Syrians to stop shooting and bombing Jordanian diplomats and assets abroad. But the entente with Syria also strongly suggested that Hussein had given up on direct negotiations or a dramatic breakthrough in the peace process. The events of 1985–6 fit into Hussein's protracted, patient Palestinian strategy, but with what seemed to Jordan to be an incompetent administration in Washington and with Likud's turn to govern within the 1984 "rotation" agreement coming in Israel in October 1986, it was no time to aspire to full and formal peace negotiations leading to a final settlement.

In the beginning of his term, Peres had believed that peace would proceed in two stages, first economic/functional and then political/diplomatic. Stage one was supposed to preface stage two, so to speak. In fact, stage two never got off the ground, which led in early 1986 to a redoubling of efforts on stage one, because that was all that was left. Before the collapse of PLO–Jordanian cooperation, functional ties had the effect of strengthening Jordan's hand in order to draw the

PLO closer to a declaration of real moderation. After the collapse, this strength was used to attack the PLO and make it as irrelevant as possible to future peace processes. Naturally those PLO elements who had opposed any movement toward conciliation in the first place were not about to allow Jordan to get away with marginalizing them. They reacted, and without delay.

LET'S CALL THE WHOLE THING OFF

In reality the high diplomacy of 1985–86 was not as close to achieving a diplomatic breakthrough as that which had collapsed in 1984. The reason, largely, was that Hussein's circumstances were less propitious. So when Arafat returned to Amman on 13 November 1985, and tried yet again to fob off the King, Hussein demanded in the firmest possible way that Arafat finally decide. Although the threat of an Israeli–Jordanian condominium over the West Bank was thick in the air, for two long months Arafat refused to commit himself. Instead, he raised new demands with respect to Jordanian–PLO cooperation that had not been present back in February 1985. Until the King promised on five points, Arafat would not say yes to UNSCR 242. Arafat demanded that a confederation allow a Palestinian parliament, flag, and currency. Hussein agreed. But Arafat also demanded an army, which the King refused. Worse, he demanded that after the Hussein "era," executive authority in the confederation alternate, or rotate, between Palestinians and Hashemites.[33]

The King absolutely refused, announcing on 19 February 1986 that the PLO was not serious about peace, and suspended the Jordanian–PLO accord. The United States, through Wat Culverius, was apprised of the negotiations and clearly sympathized with the King. In July, after another Israeli–Jordanian summit, discussed below, Jordan shut all PLO offices in the country and expelled the PLO's representatives, including the late Khalil al-Wazir, who had busied himself developing a network of cells in the occupied territories that later fed directly into the *intifada*.[34]

The February severing of Jordanian–Fatah cooperation led to a political vacuum on the ground in the occupied territories. In that context Jordan's not-so-subtle threat that it might proceed further with the peace process without the PLO garnered much attention from some quarters. It was designed in large part to get the local residents to pressure the PLO to accede to Jordanian terms; in this it had much in common with older, tried and true, tactics. It also implied a fuller operationalization of the Israeli–Jordanian condominium scheme, and this was anathema to a number of important regional actors. Indeed, soon after the collapse of the PLO–Jordanian accord, secret summitry picked up its pace. Soon after the collapse Peres's aide, Yossi Beilin, met in Paris with Rifai. Avraham Tamir went to Egypt to keep President Mubarak informed; Egypt, however, was not inclined to be helpful until the Taba dispute was settled. Taba was small but its symbolic significance was large. Still, Peres realized that unless Egypt was on his side, the initiative with Jordan would be in jeopardy. Thus one motive for Israel's settling the Taba dispute on Egypt's terms, through binding arbitration, was to get on with more important things. But it took 18 months to settle Taba, and during that period Mubarak stubbornly refused to help out. "Israel and Jordan were to pay dearly for those 18 months, wasted because of Mubarak's stubbornness," wrote Michael Bar-Zohar, and he was right.[35]

Another Peres aide, Al Schwimmer of Dead–Med Canal and Irangate fame, used his US passport to go to Jordan from time to time. On the Jordanian side, beside the King and his brother, only Rifai, bin Shaker, and Adnan abu-Odeh knew the full picture of what was being done.

The United States also was active. Thanks to Richard Murphy, a version of what later became the London Agreement was worked out by January 1986. But it was incomplete, and serious disagreements—about the Soviet role, the PLO role, and the nature of the international conference in particular—remained.[36] The collapse of the PLO–Jordanian arrangement a month later depressed the Americans as much as it cheered the Israelis, but the Americans kept working just the same.

Still, everyone involved—Peres, Hussein, Murphy and others—were all beginning to worry that the process was becoming too complex and protracted for the amount of time Peres had to work with. Worse, enemies were arising. The first to suffer from the new tensions between Jordan and the PLO was Zafir al-Masri, who was murdered in Nablus on 2 March 1986 by the Popular Front for the Liberation of Palestine. In this way, too, the Syrian government demonstrated an active presence in the occupied territory, and did it in such a way as both to undermine the Third Force elective and to undercut Fatah, for Masri had obtained Arafat's permission before taking the job and Arafat had clearly failed to protect him.

Only one thing remained wholly positive for Jordan in this period: its campaign to rebuild its patronage effort in the territories at the PLO's expense, and with Israel's help, seemed to be making some headway. The King did not buy into the condominium idea as such; he has always rejected the notion that Jordan should do the dirty work of policing the territories while Israel reaped the main advantages. But it may be, as a few Israeli observers speculated, that King Hussein agreed with the analysis of some in the Labor Party in Israel that a strictly old-fashioned territorial compromise was no longer possible.[37] If so, then some sort of novel administrative sharing was inevitable and, in that context, every planned recession of Israeli authority and prerogative created an opportunity and a danger—in short, it created a vacuum that would be filled either by Jordan or by forces unfriendly to it. That such unfriendly forces still existed was driven home by Masri's murder.

On the other hand, it was not a foregone conclusion as to where the balance of power and resolve lay for, despite Masri's murder, Israel was able to appoint more Arab mayors, and there was no lack of candidates for the positions. From February 1986 until December 1987 Jordan, bent on weakening the PLO as much as possible, continued to campaign for its own constituency on the West Bank.[38] Jordan maintained in public that there was a difference between good PLO and bad PLO, hoping to coopt as many "good" PLO types as could be found. In every imaginable way, Jordan intensified its public relations and patronage efforts in the territories.

One reason that the Jordanian effort made progress is that Shimon Peres and the Labor Party still helped; the range of Israeli–Jordanian private cooperation expanded dramatically after the collapse of the PLO–Jordanian agreement, and some of it became more public than ever before.[39] This was not despite the fact that the grand scheme of the fall of 1985 did not succeed, but in a way it was because it failed. As long as the aim of Jordan's comeback in the West Bank was to moderate the PLO, Israel's enthusiasm was tempered with great caution. Once the main point of Jordanian policy was to marginalize the PLO instead, Israel's enthusiasm became unfettered.

Peres, however, still could not bring the rest of the Israeli government along. Shamir was kept informed; he knew every detail of secret summits and functional arrangements. But he worried about them more than appreciated them. Likud did not care which Arabs were more or less popular in the territories for it had no intention whatsoever of sharing effective authority or sovereignty with them. And polls continued to show that the coalition government that united Labor and Likud was still sufficiently popular that bringing it down deliberately would be politically costly in ensuing elections. Besides, the Soviets were not being cooperative, and the Israeli–Jordanian disagreement over the PLO role was never solved, only shelved.

A LAST TRY

In the spring of 1986 Israel and Jordan made one last effort to punch a hole in the political status quo before the scheduled Israeli rotation in October. Hussein and Rabin met again near Strasbourg, France in April. The basic agenda had to do with terrorism and border security, but the Israelis hoped to arrange something dramatic—attentions focused on Gaza this time—before the rotation in order to give Peres a means of preventing his loss of the Prime Minister's office to Yitzhak Shamir.[40] This must have reminded Hussein of his meeting with Meir and Dayan in 1974, just before they were thrust from office. The talks were detailed and sincere. No political breakthrough occurred; Hussein evidently still did not like the looks of the regional environment or what the United States, mired in Irangate, might want or be able to do to help. But Hussein was eager to get more Israeli help in the territories, and if his lingering liaison with the PLO prevented that, it would have to go. When Hussein got home he ordered all remaining PLO offices closed, banished Abu Jihad (Khalil al-Wazir), Abu Iyad (Salah Khalaf), and Abu Tayeb, the commander of the PLO's Force 17, from Amman.

After the rotation of the Israeli government, the functional track maintained a momentum of its own even though the high political track became even more profoundly blocked. Among the more important continuing developments were those concerning bridge traffic, the press, manipulation of the patronage network, expansion of the Jordanian ancillary administrative presence, and the use of "development" monies to organize political support.

There was also an important psychological development; Jordanian discretion was somewhat less complete as time passed. Before the 1986–87 period most direct contact and other cooperative undertakings were based either on knowing glances, mutual benign neglect or, at most, oral pledges. Now they were more frequently committed to paper. The model for this, or the threshold event, seems to have been the afore-mentioned tussle over the Jerusalem Electric Company and dealing with its deficit, which was handled through an exchange of memoranda.[41]

Jordan changed the flow of traffic across the bridges to punish PLO supporters; Israel made it easier for average West Bankers to pass into and back from Jordan to facilitate exchange and commerce.[42] Israel allowed Jordan to open pro-Jordanian newspapers in the West Bank, and expelled or detained editors friendly to the PLO. The PLO, in return, tried to bribe editors to favor its line, and paid the editors of *al-Quds* the equivalent of $150 000 to do so.[43] The editors complied and for their trouble one of them was expelled from

Israel. He then specifically blamed the Jordanian factor for his expulsion and, in general, most observers saw the harsher Israeli hand toward PLO supporters in the territories as aimed at helping Hussein re-establish his constituency there.[44] Israel and Jordan agreed on mayors to be appointed to various West Bank towns, this in order for Jordan to be able to channel patronage funds to them.[45] Toward this end Jordan revoked the power of pro-PLO mayors to issue licenses, until they came to Amman to pay obeisance to the royal court, and Amman extended such powers to more friendly faces.[46] Jordan made up its quarrel with the Village Leagues organized earlier by Israel, and facilitated coordination between them and Jordanian politicians; indeed the head of the Israeli Village League Council and the head of Jordan's Ministry of the Occupied Territories came not coincidentally from the same family—the Dudin family.[47]

Both Israel and Jordan engaged in a "quality of life" improvement program in the mutual belief that a population waxing in wealth was not likely to be a population ready to revolt and use violence. Jordan created a (theoretically) grandiose and highly acclaimed 5-year development program for the territories.[48] Israel reduced many of its own restrictions and even asked Jordan to reduce its export quotas for West Bank produce—this in public.[49] Jordan sought aid for the territories from abroad—from Japan and West Germany—and Israel encouraged it.[50] In August 1987 Israel lifted a ban on West Bank exports to the European Community, and Amman publicly hailed the decision.[51] Agricultural projects in the West Bank, financed by Jordan and carefully placed in areas whose leadership tended to be friendly to the Hashemites or at least neutral, were announced and approved by Israel.[52] The two sides cooperated on facilitating pilgrimages to Mecca by Israeli and West Bank Muslims.[53]

Security cooperation also increased, and Israel noted publicly its benign effects. Defense Minister Yitzhak Rabin stated that terrorism had been reduced thanks to Jordanian efforts. It seems that greater coordination resulted from an incident in January 1986 when a Jordanian soldier crossed the border and killed two Israelis before he was shot dead. The Jordanians apologized for the incident, blamed it on defectors from the Jordanian army, and stressed that all measures would be taken to prevent further incidents.[54]

In addition the Jordanian administrative presence in the territories was widened. There was the opening of branches of Royal Jordanian Airlines (formerly Alia) in the West Bank.[55] Preparations for this reopening were discussed rather openly in both the Jordanian and Israeli media, and reports of Jordanian officials from Amman travelling to Jerusalem were broadcast as well.[56]

There was also the opening of the Cairo–Amman Bank branches in Nablus, and later in Ramallah, Jenin, and Hebron, to facilitate the flow of Jordanian money into the territories. From the Jordanian point of view, the bank openings were also designed to get the dinars in the mattresses and under the floorboards in the territories into general circulation, to the general benefit of the Jordanian banking system and economy on the east bank. The bank plan was the subject of long and arduous negotiations between Israel and Jordan. It also happened to be a case that Israel and Jordan could not solve by themselves, and it took the mediation of Ambassador Pickering to seal the deal. Still, direct negotiations helped too. The president of the bank, Juwadad Shasha, visited Israel several times during the negotiations to work on details. Part of the problem concerned Jordan's concern that the bank's assets not be supervised by the Bank of Israel. Thanks partly to American pressures, Israel supervises the bank deposits in Israeli currency—the least of the deposits— while Jordan supervises the dinar deposits.

Another concern, mainly in Amman, was over who would run the bank branches on the West Bank. Israel initially gave permission to Zafir al-Masri in May of 1985, but Jordan refused.[57] Khalil Karsawa, a member of a family of Nablus money-changers, was instead appointed to manage the bank.[58] The point is that technical problems, patronage, and vested interests were responsible for holding up the deal rather than obstacles having to do with honor, ideology, or politics in general.

The bank deal was finally signed, after arduous technical problems were solved, in London in August 1986. Concessions were made by both sides. Most important perhaps, this agreement was actually committed to paper and signed—the first such document ever in the history of Israeli–Jordanian relations.[59]

In addition, less significantly, Jordan agreed to open a West Bank university to cultivate a friendly local élite and Israel agreed.[60] Jordan's parliament selected some new representatives for the West Bank; and Peres suggested that West Bank residents be allowed to vote for who would represent them in the Jordanian parliament, this clearly in the spirit of the fall 1985 working paper.[61] Jordan also began broadcasting the weather for "the Western Heights," something it had not done since shortly after Rabat in 1974.[62]

This sort of talk and action evoked complaints about the re-Jordanianization of the West Bank from Ariel Sharon and his associates, but Peres pushed ahead just the same.[63] Indeed the momentum of the cooperation with Jordan was so intense that even Yitzhak Shamir made positive remarks about it.

In conjunction with the bank plan, new dialling and telex communications in the West Bank were installed so that the residents could link up with the world directly.[64] Also, a Jericho Free Market was agreed upon by Israel and Jordan, and open notice of Israeli–Jordanian agricultural cooperation increased.[65]

As all of this was going on, Shimon Peres was waxing optimistic about Jordan's agreement to direct talks, and reports were leaking out about the existence of secret negotiations—including from Peres himself and those close to him, such as Avraham Tamir[66]—technical agreements and arrangements for a condominium. Toward the end of this period, even after the rotation, Peres made some definite statements about what had been achieved:

> In the West Bank, the policy was changed seriously. There is a change in our settlement policy; in fact we brought it to an end. All mayors are Arabs. A Jordanian–Egyptian bank was opened there. Economically, many gates that were previously closed are open today, and . . . the situation is a more liberal and acceptable state of life.[67]

He also told two visiting US Senators shortly thereafter that "there is a recognizable change in the orientation of

Judean and Samarian inhabitants from pro-PLO to pro-Jordanian."[68]

In truth Peres exaggerated, mainly for purposes of domestic politics. Hussein was still reluctant to get involved in any full scale condominium-like arrangements with Israel but was unable to resist taking advantage of small favors.[69] His money in the West Bank was designed not only to buy patronage and hurt the PLO, but also to preserve the Arab character of the economy and the population, aims which in many ways ran counter to those of Israel.[70] And Peres and Tamir may very well have overestimated how much all of this cooperation would buy Hussein in the political sphere. Since the process ultimately did not produce a public breakthrough, as many local residents hoped, King Hussein's status may have decreased as a result. But even if the Israeli government did not overestimate, and even if Jordan's position deteriorated somewhat, it was still arguably the only game in town with respect to the peace process.

DENOUEMENT

Even after the October rotation the functional area maintained its own evolutionary logic. Indeed things had developed so far in 1986–87 that a tentative functional agreement, still in coordination with larger diplomatic aspirations, was worked out on paper directly with King Hussein at the end of 1986.[71] Things had reached such a stage that even officials close to the Jordanian court were admitting more openly than ever that contacts with Israel had taken place. Truly, the revelations of January 1987 marked a new stage in functional aspirations and candor, even despite the fact that the political objective of all this was as distant as it had been three years earlier when the conscious effort to use functional linkages for higher diplomatic purposes commenced.

On 21 January 1987, the Israeli daily *Al-Hamishmar* reported that an envoy of Foreign Minister Shimon Peres had travelled to Jordan and met with the King, Prime Minister Rifai and the rest of those few who really mattered in the Hashemite Kingdom. The correspondent, Uzi Mahanaymi, reported that a technical agreement had been signed involving various spheres, including joint economic projects in the Arava area and the development and use of the port of Haifa to facilitate Jordanian exports. What was peculiar and particularly interesting is that Mahanaymi's source did not come from the usual suspects in the Israeli governmental establishment, but rather from Jordanian sources in London. Mahanaymi's report included materials suitable for a novel of international intrigue and high finance. It went as follows:

> Our correspondent notes the agreement, which, as mentioned, was learned about from sources close to the Jordanian Prime Minister, Zaid ar-Rifai, was also confirmed by Saudi millionaire Adnan Kashoggi's secretary, who was a party to the secret. According to the secretary, the talks on this matter began in late 1985 during a meeting held at the Regency Hotel in New York between Adnan Kashoggi and Shimon Peres, with the participation of Avraham Tamir. The secretary, who was present at the meeting, recalled Shimon Peres conveyed to Kashoggi his proposals for Jordanian–Israeli cooperation. The proposals included a far-reaching plan for vast economic cooperation between Israel and Jordan which, if implemented, would lead to greater cooperation between the two nations and to economic prosperity.[72]

If we recall the condominium discussions of late 1985, this account has the ring of authenticity.

The rest of the dispatch also rang true, and raised familiar old problems. Mahanaymi went on:

> The Jordanian sources in London stressed that the technical agreement reached is conditional upon Israel's willingness to progress toward a peace agreement with Jordan and the Palestinians. To this end, the Jordanians suggest Israel meet with Colonel Abu al-Zaim ('Atallah 'Atallah), Jordan's substitute for 'Arafat, to get to know him and reach some arrangement with him.[73]

Later in the day, two other journalists from *al-Hamishmar* harried Peres in advance of a trip to Europe, trying to pry more information from him in a live telephone interview on

IDF radio. The exchange was fascinating as an example of raw politics and also of the timeless nature of relations between the press and politicians.

Mikha Friedman: Good morning to you, Mr Peres. Did you have time this morning to read *Al-Hamishmar*?

Peres: No.

Friedman: The paper's headline states that one of your envoys recently visited Jordan and worked out a technical agreement on cooperation which includes, among other things, joint projects in the 'Arava and the opening of Haifa to Jordan's exports. Is there any similarity between what the paper reports and what you know?

Peres: If you will it, it is not a dream, but for the time being it is only a dream . . .[74]

Friedman: Mr Peres, King Hussein is still in Europe, and people will probably once more try to find a time period that has not been accounted for in your schedule to get the two of you together.

Peres: There is no reason for me to try to do so. Europe is large enough to hold both of us, and so we need not meet at any given moment.

Friedman: So, is your timetable so full and busy that there is not a single moment for an unscheduled meeting?

Ilana Dayan: Not even for a joint ski session with the King in Austria?

Peres: I am not taking a ski trip. If I have time for vacation, I like to spend it in Israel.[75]

That was not the end of matters. The next day, Mahanaymi reported that Peres's special envoy to Jordan was none other than Al Schwimmer. Again, the source of the information was Jordanian contacts in London.[76]

On these sources, themselves a story quite apart from any technical arrangements, *Ma'ariv*, an important and prestigious Israeli daily, ran a separate item on 22 January. Shefi Gabay reported that

Jordanian–Israeli meetings did indeed take place last year between figures at different levels. Egypt, however, objects to these direct meetings, and voiced its opposition to

Jordan's King Husayn. This was stated to *Ma'ariv* last night by people close to the Royal Court in Amman, in reaction to the recent reports on Israeli–Jordanian meetings.[77]

Gabay went on to repeat Jordan's version of its argument with the Egyptians, whether true or not is hard to know but almost beside the point in this context, but ended by reporting that the Jordanians told the Egyptians as follows:

> According to the sources, the Jordanian Royal Court has made it clear (to the Egyptians) that it is a part of very old Hashemite policy to occasionally hold clarification meetings with the Israeli leadership. This policy was implemented even at the time of King 'Abdallah, King Husayn's grandfather.[78]

To say such things to Israeli journalists, knowing that they will be published in print, and quite likely picked up by the radio and broadcast throughout the entire region, was a remarkable departure from Hashemite traditions on such matters, far more bold even than committing private agreements to paper.

Throughout the first three months of 1987, Israeli–Jordanian understandings seem to have reached a new level of complexity and stability. Nor were they shorn of associated political expectations, at least on the Israeli side, of what such cooperation could accomplish. A momentum was maintained and it arguably helped lead to the famed London Agreement between Peres and Hussein of April 1987. Mr Peres and the King agreed on new and specific ground rules for an international conference and what might be termed, borrowing a term from the Camp David accord, modalities for pursuing a settlement. Details of the agreement were, as usual, leaked by the press in Israel, so we know its scope. It was impressive. Its final part, part C, meant to be kept secret, contained in its seventh and final section the referent to functional questions in the phraseology, "other issues will be resolved through mutual agreement between Jordan and Israel."[79] The continued importance, at least in the Israeli view of things, of functional matters was stressed by Shimon

Peres himself. He said in June 1987 that bilateral talks with Jordan at an international conference would focus at first on joint economic projects, such as the digging of a canal to connect the Dead Sea with the Red Sea, that is, the old *Jordanian* plan for the region. "We don't have to start at the territorial end," Peres said.[80]

ENTER THE INTIFADA

But before either Israel or Jordan could deliver enough of a constituency to proceed further—for Hussein the West Bankers and, perhaps, part of the PLO, for Peres, the other half of the Israeli government—the *intifada* derailed the whole exquisite plan. This is not to say that it would have worked had it not been for the *intifada*. In retrospect a good deal of what Mr Peres was saying about Jordan was neatly packaged wishful thinking, partly illusion, partly political currency for voters who preferred to believe such things. Still, before turning to the *intifada* and what it has wrought, it is worth reflecting on the legacy of the 1984–87 period.

Between 1984 and 1987 the functional approach to bolstering diplomacy both worked and did not work. On the one hand, by most objective measures, Jordan's position was growing stronger with Israeli help. Jordan's key constituency in the West Bank and Gaza was aided. But in the hearts and minds of most Palestinians in the West Bank, the King was growing less and less present. It was as if the King was paying his dues at the kissing booth, but not getting kissed.

This could not go on forever. Even as Hussein and the Israeli Labor Party plotted the great breakthrough, and decorated it with a deliberate and vast increase in functional cooperation on many levels, *now consciously elevated as an instrument of political change*, the flow of social power in the territories gradually passed away from the King's men into the hands of those who acted independently but in the name of the PLO. Thus the irony was that when the vaunted Third Force arrived with the *intifada*, it was neither pro-Jordanian nor was it controlled by the PLO.

The *intifada*, whatever else it did, made a mess of much of the tacit cooperation built up between Israel and Jordan in the territories. It certainly dispelled illusions that functional linkages alone could serve as a way to produce or sustain a diplomatic breakthrough.

Yet even the *intifada's* character has been influenced by the multiplicity of functional ties in the region, particularly the economic ones. Certainly Jordan's effort to limit the extent of the *intifada* by limiting the West Bank's economic resources is an example of how Jordanian and Israeli interests still coincide to some degree. It is to these matters that we now turn our attention.

Notes

1. Interviews and conversations in Moscow, November 1986.
2. Recent Soviet policy on this question is quite clear, and since 1987–88 they do not hide it from the Arabs. See "PLO Sources on U.S.–USSR Mideast Talks," Kuwait, KUNA, in FBIS–NE, 6 October 1988, p. 3.
3. See Moshe Zak, "Israeli–Jordanian Negotiations," *Washington Quarterly*, Winter 1985.
4. Moshe Zak, "The Quiet Diplomacy with Hussein," *Ma'ariv*, 29 April 1986.
5. For fuller flavor of Sharon's "Jordan Is Palestine" notion, see Daniel Pipes and Adam Garfinkle, "Is Jordan Palestine?" *Commentary*, October 1988.
6. See Meron Benvenisti, *The West Bank Data Project* (Washington: American Enterprise Institute, 1984), p. 5.
7. See "Shamir Calls on Husayn To Meet 'Face to Face'," FBIS–NE, 9 January 1987, p. 12.
8. Yossi Melman and Dan Raviv, *Behind the Uprising* (Westport, Conn,: Greenwood Press, 1989) p. 192.
9. This is detailed in my "Sources of the al-Fatah Mutiny," *Orbis*, Fall 1983.
10. Here see the details in Asher Susser, "Jordan," *Middle East Contemporary Survey (MECS)* Volume 7, 1982–83, pp. 642–3.
11. For details and sources, see Susser, "Jordan," *MECS*, Vol. 8, 1983–84, pp. 520–22.
12. In the historical shadow, always, is the traumatic episode of

19–23 September 1970, when the steadfastness of the United States in Jordan's hour of need left much to be desired, appearances to the contrary notwithstanding. See my "U.S. Decision-Making in the Jordan Crisis of 1970," *Political Science Quarterly*, Spring 1985.

13. See James MacManus, "Reagan Letter Fueled Hussein's Attack," *Washington Post*, 16 March 1984, p. 16. See also "Interview: H.M. King Hussein," *Defense & Diplomacy*, June 1984, p. 19.

14. Michael Bar-Zohar, "'Life Insurance' for Hussein," *The Jerusalem Post*, 2 June 1990, p. 11.

15. Ibid., p. 11. Melman and Raviv (*Behind the Uprising*) refer instead to a "think tank" assembled under Tamir, p. 191. These were the same groups.

16. Personal knowledge. The author is acquainted with Novik, Haig and Sicherman.

17. Zak, "The Quiet Diplomacy," mentions these points, too.

18. See Samuel Lewis, "Israel: The Peres Era and Its Legacy," *Foreign Affairs*, America and the World 1986, especially pp. 599–600.

19. See *Foreign Assistance Legislation for Fiscal Years 1988–89 (Part 2)* Hearing before the Subcommittee on Arms Control, International Security and Science of the Committee on Foreign Affairs, US House of Representatives, One Hundredth Congress, First Session, Overview of Security Supporting Assistance Programs, 3 March 1987 (Washington: USGPO, 1987), p. 87.

20. Faruq Shukri, "PLO Deposits Funds for West Bank Salaries," Manama, WAKH, in FBIS–NE, 3 October 1988, p. 5.

21. I make this case in "'Common Sense' About Middle East Diplomacy: Implications for U.S. Policy in the Near Term," *Middle East Review*, Winter 1984–85, reprinted in Michael Curtis (ed.), *The Middle East Reader* (New Brunswick: Transaction Press, 1986).

22. See Shaul Ramati, "Huseein's Plan," *The Jerusalem Post*, 10 January 1987; and also "Gaza Notables Allowed to Leave for Jordan," FBIS–NE, 9 September 1985, p. 19; and "Gaza Attorney Allowed to Depart," Jerusalem Domestic Service, FBIS–NE, 24 July 1985, p. 14. And see especially Pinhas Inbari, "Turning Off the Royal Faucets," *Al-Hamishmar*, 24 November 1985, p. 6.

23. "Energy Minister Confirms Jordan Electricity Plan," Jerusalem Domestic Service, FBIS–NE, 1 November 1985, p. 15;

"Shahal on Supply of Power to West Bank by Jordan," IDF Radio, FBIS–NE, 4 November 1985, p. 15; and Yisrael Tomer, "Israel, Jordan Negotiating Link of Electricity Grids," *Yedi'ot Aharonot*, 31 October 1985, pp. 1, 4 also in FBIS–NE, 31 October 1985, p. 14.

24. This is a very complicated issue, involving too many factors to cover here in detail. But see Dani Rubinstein, "Jordan to Help Finance Arab Electric Corporation," *Davar*, 15 December 1985, p. 6, in FBIS–NE, 18 December 1985, p. 16. For more background, see "Jordan Sets Terms to Save Jerusalem Electricity Company," *The Jerusalem Post*, 25 February 1986, pp. 1–2; and Roy Iskowitz, "Arab Electricity Company Urged to Pay 11 Million Dollar Debt," *The Jerusalem Post*, 26 February 1986.

25. Andrew Whitely, "Israel, Jordan in Secret Talks on Water Row," *Financial Times*, 15 December 1986.

26. "Israel, Jordan Cooperate in Al-Yarmuk River Project," Jerusalem Domestic Service, FBIS–NE, 3 December 1985, p. 16. For background, that makes Israel out to look maximally evil, see Thomas Stauffer, "Tightening the Squeeze on Jordan's Water," *Middle East International*, 20 April 1984, pp. 12–13. See, too, his "Arab Waters in Israeli Calculations: The Benefits of War and the Costs of Peace," in Abdul Majid Farid and Hussein Sirriyeh (eds), *Israel and Arab Water: An International Symposium* (Ithaca, Ithaca Press, 1985). Here Stauffer argues that Israel's invasion of Lebanon was motivated primarily by the desire to seize and divert the Litani River into Israel. He argues further that Israel has gone to war and will go to war again for water, and that because of water it cannot afford and does not wish to make peace. Few serious analysts accept such conclusions.

27. Rejected were Nabil Sha'ath, one of Arafat's aides, and Sheik Sayah, President of the Palestinian National Council. Sha'ath had been arrested by Israel in southern Lebanon at one point for terrorist activity and so was disqualified. Sayah, an old man, was disqualified just because of his title. Peres later said: "He is a senile old man. We were stupid enough to say no." Michael Bar-Zohar, "The Crumbling of the Jordanian Option," *The Jerusalem Post*, 9 June 1990, p. 10.

28. See "Plan in Tamir 'Working Paper'," IDF Radio, FBIS–NE, 1 November 1985, p. 15.

29. This was leaked lavishly, and apparently accurately, in the Israeli media in late October and November of 1985. See Ilan

Kfir, "PM Office's 'Top Secret' Peace Plan Detailed," *Hadashot*, 25 October 1985, p. 1; Yehuda Litani and Aqiva Eldar, "Joint Control With Jordan Over West Bank Planned," *Haaretz*, 29 October 1985, p. 11; Pinhas Inbari, "'Source' Reports Details of Husayn–Peres Contacts," *Al-Hamishmar*, 30 October 1985, p. 2; Dalya Shehori, "'Source' Confirms Discussion of West Bank Self-Rule," *Al-Hamishmar*, 31 October 1985; "More on Peres–Husayn 'Joint Rule' Document; Tehiya Discloses Details," Jerusalem Television Service, FBIS–NE, 1 November 1985.

30. I was told privately as early as May 1981 by Jordanian Foreign Ministry officials that the hoisting of the Jordanian flag near the Dome of the Rock, and other such modest symbolic gestures, could well satisfy Jordanian interests insofar as Jerusalem was concerned.

31. See Leopold Yehuda Laufer, *Western Europe and the Palestinians: The Socio-Economic Dimension* (Jerusalem: Leonard Davis Institute, Policy Study 39, May 1990), pp. 30–34.

32. Here see Adam Garfinkle, *Western Europe's Middle East Diplomacy and the United States* (Philadelphia: Foreign Policy Research Institute, 1982).

33. Bar-Zohar, "The Crumbling . . .," p. 10.

34. The King's July demarche to the PLO was probably quickened by Israeli concerns, voiced in public and in private, about the nature of al-Wazir's activities in Amman. See "Sharon on Attacking Terrorist HQ in Jordan," *The Jerusalem Post*, 30 July 1985, pp. 1–2; "Concern Evinced About PLO Entrenchment in Jordan," Tel-Aviv, IDF Radio, 31 July 1985, FBIS–NE, 1 August 1985, p. 12; and "Bar-Lev: Jordan Asked to Remove PLO Bases," Jerusalem Domestic Service, FBIS–NE, 8 August 1985, p. 13.

35. Bar-Zohar, "'Life Insurance' . . .", p. 11.

36. Bar-Zohar, "The Crumbling . . .," p. 10.

37. See Pinhas Inbari quoted in Daniel Pipes, "The Unacknowledged Partnership," *The National Interest*, No. 10, Winter 1987/88, pp. 96–7.

38. Ramati, "Hussein's Plan."

39. The occasion of Italian Defense Minister Giovanni Spadolini's visit to Israel was occasion for some juicy leaks. See "View Jordanian Cooperation," Jerusalem Domestic Service, FBIS–NE, 23 January 1987, p. 12.

40. See Ilan Kfir, "Peres Renews 'Secret' Contacts with Husayn," *Hadashot*, 25 April 1986, p. 2. The fact that this only made

page two, and that the word secret was in quotations, indicates how unsurprising this sort of news had come to be in Israel.

41. Pipes, "The Unacknowledged Partnership," p. 97.

42. "Crossing Into, From Jordan on Same Day Permitted," Jerusalem Domestic Service, FBIS–NE, 19 June 1986, p. 12; and see "The Bridges of Misery," *Al-Quds*, 19 June 1986, pp. 1,7 in FBIS–NE, 26 June 1986, p. 15.

43. Barbara Rosewicz and Gerald F. Seib, "Aside from Being a Movement, the PLO Is a Financial Giant," *Wall Street Journal*, 21 July 1986.

44. See "Deported Arab Editor Blames 'Jordan factor'," *The Jerusalem Post*, 10 January 1987.

45. See Joel Greenberg, "Jordan Pledges Aid for Palestinian-Led W. Bank Towns," *The Jerusalem Post*, 1 July 1986, p. 2.

46. Uri Nur, "Jordan to Empower Passport Officials in West Bank," *Haaretz*, 23 July 1986; and "W. Bank Mayors' Documents Not 'Recognized'," WAKH; Manama, FBIS–NE, 11 August 1986, p. F2; Pinhas Inbari, "Jordan Recognizes Action Against Arab Mayors," *Al-Hamishmar*, 10 August 1986, p. 3.

47. See "Marwan Dudin Receives Three West Bank Officials," Amman Domestic Service, FBIS–NE, 11 August 1986, p. F2; "Village Leagues Call for Speeding Up Peace Talks," *Haaretz*, 4 November 1985, p. 3; "Dudin Meets Nablus Deputy, UNRWA Official," Amman Domestic Service, FBIS–NE, 5 August 1986, p. F6.

48. Ramati, "Hussein's Plan," and Oded Granot and Sari Robert, "Jordan Plans Development Program for Territories," *Ma'ariv*, 25 June 1986, p. 5; Joel Greenberg and Yehuda Litani, "Jordanian Program for Territories Outlined," *The Jerusalem Post*, 21 July 1986, pp. 1,8; "Prime Minister Al-Rifa'i on West Bank Measures" Paris Radio Monte Carlo, FBIS–NE, 3 October 1986, p. F3; and see, too, Pinhas Inbari, "W. Bank Plan Meant to Reinforce Jordan's Status," *Al-Hamishmar*, 24 January 1986, pp. 1–2.

49. Dani Rubinstein, "Rabin: Jordan Asked to Lift Export Restrictions," *Davar*, 25 December 1985, p. 2 also in FBIS–NE, 26 December 1986, p. 14.

50. Ramati; and Yoel Greenberg, "Rabin Welcomes FRG–Jordanian Aid to Territories," *The Jerusalem Post*, 20 July 1986, p. 2.

51. Pipes, "The Unacknowledged Partnership," p. 97.

52. Pinhas Inbari, "Jordan Transfers Aid Money to West Bank,"

Al-Hamishmar, 11 November 1986, p. 3 also in FBIS–NE, 13
November 1986, p. 13. And see, from the Jordanian media,
"Agricultural Project To Be Financed in W. Bank," Amman
Domestic Service, FBIS–NE, 7 July 1986, p. F4.

53. "Muslim Pilgrimage Discussed with Jordanians," Jerusalem
Domestic Service, FBIS–NE, 23 July 1986, p. 18; David
Rudge, "Israeli Arabs Leave for Mecca Pilgrimage," *The
Jerusalem Post*, 28 July 1986, p. 2. This cooperation persists
even today, the main problem now being the reluctance of
Saudi officials to accept many West Bank Muslims for fear of
what they might do in Mecca. Jordan acts as the go between
between Riyadh and Jerusalem. See "Saudis Restrict Hajj
Pilgrims from Territories," Jerusalem Domestic Service, in
FBIS–NE, 1 July 1988, p. 21, and "Muslims Depart for
Mecca; Some Turned Back," Jerusalem Domestic Service, 25
June 1989, in FBIS–NE, 27 June 1989, p. 19.

54. Aqiva Eldar and Reuven Pedatzur, "Jordan Regrets Incident,"
Ha'aretz, 30 January 1986, pp. 1, 3; "Rabin: Terrorism
Reduced by Jordanian Restrictions," Jerusalem Domestic
Service, in FBIS–NE, 25 July 1986, p. 18; and Yosef Walter,
"Minister Rabin Outlines West Bank Policy," *Ma'ariv*, 29
September 1986, pp. 1, 9.

55. See Shefi Gabai," Jordanian Airlines Company is Interested in
Reopening its Office in Judea and Samaria and Jerusalem,"
Ma'ariv, 12 November 1986, p. 4; and "Airline Official on
Reopening W. Bank Offices," Amman Domestic Service,
FBIS–NE, 24 December 1986, p. F1.

56. See Avraham Tzohar, "Jordan Agriculture Delegation Visits
West Bank," *Haaretz*, 10 November 1985, p. 1.

57. "Approval for Bank in Territories Announced," Jerusalem
Domestic Service, FBIS–NE, 18 June 1985, p. 14.

58. "Cairo–Amman Bank to Open West Bank Branches," *An-
Nahar*, in FBIS–NE, 18 November 1986, p. 14.

59. Melman and Raviv, *Behind the Uprising*, pp. 196–97.

60. "Jordan Prepared to Open University in West Bank,"
Hatzofeh, 25 January 1987.

61. "House Elects Four West Bank Representatives," Amman
Domestic Service, FBIS–NE, 25 November 1985, p. F1; and
"Peres Proposes W. Bank Vote for Jordanian Parliament,"
Jerusalem Domestic Service, FBIS–NE, 5 August 1986, p. 13.

62. Melman and Raviv, *Behind the Uprising*, pp. 197–98.

63. "Sharon Criticizes 'Jordanianization' of West Bank," Jerusalem Domestic Service, FBIS–NE, 13 January 1987, p. 14.

64. "Jordan Okays Bank Plan for Territories," *The Jerusalem Post*, 13 January 1986. For more detail see Avinoam Bar-Yosef, "Announcement Expected on Palestinian Bank Opening," *Ma'ariv*, 27 August 1986, p. 4.
65. "Jordan Agrees on Free Market Near Jericho," *Al-Tali'ah*, FBIS–NE, 16 January 1987, p. 13.
66. See "Peres Reveals Secret Diplomacy with Jordan," Hong Kong AFP, FBIS–NE, 28 April 1986, p. 11.
67. FBIS–NE, 20 November 1986, p. 11.
68. FBIS–NE, 10 December 1986, p. 13.
69. Yehuda Litani, "Husayn's Fractured Image," *The Jerusalem Post*, May 2, 1986, p. 18.
70. Interview, Ephraim Sneh.
71. See Uzi Mahanaymi, "'Technical' Agreement Signed with Jordan," *Al-Hamishmar*, 21 January 1987.
72. Ibid.
73. Ibid.
74. This phrase in Hebrew (Eim tirtzu, ain zu agadah) is a famous aphorism spoken by Theodor Herzl, the most important Zionist founder. It refers to the dream of an independent Jewish state, which obviously came to pass. It is in that context that Peres's response takes its meaning and finds its wit.
75. "Peres Denies Agreement," IDF Radio, FBIS–NE, 21 January 1987, p. 11.
76. "Sources Name Schwimmer Envoy," *Al-Hamishmar*, 22 January 1987, p. 1.
77. Shefi Gabay, "Jordanian Sources Confirm Meetings With Israel," *Ma'ariv*, 22 January 1987, p. 9.
78. Ibid.
79. *Ma'ariv* published the text of the London Agreement on 1 January 1988. See FBIS–NE, 4 January 1988. As if it mattered after this, Avraham Tamir later confirmed that the talks had taken place. See Wolf Blitzer, "Tamir Confirms Peres–Husayn Talks in 1987," *The Jerusalem Post*, 1 September 1988, p. 1.
80. Menachem Shalev, "Peres Seeks Guarantees," *The Jerusalem Post*, 13 June 1987, p. 3.

4 The *Intifada* and Jordan's Crisis

"The future is the obsolete in reverse."—*Vladimir Nabakov*

Almost from the moment it broke out in December 1987, the Palestinian *intifada* represented a war within a war. It constituted a social revolution within Palestinian society as well as a protest against Israeli occupation. As such the biggest losers in the entire ordeal have been the West Bank notables who dominated politics and economic power in the region for most of the last three centuries.[1] Palestinians from the refugee camps and the lowest and younger strata of society—more than a few enraptured with fundamentalist Islam—became the heroes of the uprising in short order, and remained so for more than three years. At first it is not unlikely that King Hussein regarded them in rather the same light as his grandfather regarded the Palestinian activists of the 1930s, as noted in chapter 1. By the end of 1990, however, if not earlier, the King must have feared that the power of the old élite was shattered beyond repair.

Because the nobility was brought down by the *intifada*, so was Hussein. And because Hussein tumbled, so did the hopes for any form of a Jordanian Option as classically construed, entertained as the least unpalatable option both by the Israeli Labor Party and the United States Government.

Does this mean that the *intifada* proved that functional contacts and below-the-line-of-sight pragmatic arrangements are insignificant compared with the power of high politics or social trends? Maybe, maybe not.

Jordan's reduced position is not total defeat, at least not yet. More important, as noted above, even some of the characteristics of the *intifada* and the Israeli response to it take their shape from the pervasiveness of functional, especially economic, ties. For example, one possible reason, although probably not the main one, that Israel declined to use massive force to stop the uprising concerns the large number of Arabs from the territories who daily go to work in Israel. Despite the huge number of Arab workers, terrorist incidents caused by these workers have been very rare, even though the opportunity for them to cause havoc inside Israel if they really wanted to is almost infinite. Firing into crowds, it was feared, might turn such possibilities into realities.[2]

It works the other way, too. Young members of the *shebab*, forcing established merchants to close their shops and stopping construction workers from travelling to their jobs in Israel, often ran off to *their* jobs as waiters or day laborers thereafter. Strikes or no strikes, money circulated, wages were earned. After all, even revolutionaries have to eat. One can only imagine what these young Palestinian radicals would do with what many have said they want—an independent state in the West Bank, economically sealed off from Israel—other than starve to death.

The pervasiveness of functional linkages was and remains such that, after about a year of flailing about searching for a solution, the Israeli authorities sought to fight the uprising by starving it to death financially. This involved, primarily, limiting the amount of money that could be brought across the bridges, restricting bridge traffic, restricting imports and exports, collecting taxes and license fees, and using more intrusive intelligence measures.

Thus Israeli–Jordanian links were not entirely cut asunder by the *intifada*, or even by Jordan's supposed cutting of ties to the West Bank in July 1988. Things are not that simple, and a closer look at the King's dramatic moves of late July and August 1988 shows why.

JORDAN AND THE "OTHER" ARAB REVOLT, REDUX

One possible explanation for some of the instruments that the King chose to deal with the *intifada* relate directly to money. It was not only the Israelis who put the financial squeeze on the *intifada*; what Hashemite Jordan did after July 1988 reinforced the economic squeeze as well. In other words, Jordanian and Israeli interests with respect to the *intifada* were compatible at least to the extent that both endeavored to limit it by starving it of money.

The Jordanian government limited the amount of money that could be brought in to the West Bank, it curtailed bridge traffic, and it stopped paying most civil service salaries knowing that the PLO and the Arab states, even if they had the money, did not control the conduits to get it into the West Bank. They imposed strict quotas on citrus, olive oil and other commodities for which Jordan is traditionally the largest market.[3] Even though this aspect of Jordanian strategy was entirely missed by the US press, West Bank Palestinians certainly had their suspicions of what the King intended.[4] Indeed some Israeli observers believe that had Israel earlier found a way to put down the *intifada*, and thus limit the incubation period for Palestinian radicalism on the east bank, the King might never have declared the great "divorce" between the two banks.

But there was more to the King's move than that. What did King Hussein really intend by his dramatic severing of the Hashemite Kingdom from the troubles of the West Bank and Gaza? Did he mean what he said—that the PLO could have sole responsibility for the occupied territories, that Jordan's role there was ended, that it claimed no sovereignty over an area it had ruled for 18 years? Or, in the sometimes curious manner of Arab statecraft, did he mean just the opposite? The answer is: some of both.

King Hussein can never ignore developments in Palestinian politics any more than Yasir Arafat can ignore Jordan. Jordan is largely Palestinian in every way except politically; Arafat knows there are more Palestinians in Jordan than anywhere else in the world. This is why what happens on one side of the river must influence what happens on the other.

All this has a history too. As noted in chapter 1, radical Palestinian nationalism, from the days of the Mufti of Jerusalem half a century ago, has always been a threat to Hashemite rule, blocking their ambitions west of Jordan and often claiming its territory to the east. The Hashemite kings have resolutely opposed an independent Palestinian state and twice used force to prevent one or a base for one, once on the western side of the river in 1948, and once on the eastern side in the civil war of 1970.[5] Since then Jordan has competed with the PLO for the loyalty of West Bank Palestinians in order to prevent the PLO from attaining a state there.

In this, nothing essential changed after July 1988: Jordanian interests in the future of the West Bank are no more gone than a tree that sheds its leaves in winter is dead. A total severance of Jordan's links to the West Bank has always been out of the question. Jordan's formal severing was accompanied by some real severing, but in other respects basic relationships persisted or were put into escrow. True, most Jordanian salaries to West Bank public servants stopped. They could always be renewed, and some reportedly were resumed in the form of official accounts opened in Amman, which could only be accessed by West Bankers by jumping through one of a number of Jordanian administrative hoops in the territories, either a religious court or a chamber of commerce.[6]

Beyond that, most attempts at PLO substitutions for Jordanian money had to use the Jordanian-controlled banking system. It was harder for West Bankers to spend large amounts of time in the east bank, and harder for West Bankers to go to school at east bank universities. Many dozens of charitable societies and professional associations on the east bank have cut their formal associations with West Bank affiliates. The Jordanians changed their map; it no longer included the West Bank.[7] Produce coming across the bridges was taxed and controlled at a different level, as noted above in chapter 2, as if the goods were simply foreign imports. East bank Palestinians were issued green cards, spelling out their privileges in Jordan; this was the first time in a very long time such a thing had been done, and some establishment Palestinians in Jordan who were loyal to the King worried about the implications. Indeed a few dissenters within Jordan lost their jobs at the outset of this period, including editors of some prominent newspapers, and an influential member of the Jordanian Senate—Abdel Meguid Shorman—was relieved of his position. West Bank Palestinians with their yellow cards were entitled to qualitatively less service from the government.[8] They did not exactly become non-Jordanian citizens, but they were clearly thrust into a limbo designed to generate just the right amount of discomfort and re-thinking about loyalty to Jordan.

But, on the other hand, the bridges across the Jordan remained open, trade continued under selective impediments, the banks and courts still worked, and Jordan's currency, passports and professional licenses remained valid, albeit in adumbrated form with respect to passports, which became two-year travel documents instead of passports. Some development funds never stopped flowing. Jordan stressed early on that the Cairo–Amman bank branches would remain open, and it went forward as well with the opening of an additional branch of the Cairo–Amman Bank in Gaza.[9] In December 1988, some Jordanian pre-disengagement functions resumed quietly.[10] In June 1989 Jordan prepared to hold the general secondary school certificate examination for West Bank students and, in the fall, these were indeed held, albeit under strained conditions.[11] Besides, if the King had been looking for a real and final "divorce" from the West Bank at the time, he could have abrogated the 1950 "union" agreement which is the legal basis in the Jordanian context for the Jordanian claim to the West Bank. He could have reorganized the parliament and changed the constitution governing it instead of merely delaying new elections. He could have formally suspended West Bankers' Jordanian citizenship. He did none of these things at the time, and only the constitutional reorganization—which is both theoretically and practically reversible—has been done since.

IS THERE STILL A JORDANIAN OPTION?

As of August and September 1988, one could have seen the Jordanian Option glass as either half empty or half full. Those for whom the idea was either too heady (the Israeli right) or not heady enough (the far left) were quick to cite Hussein's pronouncements as proof that Shimon Peres was a man without an idea. Naturally Peres saw things differently. The day after Jordan announced the end of the development plan, but before the 31 July speech, Peres lectured a newspaper reporter as follows:

> All residents of Judea and Samaria have Jordanian passports. When these are taken away, then there will be no more Jordanian option. The open bridges on the Jordan River are the central economic factor. If the situation changes, they will be closed.[12]

Even many months later—indeed by the end of 1990—things were not much clearer. Did West Bankers still have Jordanian passports? Yes and no. Were the bridges open? Yes, but not quite as wide open as before. Was the King interested in a diplomatic process? He seemed distant, but every so often reports trickled out that left another impression. In March 1990, for example, *al-Quds* reported that Egypt and Jordan had agreed that if a Palestinian–Israeli meeting convened in Cairo, under US auspices, a Jordanian "observer" would participate in the talks.[13]

So, Mr Peres's hopes for a Jordanian connection to peace were not shown to be wrong. Up through the Kuwait crisis, which began on 2 August 1990, a close look revealed that most of the King's specific tactics, symbols, and timing turned necessities into advantages. He ended a $1.3 billion development fund for the West Bank in 1988, but he did not have the money then anyway and he has had even less since. He dissolved the lower house of Jordan's parliament, but it had only reopened in 1984 and parliament was, until after the November 1989 elections, only a rubber stamp for the royal autocracy. And he stepped back from the US Shultz "peace initiative" of 1988, but no initiative could have moved forward before the US and the Israeli elections in November 1988 anyway.

The only serious, probably unanticipated, consequence of Jordan's move was the plummeting value of the Jordanian dinar, which occurred only partially because of changes concerning the West Bank. West Bankers feared that the currency might not long be legal tender, and tried to dump it for dollars and even Israeli shekels.[14] But the main reason for the dinar's difficulties had to do with Jordan's own financial and balance of trade problems.

But something has changed since the summer of 1988. For Hussein to have survived on his throne for 38 years, Jordan has had to identify rhetorically with Palestinian aspirations in order to win allies among them and thus stabilize life in the Kingdom. The regime's reaction to the outpouring of Palestinian support for Saddam Hussein in the Kuwait crisis is a case in point. And, as noted in chapter 1, even while the King simultaneously managed regime security and built a quiet, pragmatic relationship with Israel, he also sought to integrate Palestinians into the mainstream of Jordanian society, giving them a stake in the prosperity and future of the country. It was not easy, but the process worked well enough, at least through 1990. Otherwise Hussein could not have done what he did in the summer of 1988 without shattering the country's domestic peace. This is what was new: Hussein could shout out loud, right in the midst of the *intifada*, that "Jordan is not Palestine," that it had a separate, prior agenda of its own, and while many Palestinians on the east bank did not like it, there was not much that they could or really wanted to do about it. At that time, the King worried far more about the implications of being associated too closely with the mayhem on the West Bank rather than being not closely associated enough. This represented a real change, made possible in part by the increasing sophistication of east bankers whose rising talents have made Palestinians less needed than they once were to run the country.[15] In this sense Jordan has separated itself from the torments of the Palestinian issue, but hardly in full. At the same time, as the riots in the south of Jordan in April 1989 showed, the east bank constituency that the King more or less took for granted in the past now has a new trans-tribal identity that will never again be as quiescent as before.

The enhanced internal stability of Jordan, at least as far as Palestinians were concerned, though far from perfect, allowed King Hussein new tactics in the old struggle with radical Palestinian nationalism. Hussein intended by his formal severing of the West Bank from Jordan to force the PLO to a decision. And the Jordanian press made the most of its opportunity: it attacked the PLO relentlessly. For example, Raja'i al-Dajani, Jordan's Interior Minister, attacked the PLO in the Jordanian daily *Al-Ra'y*.

First, al-Dajani restated old Arab propaganda positions that, seemingly, had been left behind in Hussein's 31 July speech when the King said that Jordan was not Palestine.

> We are a natural demographic and geographic extension of the West Bank, and they are an extension of us. We are one nation and one people. We do not allow anyone to bargain over us . . . We are one people regardless of what is said. His Majesty King Husayn stressed this and was careful to highlight it.[16]

Next, al-Dajani baited the PLO by questioning its judgment in a most annoying way, by disclaiming any conflict of interest between Jordan and the PLO, and then mentioning the "United Kingdom" plan which, to the PLO, was short-hand for Jordanian domination over them. "The PLO's problem," he said,

> is that they have a complex that Jordan is competing with them . . . Jordan is not competing with the PLO over the West Bank, and we have no designs on or interests in the West Bank. It is in our interests that the Palestinian Arab people return, and that the Palestinian land be returned to the Arab nation and Arab order. When this happens, we will congratulate you. Yasir 'Arafat had a complex that this talk was untrue and that we wanted to cheat him and go to the international conference. Is it possible that Jordan, going to the international conference with such international legitimacy, should come away empty-handed? Naturally, for us this was out of the question, and there are many clear Jordanian approaches, one of which is the United Arab Kingdom plan.[17]

Nor was al-Dajani finished. As if to address the PLO directly, he said:

> When you come and boast that you will pay their salaries, you mean that you will replace Jordan, which abandoned

them. I can say that this is naive talk that shows lack of knowledge of the reality of things. I say and challenge that no one in the Arab world knows this and the nature of affairs in the occupied territories as Jordan does. There have been 40 years of merger in this homeland in this part of the Arab world . . . O Yasir 'Arafat . . . you want to pay the salaries that we used to pay as an assistance to the employees that receive their salaries from Israel; that is, you want to share power with Israel? Helping this people is considered by the PLO as power sharing. I want to know what they will call the new reality, when Israel and the PLO pay salaries and assistance. Will they call it sharing power with Israel or assistance? Here, things will become clear, and we will see what will happen to the names and headlines that were given as part of the campaign against Jordan—power sharing, relations of annexation, relations of subordination.[18]

So, Jordan is not Palestine, but it is. Jordan says it does not compete with PLO, but it does. Jordan leaves the West Bank to the PLO, but it does not. Even the basic question, as to whether Jordan will or will not negotiate over the West Bank is not nearly so clear as some Western observers have assumed. One must read these statements carefully. King Hussein has put it very cleverly, and more than once: he will not negotiate over the West Bank, not unless the Palestinians ask him to do so. But all Palestinians, or just some Palestinians? If some, how many, and which ones? Clearly this is a formula that allows a reassertion of the Hashemite voice in the West Bank under any number of circumstances.

As can be inferred from the above passages, the PLO was in a bind. Hussein put it there, and there it remained despite the November 1988 Algiers PNC, the actual agenda of which was established as much by the Unified Leadership of the Uprising and by the King of Jordan as by the PLO. The Jordanians repeated over and over that they did what they did because this is what the PLO had been asking them to do for years. It is as if they had read *Faust* and applied its wisdom to the PLO: beware of what you wish for in youth, for you will get it in middle age. The PLO suddenly "got" what it claimed it had always wanted, and because of that, it had some very difficult decisions to make as of the end of 1988.

If the PLO had chosen to "accept" the West Bank only more effectively to terrorize Israel, the residents of the territories would have suffered most and the PLO would certainly have failed. It would then have been clear to all that the only way to end the occupation was through Jordan, and the King might well have been begged, at least in private, to revive his connections to the territories. But if the PLO genuinely decided to moderate its extreme demands in hopes of a lasting political compromise with Israel, Jordan would win too. The PLO would then for the first time have accepted the residents of the West Bank and Gaza as its core constituency instead of Palestinians in Lebanon and elsewhere who yearn, not for the occupied territories, but for Israel itself. If the PLO were to opt for genuine political compromise, it would have to find a way to replace Jordan's considerable role in the West Bank and a way to pay for it. To negotiate peace and establish itself in the territories, it would have to convince Israel that its moderation was sincere. Neither one of these things would be easy; a "new" PLO would need King Hussein to approach Israel, to negotiate with it, and to make peace with it, and the King's help would have a price. Even if a compromise, circumscribed Palestinian state should come into existence, it would need Jordan as a shield to protect it from the predations of Syria, Iraq, and other rejectionist elements, and it would need Jordan's markets and access to the Arab world. The King knew all this and so, in short order, did the PLO.

At base this is partly why Jordan publicly recognized the PLO's legitimacy and the "independent" Palestinian state that was declared in November 1988. It is not because the King had any affection for either, but because he has always feared the implications of successful Palestinian nationalism for Jordan and wishes to influence its future in order to make it less dangerous to the Hashemite monarchy. If there has to be such a state, and perhaps that has become Hussein's conclusion, better west of the river than east of it.

If the PLO as a whole ever finally chooses genuine

moderation and retains organizational coherence, it would become an expression of Palestinian nationalism that Hussein can both live with and effectively coopt. To the extent that the PLO rejects moderation, Hussein is disappointed, but his risks are limited because there is no chance that a radical PLO can achieve an independent state in the West Bank. In 1988 the King sacrificed little, risked little, and stood to gain much because the perduring Jordanian role in the territories doomed to failure the PLO's attempt to subvert and seize the Hashemite role on its own terms.

Between the summer of 1988 and mid-1990 the PLO clearly moved toward a *posture* of moderation, and the King encouraged this. But this posturing did not imply that a firm step was taken, as later became clear when Iraq invaded and annexed Kuwait. The PLO all the while struggled to keep itself together; that is why it insisted that it would make no more concessions to Israel or the United States: no direct negotiations outside an international conference, no stopping the uprising, no joint delegation with Jordan, no cooperation with "autonomy" schemes.[19] Jordan's interests were the opposite in every case. Jordan supported the concept of direct negotiations, and the King knew there could be no solution without them. The King wanted to stop the uprising. He wanted a joint delegation, the better to control the Palestinian factor. And interim autonomy schemes were not necessarily bad ideas because Hussein understood that the implementation of any such scheme would require an elevating role for Jordan. This meant that if the United States chose patiently to reduce all four of the PLO's "nos," it would have an ally in Amman.

It also meant at the time that it was wrong to see the options before Israel and the United States as either negotiating with Jordan or negotiating with the PLO. Both the PLO and Jordan (as well as the West Bankers) would have to be involved in any settlement or movement toward it, this despite the fact that their own relations were largely antagonistic. The real questions were, and remain: what is the center of gravity in the Jordanian–PLO relationship, how stable is that center, and what does it imply about the limits of concessions that the Arab side can make?

In this, too, little changed between July 1988 and August 1990 despite Jordan's insistence that what it did was "not tactical." In a way, surely, what the Jordanians did was irreversible, if not administratively then psychologically. But in the basic sense it was tactical because there was no choice. Despite its growing weakness, Jordan continued to use its clout in the area and its welcome mat in both Washington and Jerusalem to put pressure on the PLO. The PLO used its regional and international image, as well as its capacity to irritate Israel and the United States, to put pressure on Jordan. And while all this was going on, the Israeli Likud pointed to the PLO to put pressure on Labor, and Labor pointed to Jordan to put pressure on the Likud. That was, in brief, the true state of play at the time; anything simpler distorts reality.

Because of this basic architecture in the Jordanian–Palestinian relationship, it was no surprise that King Hussein and Yasir 'Arafat met in Aqaba on 22 October 1988, less than two months after Hussein's dramatic announcement. Arafat agreed to "coordinate" strategy with Jordan, and the King announced himself fully satisfied with the results.[20] The Jordanian pressure on the PLO had worked in record time; it could not have been put better than it was put by Khaled al-Hassan when he said that coordination between Jordan and the PLO "was a necessity that can't be ignored."[21] This was a plain admission both that the PLO could not go it alone, and that needing Jordan carried with it a price "to be determined." Soon thereafter, Arafat spoke of hoisting the Jordanian flag over Jerusalem as well as the Palestinian flag.[22] This was not loose talk or pan-Arab persiflage; it indicated that PLO moderates understood that they needed Jordan to such an extent that their state or entity could not be completely independent.

JORDAN'S TROUBLES

However it would be wrong to see the *intifada* as something positive from the Jordanian perspective, just because the King figured out an intelligent way to parry it. There has been another side to the *intifada*, with painful lessons for Jordan to learn from it.

First, it may have been that the plan to improve the quality of life in the territories backfired badly, but not in an obvious way. From the data, such as that which shows that industrial and economic growth in the territories shot up after 1985, one can conclude that the quality of life programs, especially the economic sections of them, worked as planned. People did better, or at least some of them did. The actual effect of the growth spurt, however, was to accentuate the perception of inequality within the territories that had been growing for more than a decade, and while, arguably, it made the local aristocracy more pliant and pro-Jordanian, it had precisely the opposite effect on those who came to lead the *intifada*. Again, the uprising was not just a war against Israel, but a class war, too. The Jordanians will probably think twice before they make similar assumptions about what money can and cannot buy the next time around.

Second, as (bad) luck would have it, in January 1988, just days after the outbreak of the *intifada*, the London Agreement was published verbatim in the Israeli press. It had nothing to do with the *intifada*; it was no doubt leaked by Shimon Peres's political allies as a way to make the Likud appear to have blown an opportunity for peace. Still, as noted in the previous chapter, the profile of Jordanian–Israeli contact had risen above the surface for the first time. This turned out to have been the wrong sign for the times after the *intifada* erupted, and the Jordanian government must have wondered what new liabilities there would be for having been indiscreet. The care with which the Jordanian *mukhabarat* patrolled the refugee camps was some indication of the level of nervousness in Amman. So was the effort to limit the number of West Bankers who could travel to the east bank.[23] Indeed the decision to reduce the money sent to the West Bank may well have been promoted by a perception that more funds were needed to calm Palestinian energies on the east bank. Since then dealings with Israel have returned to their more discreet forms, and they are likely to stay that way. Indeed, after the blossoming of Jordanian *glasnost* after the November 1989 elections, Jordanians have been more reluc-

tant than ever to be associated with anything smacking of
face-to-face contact with Israel.

Clearly, then, the King concluded, as of the summer of
1988, that the dangers of a titularly independent Palestinian
state were not appreciably worse than a confederated
arrangement, or a "United Kingdom" arrangement such as
the March 1972 plan that for many years was the signature of
Jordanian policy aspirations toward the West Bank. Besides,
that was all that was available, and the Jordanian élite would
have failed miserably and publicly in trying to buck the tide.
This did not mean, as some American commentators concluded, that there was no more Jordanian Option in any
form.[24] It did mean that the directness and the instruments of
Jordanian influence looked much different than in the
classical Jordanian Option scenario of 1968–71, or the
abridged United Kingdom notion of 1972–74, or its still
further reduced post-Rabat version, 1975–86. Certainly it is
true that the total recontainment of the West Bank under
Jordanian aegis is a thing of the past. The Jordanians began
to speak of "constructive pluralism" in the post-disengage-
ment period, a clear indication that the Hashemite élite
understood that there had been a further weakening of their
general position.[25]

The main implication of Jordan's relative weakness for
Israeli–Jordanian relations is somewhat ironic. In essence, the
intifada meant that any even minimal Jordanian re-assump-
tion of influence or authority would have to be coordinated
much more closely with Israel in order to make sure that any
small Palestinian state or entity did not "get out of hand."
This reflects, once again, the strange local triangle in which
Jordan and the PLO are allied against Israel's presence in the
West Bank, but in which Israel and Jordan are allied against
the PLO's getting control of it should Israel ever leave. Thus it
should come as no surprise that, the formal divorce of the
West Bank from Jordan notwithstanding, direct contact
between Israel and Jordan went on more or less as usual in
1988 and most of 1989.

Some days before the King's 31 July blockbuster, Peres
received a message warning him not to front the "Jordan
Option" in the upcoming Israeli election campaign.[26] A few

days later, Peres got another message from the King affirming that the terms of the London Agreement were still in force.[27] Odder things happened, too. The Israeli Agricultural Minister, Arye Nehamkin, threatened West Bank farmers that Israel would violate standing agreements that facilitated exports of their produce to Jordan and the Arab world if they went out of their way to help and finance the *intifada*. Of course this revealed, first, that such arrangements existed, and second, that the Jordanian side had done nothing to change them, divorce or no divorce.[28] Perhaps most astonishing of all, the *New York Times* revealed that when King Hussein appeared on *Nightline* on 20 October 1988, Mr Peres's office helped arrange the appearance![29]

By the end of the *intifada's* first full year, the best that King Hussein probably hoped for was that the uprising would have the effect of empowering Palestinians within the territories at the expense of the core constituency of the PLO outside the territories—this despite their ostensibly pro-PLO affiliation. The Algiers meeting of the Palestine National Council in November, and Arafat's statements in Geneva in December 1988, indicated at the very least that the PLO was bending toward its West Bank constituency, which is assumed by most observers to be an inherently more moderate one, seeking Hebron and Nablus, than that constituency which longs for Jaffa and Haifa. But, as the Palestinian reaction to the Kuwait crisis showed, the PLO is far from ready to make real peace with Israel.

In the meantime, as Zionist and Palestinian nationalists dig their political trenches for a long struggle, the Israel–Jordanian relationship will continue to have its ups and downs too, like any reasonably normal political relationship does. Jordan's financial weakness, growing to the level of a major crisis in the spring and summer of 1989, for example, had an important effect on Israel–Jordanian ties. In August 1989 Jordan agreed to reopen offices of the Palestine National Fund in Amman because Yasir Arafat had promised in return that he would desposit up to $1 billion in PLO funds in Jordanian banks to reinstill confidence in the Jordanian economy and its sagging currency.[30] Arafat also urged West Bankers to use the Jordanian dinar.[31] And part of the

Jordanian campaign to extract money from Saudi Arabia and other wealthy Arab states consisted of blaming Israel for manipulating the dinar market deliberately to injure Jordan.[32] This was untrue, and Israeli Radio broadcasting in Arabic returned the compliment by accusing the PLO of having sabotaged the dinar by moving its funds out of Jordanian banks.

Even more dramatic, and annoying from the Israeli perspective, was that in the same month Jordan allowed Iraqi aircraft to overfly the Israeli–Jordanian frontier to photograph Israeli installations. Israel reacted harshly to this in public and protested privately through the United States, and perhaps also directly to Jordan, to let King Hussein know the gravity with which Israel viewed this act.[33] Probably Jordan's debts to Iraq on a number of accounts, and its alliance with Baghdad against Damascus with respect to the then deepening crisis in Lebanon, had something to do with the Jordanian decision.

These policy matters coincided with three incursions from Jordan into Israel in the late summer of 1989, one in which two Israeli soldiers were killed, one in which a renegade Jordanian soldier was killed after taking a hostage at a kibbutz, and another involving the first missile attacks against Israel from Jordanian soil in more than twenty years.[34]

As all this was going on, the Israeli government was causing trouble for Jordan as well. Both the Arabic and Israeli press suggested that Prime Minister Shamir, as his elections initiative fell on ever-harder times, began voicing the standard Likud view that the east bank of the Jordan might satisfy Palestinian nationalist aspirations first, and that then talks about the West Bank could begin some time after.[35] This sort of talk, combined with threats from politicians to "transfer" large numbers of Palestinians across the river into Jordan, always sends shivers up and down the spine of the Hashemite throne, as well it should. Taken together, the general tenor of Israeli–Jordanian relations was much depressed as of the fall of 1989, but it was a testament to the solidity of the relationship that no one, at least on the Israeli side, got very excited about these developments.[36] As for the Jordanians, .once it was established that Islamic fundamentalists were responsible for some or all of the border incidents, the government worked hard to increase security by repairing roads and reducing obscuring foliage along the border.[37] Israeli radio made special mention of the fact, too, that Jordan had foiled an attempted terrorist incursion near Elat.

As the winter of 1989 went forward, the Islamic and trans-border elements of the Israeli–Jordanian environment began to mix. There were more incidents, or attempted incidents, and again the Israeli military and press praised Jordanian efforts to keep the border pacified.[38] At the same time it became ever clearer that Islamic fundamentalists both inside the territories and in Jordan proper were developing closer ties, and that the spate of violence or attempted violence had this new conjunction at its source. The Jordanian elections of 6 November revealed strong support in Jordan for funda-mentalists grouped around the Muslim Brotherhood. More revealing, Palestinians in Jordan supported fundamentalist candidates in large numbers, some of whom were themselves Palestinians.[39] Indeed some of those elected to the Jordanian parliament were linked to efforts in 1983 and thereafter to fund the radical Islamic group HAMAS, and in particular, to help the spiritual leader of HAMAS in Gaza, Sheik Ahmad Yasin.[40]

There were a number of reasons for Palestinian support for the fundamentalists in Jordan. First and most important, Palestinian rage is more acceptable in the Jordanian context when expressed in religious as opposed to nationalist terms. In the former mode, alliances are created; in the latter, concern with "separatism" creates enemies. Second, the fundamentalist platform was most uncompromising about the Palestine issue, most anti-establishment, and most roman-tic—all positions appealing to the least advantaged sectors of society. And third, as noted above, some of the candidates were Palestinian.

Some of the attempts at crossing the border in the period just prior to the election must be seen as part of the election campaign in Jordan. The Islamists were appealing to the Palestinians by saying, in effect, that while the corrupt, pro-Western establishment headed by the King wants to keep the border quiet to help Israel, "we" want to keep the border hot and loud to help the *intifada*. This worked fairly well, judging by the election results.

More interesting, and ominous for both the Israeli and Jordanian governments, were the clear signs that HAMAS in the territories and the Muslim Brotherhood (Ikhwan) in Jordan proper were ever more closely linked. As reward for this improved cooperation, in fact, the Iranian government agreed in November 1989 to increase financial and other aid—the form of which was unspecified—to both.[41] This must have raised the prospect in the minds of Jordanian leaders that the new fundamentalism in Jordan, far to the radical side of the Ikhwan, would try to arm itself in order to create a secret militia in the style of those in Lebanon. With the violence of the *intifada* next door, the temptation was all the more strong. And clearly the potential emergence of such a para-military, militant fundamentalist power in Jordan, that would coordinate with and assist HAMAS, would get the attention of Israeli authorities too. All things being equal, the level of quiet Israeli–Jordanian cooperation to fight this new fundamentalist power should have been expected to grow as the threat grew. But all things are not equal.

INTO 1990

With the advent of 1990 the mixed nature of Israeli–Jordanian relations found much illustration. Terrorist raids across the border continued episodically, but again, at least before the collapse of the national unity government in March, Israeli officials downplayed their significance. They even downplayed stories about an Iraqi squadron of fighters being based in Jordan. Defense Minister Yitzhak Rabin said there was "no need to worry" about these developments, and he defended Jordan against right-wing Israeli politicians who seized on every problem to push their "Jordan is Palestine" position. He went out of his way, in fact, to "understand" the Jordanian point of view. "The economic situation in Jordan has become somewhat more difficult," Rabin explained:

The recent parliamentary elections have proven the radical Islamic element's strength. At the same time, voices were heard in Israel saying that Jordan is the Palestinians' homeland. So both internal factors and the fear that some Israelis may have devious intentions provided a sufficient background for the accelerating cooperation between Arab countries. We are now witnessing the manifestations of this cooperation.[42]

A few days later, Rabin was even more explicit:

We must not gloat over or assist in the toppling of the Hashemite regime in Jordan. All the alternatives are far worse . . . I would prefer to see the incumbent administration in Jordan more stable, because I know what can replace it.[43]

At the same time rather old-fashioned functional topics continued to arise from time to time. Energy and Infrastructure Minister (Labor) Moshe Shahal called on the Jordanian government to work with Israel to build a canal from the Dead Sea to the Red Sea—this being, of course, an old idea formerly discussed in private years ago.[44] Arrangements for Israeli Muslims to make pilgrimage to Mecca went forward as usual. Israel announced that the dates to cross the Allenby Bridge for the journey would be 8 and 9 July instead of 4 and 5 July, and the press reported that this had been agreed between Israeli and Jordanian officials directly during a meeting on the bridge.[45] In addition, the water, agriculture and intelligence liaisons all went forward as usual without interruption.

Still, Jordan's general predicament and the King's nervousness gave rise to untoward events. As the Arabic press was almost daily predicting Israeli attacks on Jordan,[46] in early May an Israeli patrol boat in the Gulf of Aqaba got too close to King Hussein's yacht, and fired a shot too close to it, as well. The King had a foreign guest on board and was humiliated by the action. Israel claimed that the shot was just a normal weapons' testing procedure, and that the King should not have been alarmed.[47] The truth, however, is that the Israeli ship acted in an indisciplined manner; its crew was punished and Rabin apologized, by telephone, to the King.[48]

WATER AGAIN

By far the most illustrative example of the mixed condition of Israeli–Jordanian cooperation in 1989 and 1990 concerned water, a subject around which both conflict and cooperation have swirled since 1953. It is a story about which a few details must be omitted, but worth telling anyway. Figure 4.1 shows the Yarmouk and Jordan River basins.

Israeli–Jordanian cooperation on water issues over the years has been concentrated many times by a common fear of Syria. The original Johnston Plan of the middle 1950s foundered over Syrian opposition, but aspects of the plan have been followed ever since. As noted above, Johnston came so close to getting agreement that he fudged the numbers, showing different figures to different sides. Ever since, Israel has been taking roughly 40 million cubic meters (mcm) on average from the Yarmouk each year. According to figures shown to Jordan, Israel should take only 25 mcm. The two countries have never agreed over this, but aspects of cooperation in other fields has made it unprofitable for the Jordanians to press the point. Still, other disagreements do surface, all the more as the need for water brings the two sides close to a zero-sum competition. Douglas Davis expressed it well:

> [T]he subject of water allocation from the river is a matter of constant haggling between Israeli and Jordanian officials. According to sources in London, the flow is so meticulously monitored and the supplies so carefully allocated that the debate between the two sides became overheated when Israel reportedly removed a large boulder in the river that slightly increased its share of the water flow.[49]

In 1986 Jordan became particularly concerned, as did Israel, that Syrian water projects would reduce the flow of the Yarmouk to the detriment of both downstream countries. More than 80 per cent of the catchment basin for the Yarmouk lies on Syria's side of the border, and nothing could stop them—save force—if Damascus decided to proceed unilaterally. Syria currently uses about 38 per cent of the Yarmouk waters; aggressive water projects done unilaterally could double that number, however. Both Israel and the United States provided intelligence to Jordan about Syrian activities, and it alarmed the King very much. It did more than that; it propelled the Jordanians to make a deal, very advantageous for Syria,[50] to build a dam, the Wihda or Unity Dam—also called the Maqarin dam—along the Yarmouk in order to control the flow. Not only did Jordan agree to pay for the great majority of the dam, but it also gave Syria 140 million cubic metres (mcm), more than Syria was allocated under the Johnston Plan (90 mcm) and in the traditional understanding that evolved thereafter.

Israel uses about 15 per cent of the river's flow, amounting to only about 3 per cent of Israel's annual water consumption. 3 per cent does not sound like much, but as Israel's needs increase, every drop is precious.

Of the three countries that use the Yarmouk, Jordan is by far the most dependent on this source. Jordan uses about 30 per cent of the Yarmouk waters for irrigation and this is, in turn, a very high percentage of Jordan's total irrigation usage. The dam, optimally, could increase its share to about 45 percent. The reason lies in geography and hydrology.

The Yarmouk flows strongest in the winter when the rainy season comes, and without a way to store the water, about 17 per cent of the roughly 430 mcm per year flows into the Dead Sea and evaporates. The dam would minimize the loss of water from winter floods, alleviate the summer shortages that plague the region, especially in Jordan, and also alleviate the crunch between Israel and Jordan should water become so scarce that current arrangements no longer minimally satisfy all sides. Those current arrangements, by the way, include a secret summer sharing arrangement, negotiated in 1979–80 through the mediation of Ambassador Philip Habib. In that agreement, Israel agreed that 25 mcm was the correct figure to which it was entitled (even though it still took more) in return

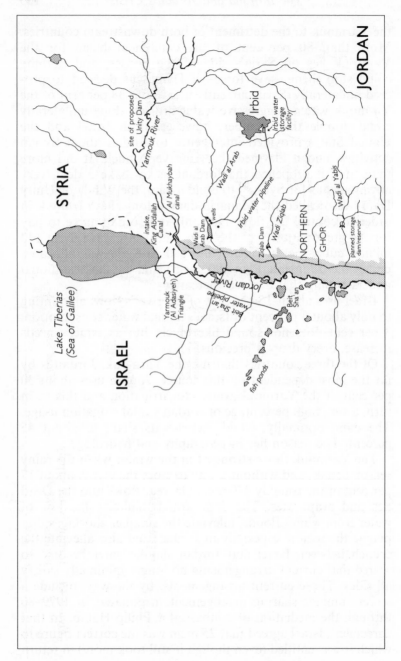

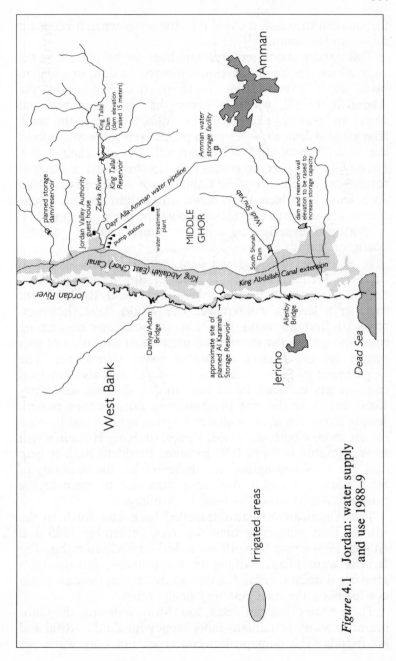

Figure 4.1 Jordan: water supply and use 1988–9

for an assurance that it could take the water when it needed it most—in the summer.[51]

This arrangement requires sandbags to be placed in the river where the Yarmouk flows into the Jordan, in order to push water toward the mouth of the Ghor, now the Abdallah, Canal, which is lower than the river bed and works by gravity. The place where this is done is the small triangle at Adasiyeh, where, at a picnic table a few yards from the river, Israeli and Jordanian officials do their work. Eventually the current erodes the sandbags and a sandbar forms near the mouth of the Canal. Every so often Israeli and Jordanian crews have to go down with bulldozers and dredge the area in order to control the flow. The problem, in reality, is thus not exactly "natural" as most accounts of this operation imply.

In any case, to build the dam, which Jordan agreed to finance, Jordan required a loan of approximately $350 million. To get it Jordan asked the World Bank to put together a lenders' conference. The World Bank, however, required first an assurance that all questions concerning riparian rights downstream had been taken care of, and that meant solving finally the water issue with Israel. The Department of State undertook low-keyed and also low-level negotiations between Israel and Jordan in 1988 and early 1989, but these did not progress very far. As time passed, Jordan's concern about unilateral Syrian actions and its need for the money both increased. Hence, on King Hussein's visit to Washington in April 1989 he asked President Bush to help out. The President agreed and in September the Secretary of State named a senior American diplomat to mediate the problem: Ambassador Richard L. Armitage.

The American mediator travelled back and forth to the Middle East numerous times between September 1989 and August 1990 trying to work out a deal on riparian rights. The Israelis were pliant, willing to compromise, but Jordan's growing domestic crisis became so acute that Jordan could not focus on the issue one way or the other.

There were other problems, too. More water for the Ghor meant to many Jordanians more money for Zaid al-Rifai and his friends. The dam project concerned not only water for irrigation, but also water for residential and industrial use; indeed, the World Bank stipulated that it would not loan money unless a systematically sound project was envisaged with respect to usage as well as supply. The more water used for drinking and industrial processes, however, the less is left for cheap irrigation. Moreover some Jordanian lands stood to be flooded by the dam. Without the dam, those lands are barren and worth little. But rumors spread that some of Jordan's wealthier, well-connected families were buying up the land as speculators, waiting for a windfall profit. The project, therefore, has pitted some powerful and wealthy élite families against others. But it is no longer so easy to hide graft and corruption in Jordan, and the entire affair threatened to expose more corruption and hidden wealth than Jordan's political nerves could have stood in 1990.

Despite the dangers of a full revelation of what is behind the Jordanian view of the project, the issue nevertheless rose in visibility thanks in part to Jordan's press *glasnost*, and in part to the unusually dry winter of 1989–90 which occasioned shortages in the summer of 1990 and hence a greater than average interest in water.[52] Naturally the little that the Jordanian press had to say about the issue blamed Israel for the delay;[53] but this was not so. The Israeli press took up the complaint, and made the point that Israel's insistence on a deal between Israel and Jordan put Jordan at the mercy of Syria.[54] In March 1990 Syria began flexing its muscles in that regard, pumping water from the Yarmouk in violation of the 3 September 1987 agreement—information relayed to Jordan by the US mediator within days of discovery.

ENTER THE KUWAIT CRISIS

The Kuwait crisis that broke out in August 1990 illustrated a number of the constants and variables of Israeli–Jordanian relations. Throughout the first month of the crisis, Jordan adopted an almost perfect equivocation. It verbally supported Iraq's invasion, but refused to accept Iraq's annexation. It voted within the Arab League to send Arab forces to Saudi Arabia (but not Jordanian forces), but with reservations. It told the United States that it would abide by UN economic sanctions against Iraq, but in fact it did not and set about "studying" the matter—a reasonable conclusion given Jordan's acute dependence on Iraqi oil and export markets. King Hussein visited Saddam Hussein, but flew to the United States to meet with President Bush in Kennebunkport, Maine a few days later. In late August and early September, he flitted from capital to capital in search of an Arab or a wider diplomatic solution to the crisis, and also a solution to Jordan's special burden of dealing with hundreds of thousands of stranded refugees from over thirty countries.

Clearly, the Iraqi invasion of Kuwait put Jordan in a terribly difficult position. Jordan had gravitated toward an Iraqi orbit for about two years: the reasons were economic and geostrategic. The Gulf War had helped orient Jordan's economy toward Iraq, and with the bottom falling out of the oil market, Jordan saw its economic future increasingly bound up in regional schemes in which Iraq played a major role. As for geopolitics, despite claims that King Hussein and President Hussein had a genuine friendship and rapport, more likely the king was simply following a tested pattern of dealing with Pan-Arabist challenges to the political status quo in the region. As with Nasser's Egypt after Suez, and Assad's Syria in the late 1970s and early 1980s, King Hussein's general view has been that if you cannot beat them, better to join them for protection's sake. One is reminded of a William Saroyan witticism from *My Name is Aram* that if you give to a thief, then he cannot steal from you, and therefore he is no longer a thief.

In any case, Jordan's support for Iraq proved extraordinarily popular among Palestinians in Jordan, most of whom enthusiastically supported the Iraqi position. The King enjoyed being popular, but the price was steep. Jordan's natural constituency is with Saudi Arabia, Egypt and the United States. Moreover, the King must have realized that Palestinian and PLO enthusiasm for Iraq's rabidly anti-moderate attitude toward all matters Arab–Israeli seriously set back prospects of Arab–Israeli conciliation, a conciliation for which King Hussein has striven for more than three decades.

If that were not enough, the crisis brought still more problems for Jordan. Remittances from workers in the Gulf dropped suddenly and dramatically, deepening Jordan's economic crisis. Refugees, Palestinians and others, moved into Jordan by the hundreds of thousands. Returning Palestinians were unemployed and raised the hackles of already disgruntled young east bankers. The others raised practical problems but here, at least, an international relief effort headed by the United States and Japan promised funds beyond those needed immediately for the refugee crisis.

Even worse, as the crisis dragged on, virtually every observer expected Saddam Hussein to bring the crisis westward, to turn it from a Gulf crisis into an Arab–Israeli crisis. Few believed that Iraq wanted war with Israel, but the chances of blundering into one anyway was of special concern to Jordan. An Iraqi–Israeli battle would be fought over, and possibly in, Jordan, and might be occasion for massive foreign intervention—and even eventual partition of the country. Jordan's border became the most porous one Iraq had, and the chances that Iraq might try in desperation to break out of diplomatic strangulation through it also caused great anxiety. With Jordan acting publicly as Iraq's ally, how would King Hussein have refused a request for "fraternal" Iraqi troops on his soil?

As Jordan mobilized its military in mid-August, Israeli officials seemed confused. Ostensibly, the mobilization was directed against the possibility that Israel might attack Jordan, or respond to Iraqi threats through Jordan. In truth, Jordan's mobilization might well have been aimed at discouraging any Iraqi thoughts about moving in, for despite the differences on paper between Iraqi and Jordanian military capabilities, the Jordanians could put up a very effective resistance if the will were there to do it.

In any case, the crisis had sobering effect on much of the Israeli right. With Palestinians the world over rooting for Iraq, the importance of Jordan as a buffer between the distempers of the Gulf and those of the Levant became too obvious to ignore. Were Jordan to have become a Palestinian state before the crisis, as many Israeli right-wingers desired, what would have stopped the creation of a real, as opposed to a limited and largely phony, Iraqi–Jordanian alliance? As this lesson sunk in, and as the most right-wing government in Israeli history, in every way it knew how, passed along assurances to King Hussein that Israel would do nothing to jeopardize the stability of the monarchy, a new reality was driven home: Israel's strategic interests required a stable Jordanian buffer, and the Hashemites provided the best means to that end.

Israel's new awareness of the importance of Jordan persuaded both Israel and the United States that the water mediation was perhaps more important than ever, both for its own sake, and for the sake of using that channel to manage this particular aspect of the crisis. It was fortuitous in a way that Ambassador Armitage had been laboring in the region for he provided a special link between the two sides when the crisis struck. He had been carrying separate back-channel messages to the president in any case, and now his recent contacts with both sides proved invaluable. Armitage met with Under-Secretary of State Robert Kimmit—the man who more than anyone else was the "technician" of the crisis management team—and sent some of his aides to Jordan during the crisis to keep abreast of developments in the palace separate from the US embassy.[55] Water negotiations, however, were frozen.

Not all Israeli–Jordanian interaction in the Kuwait crisis was amiable. Given the return of the street in Arab and Jordanian politics, it became more important than ever not to let any direct contacts with Israeli officials leak out. Israel offered its own territory as a way station to refugees stranded in Jordan, but in order to do that massive use of the Jordan river bridges would be required, or more direct flights from the Jordanian desert into Israeli air space. Either method would require tacit and explicit cooperation, and Jordanian officials were loath to risk it.

In addition, finally, Israel tried to do what it could to enforce the embargo against Iraq which, in Israel's case, meant preventing exports of foodstuffs from the West Bank and Gaza into Jordan bound for Baghdad. It was not immediately clear how the Israeli authorities could do this, and how they could distinguish produce headed for Iraq from produce headed elsewhere, but officials insisted, probably rightly, that they indeed knew what was going where.[56] The Israeli authorities did proceed to stop selected exports across the bridges.

Palestinians in the occupied territories, already set to suffer greatly from the invasion of Kuwait,[57] saw Israel's announcement as a cover to hurt the Palestinian economy generally so as to deal a death blow to the already staggering *intifada*. They may well have been correct about the Israeli government's intentions. But Jordan, suddenly beset with a massive refugee problem, needed all the foodstuffs it could get. Unfortunately, there did not seem to be available any Israeli tactic that could put pressure on the *intifada* without also causing some inconvenience to Jordan.

Finally, and not without special interest in the context of this essay, there is evidence that Israel and Jordan maintained direct communication in the crisis, and that Jordan acted as a go-between to exchange messages between Israel and Iraq. Inexperienced Foreign Minister David Levy gave away the basic matter on 15 August when he said on IDF radio that: "We have from the beginning transmitted directly and indirectly Israel's desire for stability in Jordan as its security interest . . . He [Saddam] understood our message."[58]

Moreover, Moshe Arens and King Hussein both happened to be in Bonn at the same time, 2–3 September. Barraged by inquiries from journalists, the Israeli and Jordanian embassies in Germany of course denied that the two had met.[59] No one believed them.

Even after the war ended and the peace process creaked forward, the legacy of Israeli–Jordanian cooperation broke through. Amid expectations of an Israeli–Syrian dialog, Prime Minister Shamir told visiting Canadian Foreign Minister, Joe Clark, that he anticipated future cooperation with Jordan on water, tourism, and environmental issues. Shamir even said that he expected Jordan to be the next country with which Israel would achieve peace.[60]

Notes

1. Their power declined before the *intifada* too, as the 1976 municipal elections showed, but the *intifada* was a harder blow. Nevertheless, withal, their influence is not completely gone.
2. Interviews, Clinton Bailey and others.
3. See for example, David Rosenberg, "Jordan Cuts Farm Import Quota from West Bank," *The Jerusalem Post*, 19 January 1989, p. 8.
4. See "Difficult Questions at a Critical Stage," *Al-Quds*, 6 December 1988, pp. 1, ll, in FBIS–NE, 8 December 1988, p. 31–2.
5. There was a difference between the two occasions, admittedly. In 1948, the Palestinians sought a state and the Hashemites stopped them. In 1970 the Palestinians sought control of the east bank in order to establish a state on the west bank, but the Hashemites stopped that, too.
6. See the report in *Al-Sha'ab*, 28 February 1989, p. 1.
7. Randa Habib, "Country Map Modified To Exclude West Bank," Radio Monte Carlo, FBIS–NE, 1 September 1988, p. 44.
8. For the most easily obtained summary, see Youssef M. Ibrahim, "Jordan's West Bank Move Upsetting Daily Life," *New York Times*, 18 October 1988, pp. 1, 12. For more details, see FBIS–NE for Jordan throughout August and September 1988. Almost every day contains some new measure and an official explanation for it.
9. See "Cairo–Amman Bank Branches to Remain Open," *Al-Ra'y*, in FBIS–NE, 10 August 1988, p. 27; "'Some' West Bank Projects Reportedly To Continue," Abu Dhabi, *Al-Ittihad al-Usubi'i*, in FBIS–NE, 27 September 1988, p. 25; and "Cairo–Amman Bank to Open Branch in Gaza," Dubayy, *Al-Bayan*, in FBIS–NE, 28 September 1988, p. 5.
10. See the report in *An-Nahar*, 1 December 1988, pp. 1, 11, also in FBIS–NE, 6 December 1988, p. 31.
11. "King Confers on West Bank School Examinations," *Al-Ittihad al-Usbu'i* Abu Dhabi, June 8, 1989, p. 21, in FBIS–NE, June 14, 1989, p. 44.
12. "Peres Cited on Moves by USSR, Jordan, U.S.," Jerusalem Domestic Service, in FBIS–NE, 29 July 1988, p. 19.
13. "Jordanian 'Observer' to Participate in Cairo Talk," *Al-Quds*, 19 March 1990, p. 1, in FBIS–NE, 21 March 1990, p. 5.

14. The Jordanian media explained the drop instead as an Israeli "conspiracy," an ever-popular theme in the Arab world. See "'Israeli Conspiracy' Blamed for Lower Dinar Rate," *Sawt al-Sha'b*, in FBIS–NE, 31 August 1988, p. 35.
15. The case is made in some detail in *The Next Generation in Four Key Arab Societies*, Office of Near East and South Asia Analysis, Office of Leadership Analysis, Central Intelligence Agency, March 1989, chapter 4, "Jordan."
16. al-Dajani in *Al-Ra'y*, 10 September 1988, in FBIS–NE, 14 September 1988, pp. 27–32.
17. Ibid.
18. Ibid.
19. Salah Khalaf was quite explicit on these points. See Alan Cowell, "P.L.O. Goes Back to Debating How to Create Its Exile State," *New York Times*, 26 January 1989, p. A8.
20. See Alan Cowell, "Arafat Confers With Hussein on Ending Split," *New York Times*, 23 October 1988, and Alan Cowell, "Parley in Jordan Is Said to Narrow Split with PLO," *New York Times*, 24 October 1988.
21. See Alan Cowell, "PLO Appeals to Israelis to Vote the 'Peace Choice'," *New York Times*, 25 October 1988.
22. "Flags Hoisted: 'Arafat Speaks," Amman Television Service, 7 January 1989, in FBIS–NE, 9 January 1989, p. 42.
23. See here Dan Avidan, "Jordan Taking Steps to Curb Spread of 'Uprising'," *Al-Hamishmar*, 15 July 1988, p. 4, in FBIS–NE, 19 July 1988, p. 40; "Jordan Said Banning Entry of West Bank Youths," *Al-Tali'ah*, 21 July 1988, p. 1, in FBIS–NE, 22 July 1988, p. 28; and Roni Sheqed, Tzvi Singer, Orli Azulay-Katz, Uzi Mahanaymi, and Erol Guiney, "Possible Uprising in Jordan," *Yedi'ot Aharonot*, 5 August 1988, pp. 1, 6, in FBIS–NE, 5 August 1988, p. 20. In one instance, a particular individual was turned back at the bridge despite having received an exit permit from the Israelis. See the dispatch about Ahmad Hamdi al-Natshah, a PNC member, in "Jordan Denies Entry to Palestinian Activist," Jerusalem Domestic Service, in FBIS–NE, 19 July 1988, p. 41.
24. Two examples include Arthur Hertzberg, "This Time, Hussein Isn't Being Coy," *The New York Times*, 9 August 1988, p. 19; and Trudy Rubin, "Hussein's had enough of West Bank mess," *The Philadelphia Inquirer*, 11 October 1988. A somewhat weightier expression of the same view is Don Peretz, "Intifadeh: The Palestinian Uprising," *Foreign Affairs*, Summer 1988, p. 978.

25. Crown Prince Hassan's coinage. See his interview in *Wochenpresse*, an Austrian magazine published in Vienna, on 12 May 1989, p. 38.
26. See Pinhas Inbari, "Peres Warned to Temper 'Jordanian Option' Talk," *Al-Hamishmar*, 24 July 1988, p. 1.
27. See "Peres Implies Possession of Message from Husayn," IDF Radio, FBIS–NE, 4 August 1988, p. 37.
28. "Nehamkin Warns of Interference With Arab Exports," Jerusalem Domestic Service, 22 August 1988, in FBIS–NE, 22 August 1988, p. 32.
29. Joel Brinkley, "Arab Intrusion in Israeli Politics Dominates an Election Debate," *New York Times*, 24 October 1988, p. A8.
30. Said al-Silawi, "Arafat's Instructions," *Sawt al-Sha'b* (Amman), 16 August 1989, pp. 1, 13, in FBIS–NE, 16 August 1989, p. 5.
31. "'Arafat Asks Palestinians to Use Jordanian Dinar," Cairo Domestic Service, 15 August 1989, in FBIS–NE, 16 August 1989, p. 5.
32. For examples, see "Goebbels' Students," *Al-Ra'y*, 24 July 1989, pp. 1, 24, in FBIS–NE 24 July 1989, p. 26, and "Arab Citizens Arrested in Israeli Dinar Plot," Manama WAKH, 28 July 1989 in FBIS–NE, 28 July 1989, p. 25.
33. See Zeev Schiff, "The Iraqis Are Provoking Israel and the United States," *Haaretz*, 21 August 1989, p. 2, and "'Strong Protest' Over Iraqi Flights Over Jordan," *Davar*, 20 August 1989, p. 1.
34. Joel Brinkley, "Jordanian Killed at Israeli Border," *New York Times*, 9 August 1989, p. A7; and "Several Missiles Fired at Israel From Jordan," *New York Times*, 8 September 1989, p. A6.
35. Speculations appeared in both *Al-Hamishmar* and in the UAE press. See Pinhas Inbari and Moti Bassok, "Shamir Offers Palestinian State in Jordan," *Al-Hamishmar*, 26 July 1989, p. 1; and Khalid 'Alawiniah "Plan for Palestinian State in Jordan Cited," *Al-Bayan* (Dubayy), 10 July 1989, pp. 1, 16, in FBIS–NE, 27 July 1989, p. 24.
36. "Shamir: Ties with Jordan Normal; Incident Unusual," IDF Radio, 8 August 1989 in FBIS–NE, 9 August 1989, p. 27.
37. See "Jordan Captures 3 Islamic Jihad Terrorists," Jerusalem Domestic Service, 10 September 1989, in FBIS–NE, 11 September 1989, p. 29; and "Jordan Clearing Foliage, Repairing Road on Border," Jerusalem Radio in Arabic, 17 September 1989, in FBIS–NE, 18 September 1989, p. 26.

38. See, for example, Dan Segir, "Crossing Attempts Aborted on Jordanian Border," *Haaretz*, 29 November 1989, p. 2.
39. Most important of these is Sheik Abd-al Munim Ra'fat Abu-Zant, who was born in Nablus and was expelled to the east bank in 1967. See an interview with him by Mariam M. Shahin, "Without Malice," *The Jordan Times*, 16–17 November 1989, p. 5.
40. Including Layth Shubaylath and Yusuf al-Azm. See Yehuda Litani, "Jordanian Muslim Brotherhood MP's Funded Arms," *The Jerusalem Post*, 13 November 1989, p. 1.
41. Eytan Rabin, "Iran Pledges Financial Assistance to HA-MAS," *Ha'aretz*, 26 November 1989, p. 2.
42. Rabin, Jerusalem Domestic Service, 18 February 1990, in FBIS–NE, 20 February 1990, p. 30.
43. Rabin, IDF Radio, 21 February 1990, in FBIS–NE, 22 February 1990, p. 27.
44. Jerusalem Domestic Service, 14 February 1990, FBIS–NE, 16 February 1990, p. 27.
45. Jerusalem Domestic Service, 22 June 1990, FBIS–NE, 25 June 1990, p. 35.
46. One example of many was Muhammed Haqqi and Fathi al-Barqawi, "Israel to Invade Jordan in June," *al-Anba* (Kuwait), 4 February 1990, pp. 1, 30, in FBIS–NE, 6 February 1990, p. 1.
47. "Vessel 'Got Too Close' to King Husayn's Yacht," Jerusalem Television, 7 May 1990, FBIS–NE, 8 May 1990, p. 21.
48. Interviews, Washington, June 1990.
49. Douglas Davis, "Water shortages could lead to war: scientists," *The Jerusalem Post*, 9 June 1990, p. 9.
50. See Appendix E.
51. See Thomas R. Pickering, "Water Scarcity and Political Stability in the Middle East: A Lecture Before the U.S. Congress," 14 September 1989, United States Global Strategy Council, pp. 8–10.
52. See "Steps Implemented to Deal with Water Shortages," *The Jordan Times*, 4 June 1990, p. 3.
53. Randa Habib, Radio Monte Carlo from Amman, "Israel Held Responsible for Stalling Dam Project," in FBIS, 16 July 1990, p. 28.
54. Ze'ev Schiff, "Jordan Water Allocation Agreement Needed," *Haaretz*, 16 July 1990, p. A2, in FBIS–NE, 17 July 1990, p. 28.
55. Interviews, Washington, August 1990.

56. Joel Brinkley, "Israel Says It Will Block Exports Bound for Iraq at Jordan's Border," *New York Times*, 27 August 1990, p. A8.
57. According to Palestinian economists, approximately 30 000 West Bank and Gazan Palestinians worked in Kuwait, and over 100 000 people out of 1.7 million in the territories depended on their forwarding remittances home.
58. "Minister Levi Interviewed: Comments on Jordan," FBIS–NE, 15 August 1990, p. 28.
59. "Arens Returns from FRG; Husayn Meeting Denied," in FBIS–NE, 5 September 1990, p. 30.
60. "Shamir on Talks, Regional Cooperation With Arabs," Jerusalem Domestic Service, 8 March 1991, in FBIS–NE, 11 March 1991, p. 52.

5 Epilogue: Of the Future

To the extent that Palestinian nationalism manages to come to terms with the existence of both Israel and Jordan, the legacy and depth of functional cooperation between Israelis and Palestinians and Jordanians becomes at least potentially more important than ever. Day-to-day coexistence, if it is ever to be changed from a begrudged fact of life to a mutual desire, would depend on the knowledge and experience of West Bankers who have dealt with Israel and Israelis for many years—all of this, it must be remembered, in a Jordanian context.

This has yet to happen and, for all anyone knows, it never will. The Palestinian man-on-the-street level of reaction to the Iraqi conquest of Kuwait suggested strongly that Palestinian society in the territories will cling to its radicalism and romanticisms of suffering for a long time. It is not so much a matter of whether they are rational or irrational, but rather a matter of their sense of historical time, which most Westerners find difficult to fathom. Is it rational to hope that by waiting, perhaps for centuries, one will get what one wants? That depends on whose rationality you are talking about.

If the Palestinians, or rather their originally self-appointed leaderships, ever do settle down and come to see that half a loaf is better than none, then the Jordanian role in any transition to a new political order will be crucial, and the legacy of Israeli–Jordanian cooperation over a variety of functional subjects, and the many human agents of that cooperation, will form an army for peace against that fateful day.

Whether one is talking about agriculture, industry, health, transportation, tourism, water, electrical grids, air traffic control or any number of other things, it is obvious that Israelis, Palestinians and Jordanians all benefit from cooperation and are injured by enmity and violence. But the

179

preconditions for a bright future include not only an Israeli government willing to compromise and a Palestinian national movement both willing and able to do the same, despite possibly strong opposition from the Arab and Muslim world, but it also requires a Jordan strong and stable enough to play its part. It is not entirely clear that Jordan will be able to do so.

Speculations over the future of Israeli and Palestinian politics are widespread; much less attention is devoted to Jordan. Indeed, as noted at the beginning of this volume, many analysts count Jordan out of the Arab–Israeli equation nowadays. This has always been, and remains, a mistake. That said, the Hashemite Kingdom is in trouble, far deeper trouble than ever before. Many analysts have long under-estimated the staying power of the Hashemites, but now, quite possibly, the wolf is really here. This was the case before the Kuwait crisis; now, after it, things look even worse.

Jordan's crisis is a composite crisis and that is what makes it so dangerous. First, Jordan's economy is in very poor shape. Currency reserves are low, unemployment and foreign debt per capita are high, income distribution is skewed. Worse, the problem is not just temporary, it is not a matter of adjustment to a post-oil-boom age. The mean population age is 15, and the carrying capacity of the land has long ago been exceeded. Jordan can no longer count on exporting labor to the Gulf and collecting remittances from abroad because the dinar is as soft as the oil market, and many Jordanian workers abroad are not sending their discretionary money home any more. With the Kuwait crisis, this element of the economic crisis has more than doubled in severity.

Jordan's work force is well educated but there are few natural resources. Jordan has never been able to survive without external subventions, and it is no longer clear where those subventions will come from. Jordan must strive to turn emergency crisis aid from the Kuwait affair into permanent aid packages. This is not beyond the King's talent, but it will not be easy.

The 1970s and early 1980s touched off a revolution of rising expectations that is now being brutally disappointed. Refu-gee-camp Palestinians can no longer be brought quickly into the economic mainstream, and the wealth of Palestinian plutocrats in Jordan is resented by east bankers and less fortunate Palestinians alike. Islamic fundamentalism is sowing this fertile field, and it is already producing a harvest.

Moreover east bankers are more educated, more ambitious, and more resentful of Palestinians in their midst as time passes. The younger generation, in particular, tends to see Palestinians as usurpers and interlopers. They resent Palestinian power in Jordan, and they resent what they believe to be the Palestinian oligarchs dragging Jordan's government into hopeless and enervating struggles with Israel. East bankers also want there to be a Palestinian state west of the Jordan River, not because they support their Pan-Arab cause, but because they want to get rid of them. If right-wing Israelis and newly nationalistic east bankers in Jordan got their way at the same time, they would compete with one another to see how many Palestinians they could stack shoulder upon shoulder in the middle of the Jordan River.

There is more: King Hussein is ageing and may well be ill. He is a well-known hypochondriac, and has been for years. But that does not mean that he is not really ill as of 1990. Some reports say he has cancer. Others, more credible, speak of heart disease. The King is smoking heavily in private, trying to stay on a strict diet. He sees his London physicians frequently, and he has grayed noticeably since 1988. According to American diplomats who have seen him with some regularity in 1990, he has lost his "zest for the game" and seems tired and even confused.[1]

His brother Hassan is the Crown Prince, but he is not well respected by Jordanians or Americans despite his mastery of economic matters. Hussein's eldest son by a Muslim Arab wife, Ali, was born in 1975 and is too young to count on. Some sort of constitutional devolution which reduces the role of the monarchy is likely, and that is what King Hussein has already been planning for. The November 1989 election, increasing political liberalization, and work on a new National Charter in 1990 were all steps in this direction, aiming to solidify the state in the east bank while there is still time. The cost of these experiments, however, has been a clear reduction in political stability and order in the short term. Before 1988 the King and his court controlled 95 per cent of the high political action in Jordan; by mid-1990 a generous estimate put it closer to 65 per cent. In the past, in 1956–57, for example, the King toyed with similar experiments, and when things got out of hand, he did a *volte face* and restored his power. Will he be able to do so again under current conditions? It is not at all clear that he can, even if he wants to, and it is not even clear if he wants to.

The King's health and the state of the monarchy matter because the monarchy has acted as a sort of corpus collosum for the country, separating and mediating between Palestinians on the one side and east bankers on the other. To the extent that the state becomes ever more transparent in the lives of the people, this buffer erodes and Palestinians and east bankers find themselves standing eyeball to eyeball in a deteriorating economic and social environment. Civil war in one form or another is not out of the question. If Islam binds the two sides together well enough, then mere social revolution instead of civil war looks more likely, but that is hardly a choice to relish either for Israel, the Hashemites, or the United States.

Finally, and perhaps critically, Jordan has always been able to count on Israel in a pinch. In both the 1957–58 and the 1970 crises in Jordan, Israel was tacitly on Jordan's side and acted to help the King. At least before the sobering impact of the Kuwait crisis, Israel had become more a part of the problem as far as the King was concerned, not part of the solution. Many members of the Israeli government argued that Jordan is Palestine, and discounted the legitimacy and utility of the Hashemites. Jordan's fears that Israel intends to thrust up to a million Palestinians across the river into Jordan grew markedly in the wake of greatly increased Soviet Jewish immigration and the advent of the most right-wing government in Israeli history in June 1990. Jordanians talked openly of how the Israelis intended to strike across the river, set up a fake Palestinian entity, and then expel West Bank Palestinians into it by the tens of thousands. There is no hard evidence that such a scheme existed, but before the Kuwait crisis of August 1990, a strong fatalism had taken hold of Jordan, not unlike the fatalism that chased Arab capital and people out of

Palestine in 1947–48. It is partly because of such fears, and also economic dependency, that Jordan moved ever closer to Iraq in 1989 and 1990—just in time to be caught beneath the falcon's wing when crisis came in August.

When the main players of the Arab world came around slowly, tentatively and carefully to oppose Iraq, Jordan tried at least to walk ever so slowly away from Saddam Hussein and back toward his more natural friends. The fact that Yasir Arafat went to Baghdad, and stayed there, no doubt provided added incentive for the King to fly to the United States on July 15. As noted above in chapter 4, Jordan sided with Iraq at the outset, but then refused to acknowledge the Iraqi annexation of Kuwait, and then a few days later announced that it would abide by United Nations sanctions. Since Jordan was at the time the only "safe" border for Iraq, and since the Jordanian port of Aqaba was the only way to get much needed foodstuffs into Iraq past the UN sanctions, even saying this required some bravery. But it could not solve Jordan's longer range, deeper problems, and it did not eliminate Jordan's fears of what Israel might do, taking advantage of the Gulf crisis to work its will with the Palestinians.

Taken together, Jordan's demographic, economic, and social problems are probably lethal to stability. Add to that a likely royal transition in the not-too-far-distant future, all this in the midst of an unfriendly regional environment, and in the absence of a trustworthy superpower patron, and the conclusion almost draws itself. If one adds, finally, the absence of a vigorous and hopeful Arab–Israeli peace process —if efforts put in motion after the Gulf War, in March 1991, fail—which generally has the effect of boosting Jordan, and there appears to be no solid, substantial and sufficient help from any quarter. Such a shame, then, that when Jordan had a chance, however risky, to make a deal with Israel in public and defuse the conflict to the best of its ability, in 1971–73, and again in 1978–79, it failed to act boldly. Time really was not on Jordan's side, and regional realities, it seems, might finally be about to catch up with what Winston Churchill created one Sunday afternoon in 1921 over cigars and brandy.[2]

DOES THE MIDDLE EAST HAVE A DREAM?

Even if Hashemite Jordan in its present form does not last out the next few decades that will probably be required for any Arab–Israeli settlement to come about, the future disposition of what is today Jordan will remain important—if only for functional reasons. To give one example out of many, consider again the problem of water.

As sketched above, building the Unity, or Wihda, Dam has proven difficult. Economic and technical problems have been added on to the political ones that have bedevilled the solution of riparian legal issues concerning the Jordan and the Yarmouk for nearly forty years. But few stop to ask whether the equation of the Unity Dam plus downstream sharing agreements is the best approach to the functional problem. Almost surely, it is not; if politics were willing, there is a much better way to deal with the water problem.

As noted above, the waters of the Yarmouk cannot be effectively utilized unless the flow of the water in the winter can be stored for use during the summer. Building upstream dams is one way to achieve this, and that is what the Wihda project is all about. Of course, building a dam closer to the exit of the Yarmouk into the Jordan on the Israeli–Jordanian border would be cheaper and more effective, but only if Syria did not unilaterally interrupt the flow by building its own waterworks in the north. But there is another way, objectively neater for everyone, and that involves building a canal from the Yarmouk to the Sea of Galilee, to store its waters there, and a pumping station to pump the waters back to the river in the summer when they are most needed. According to technical estimates, the total cost of the Wihda Dam, now estimated at $350 million, is more likely to be $500 million and up. By contrast, the capital investment for a canal and pumping station using the Galilee alternative is estimated (perhaps somewhat low) at $21 million. Moreover, using Galilee as a storage area promises to capture 180 million cubic meters of the Yarmouk's flow; the Wihda Dam would be lucky to capture 100. This means there would be more to share downstream, and that upstream diversions would matter less. The full potential of the Galilee scheme could not be realized unless the storage capacity for Galilee itself were enlarged from the present 500 million cubic meters to around 740 million cubic meters, but even without expansion, the quality and quantity and price of water for Jordan would all be better than under the Wihda scheme. Jordan currently takes about 100 million cubic meters per year; under the Galilee plan, that amount could double.

There are other benefits as well. Electricity generation would be cheaper from the canal than from the dam. The salinity of Galilee, and hence of the flow into the Ghor Canal, would be reduced, making treatment for agricultural and residential use much less expensive. It might also be possible to pump the water that Galilee cannot hold into aquifers that Israel and Jordan share. This would increase the amounts available in absolute terms, but it might increase the risk of dry summers for Jordan, and so compensatory cooperative arrangements would be required.[3]

The point of all this is to show that if geography alone, rather than political geography, were the starting point for functional projects concerning not just water, but other issues as well, mutually beneficial solutions would be far easier to come by. To look at this region of the world today with such schemes in mind may seem mad, or, to be charitable, unrealistic. If one assumes that a less pragmatic government will be in Jordan in the future, not to speak of an Israeli government indisposed to conciliation, then all of this must seem madder than mad. But someone must dream these dreams, or there is no chance at all that they will ever come true.

A MODEST CONCLUSION

For all the good news, and there has been much of it over the years in relations between Israel and Jordan, the notion entertained by some that functional condominium-like arrangements can by themselves create a momentum that will lead to peace, or to significant degrees of political normalization, is likely to be disappointed by the harsh realities of local hatreds. Unpleasant as it is to contemplate, people often spite themselves, and it is not up to outsiders to "explain" to the peoples of the Middle East what their "real" interests are. It is like trying to explain to a dog that it's his tail that he's trying to catch, and woe unto him if he ever succeeds. Politics is still primary in the Middle East, and will remain so.

Nevertheless there will be functional cooperation if only because there is no way to avoid at least some of it in such tight quarters—no matter what future governments east and west of the Jordan River think of one another. And functional coordination can be useful to diplomacy, even if not decisive, and it can be useful to ordinary people as long as desperate diplomats either in the region or outside it do not expect too much from it. Beyond that, functional cooperation can help prevent a generally misanthropic situation from getting even worse.

It may well be that Israeli–Jordanian relations have been about as good as they can get throughout most of the 1970s and 1980s, given the depth of hostility between Israelis and Palestinians, the inherent political weakness of Jordan, and the absence of clear consensus on issues of war and peace within Israel. It may be, even if Hashemite Jordan survives more or less intact, that attempts to transform Israeli–Jordanian pragmatism into something more public, more formal, and more legal would set relations back, and drive away the chances for social accommodation. As Moshe Zak has put it: "The many agreements that have been achieved over the years between Hussein and Israel were partial; they related to specific, well-defined problems that did not require any publicity, and therefore they could be kept secret. A peace treaty cannot be kept secret."[4]

This is not to say that the United States, or Israel, or Jordan, should dismiss the visible spectra of the peace process as necessarily counter-productive. But all principals involved in policymaking and evaluation must understand that the relations between Jordan and Israel are not so bad that there is nothing to lose by tampering with them. All human beings, it seems, at one level or another, have trouble distinguishing between the symbolic and the real, between the thing and the name for the thing. It would be a shame if diplomats in the region and outside of it become responsible for wrecking a tense but tolerable situation in the pursuit of an ideal, but unreachable, improvement upon it.

Notes

1. Interviews, State Department, June 1990.
2. Pessimism has been widespread. See Karen Eliott House, "How Jordan's King Hussein Was Played for a Fool," *Wall Street Journal*, 14 August 1990.
3. See Meir Merhav (ed.), *Economic Cooperation and Middle East Peace* (London: Weidenfeld & Nicolson, 1989), pp. 66–70.
4. Moshe Zak, "The Ambivalent Diplomacy of King Hussein," *Global Affairs*, Spring 1989, pp. 113–14.

Appendix A: The Faisal–Weizmann Accord, 3 January 1919

AGREEMENT BETWEEN THE KING OF THE HEDJAZ AND THE ZIONISTS

His Royal Highness the Emir Faisal, representing and acting on behalf of the Arab Kingdom of Hedjaz, and Dr Chaim Weizmann, representing and acting on behalf of the Zionist Organization, mindful of the racial kinship and ancient bonds existing between the Arabs and the Jewish people, and realizing that the surest means of working out the consummation of their national aspirations is through the closest possible collaboration in the development of the Arab State and Palestine, and being desirous further of confirming the good understanding which exists between them, have agreed upon the following articles:

Article I

The Arab State and Palestine in all their relations and undertakings shall be controlled by the most cordial goodwill and understanding and to this end Arab and Jewish duly accredited agents shall be established and maintained in the respective territories.

Article II

Immediately following the completion of the deliberations of the Peace Conference, the definite boundaries between the Arab State and Palestine shall be determined by a Commission to be agreed upon by the parties hereto.

Article III

In the establishment of the Constitution and Administration of Palestine all such measures shall be adopted as will afford the fullest guarantees for carrying into effect the British Government's Declaration of the 2nd of November, 1917.

Article IV

All necessary measures shall be taken to encourage and stimulate immigration of Jews into Palestine on a large scale, and as quickly as possible to settle Jewish immigrants upon the land through closer settlement and intensive cultivation of the soil. In taking such measures the Arab peasant and tenant farmers shall be protected in their rights, and shall be assisted in forwarding their economic development.

Article V

No regulation nor law shall be made prohibiting or interfering in any way with the free exercise of religion; and further the free exercise and enjoyment of religious profession and worship without discrimination or preference shall forever be allowed. No religious test shall ever be required for the exercise of civil or political rights.

Article VI

The Mohammedan Holy Places shall be under Mohammedan control.

Article VII

The Zionist Organisation proposes to send to Palestine a Commission of experts to make a survey of the economic possibilities of the country, and to report upon the best means for its development. The Zionist Organisation will place the aforementioned Commission at the disposal of the Arab State for the purpose of a survey of the economic possibilities of the Arab State and to report upon the best means for its development. The Zionist Organisation will use its best efforts to assist the Arab State in providing the means for developing the natural resources and economic possibilities thereof.

Article VIII

The parties hereto agree to act in complete accord and harmony on all matters embraced herein before the Peace Congress.

Article IX

Any matters of dispute which may arise between the contracting parties shall be referred to the British Government for arbitration.

Emir Faisal
Chaim Weizmann

Given under our hand at London,
England, the Third day of January,
One Thousand Nine Hundred and Nineteen.

Appendix B:
Faisal–Frankfurter Correspondence

Delegation Hedjazienne,
Paris,
March 3, 1919.

Dear Mr Frankfurter:

I want to take this opportunity of my first contact with American Zionists to tell you what I have often been able to say to Dr Weizmann in Arabia and Europe.

We feel that the Arabs and Jews are cousins in race, having suffered similar oppressions at the hands of powers stronger than themselves, and by a happy coincidence have been able to take the first step towards the attainment of their national ideals together.

We Arabs, especially the educated among us, look with the deepest sympathy on the Zionist movement. Our deputation here in Paris is fully acquainted with the proposals submitted yesterday by the Zionist Organization to the Peace Conference, and we regard them as moderate and proper. We will do our best, in so far as we are concerned, to help them through: we will wish the Jews a most hearty welcome home.

With the chiefs of your movement, especially with Dr Weizmann, we have had and continue to have the closest relations. He has been a great helper of our cause, and I hope the Arabs may soon be in a position to make the Jews some return for their kindness. We are working together for a reformed and revived Near East, and our two movements complete one another. The Jewish movement is national and not imperialist. Our movement is national and not imperialist, and there is room in Syria for us both. Indeed I think that neither can be a real success without the other.

People less informed and less responsible than our leaders and yours, ignoring the need for cooperation of the Arabs and Zionists, have been trying to exploit the local difficulties that must necessarily arise in Palestine in the early stages of our movements. Some of them have, I am afraid, misrepresented your aims to the Arab

193

peasantry, and our aims to the Jewish peasantry, with the result that interested parties have been able to make capital out of what they call our differences.

I wish to give you my firm conviction that these differences are not on questions of principle, but on matters of detail such as must inevitably occur in every contact of neighbouring peoples, and as such are easily adjusted by mutual goodwill. Indeed nearly all of them will disappear with fuller knowledge.

I look forward, and my people with me look forward, to a future in which we will help you and you will help us, so that the countries in which we are mutually interested may once again take their places in the community of civilised peoples of the world.

Believe me,

Yours sincerely,
(*Sgd*) Faisal.
5th March, 1919.

Royal Highness:

Allow me, on behalf of the Zionist Organisation, to acknowledge your recent letter with deep appreciation.

Those of us who come from the United States have already been gratified by the friendly relations and the active cooperation maintained between you and the Zionist leaders, particularly Dr Weizmann. We knew it could not be otherwise; we knew that the aspirations of the Arab and the Jewish peoples were parallel, that each aspired to re-establish its nationality in its own homeland, each making its own distinctive contribution to civilisation, each seeking its own peaceful mode of life.

The Zionist leaders and the Jewish people for whom they speak have watched with satisfaction the spiritual vigour of the Arab movement. Themselves seeking justice, they are anxious that the just national aims of the Arab people be confirmed and safeguarded by the Peace Conference.

We knew from your acts and your past utterances that the Zionist movement—in other words the national aims of the Jewish people—had your support and the support of the Arab people for whom you speak. These aims are now before the Peace Conference as definite proposals by the Zionist Organisation. We are happy indeed that you consider these proposals "moderate and proper," and that we have in you a staunch supporter for their realisation. For both the Arab and the Jewish peoples there are difficulties ahead—difficulties that challenge the united statesmanships of Arab and Jewish leaders. For it is no easy task to rebuild two great civilisations that have been suffering oppression and misrule for centuries. We each have our difficulties we shall work out as friends, friends who are animated by similar purposes, seeking a free and full development for two neighbouring peoples. The Arabs and Jews are neighbours in territory; we cannot but live side by side as friends.

Very respectfully,
(*Sgd*) Felix Frankfurter.

Appendix C: Initialled Non-Aggression Pact Between Israel and Hashemite Jordan, 24 January 1950

DRAFT AGREEMENT BETWEEN ISRAEL AND JORDAN,
24 FEBRUARY 1950

A special agreement will be signed, pursuant to the Armistice Agreement, bound to the latter and reinforcing it. The agreement will include the following principles:

(1) Non-aggression for a period of 5 years.

(2) Maintenance of the existing armistice borders and a search for acceptable solutions for the abolishment of areas of no-man's-land by their division, wherever possible, between both parties.

(3) In order to reach a comprehensive agreement between the two parties, Special Joint Committees will be appointed to study and discuss each of the fundamental issues. These will include territorial and economic problems as well as other issues to be included in the agreement, with a view to replacing the temporary lines and arrangements comprised in the Armistice Agreement by permanent lines and arrangements, including Jerusalem and the question of a port and access to the sea for Jordan, under her full sovereignty.

(4) Measures are to be taken by both sides to safeguard the Holy Places and to ensure freedom of prayer and access, while eliminating the possibility of military disputes between the parties over those sites, and providing the UN authorities with satisfactory guarantees in this matter.

(5) One of the first tasks to be imposed on one of the Committees mentioned in Paragraph 3, will be to devise arrangements for payment of monetary compensation to owners of property in Jerusalem without affecting the territorial settlement in the city of Jerusalem referred to in Paragraph 3.

(6) Measures are to be taken grant to Jordan a free zone in the port of Haifa in order to implement the principle of commercial cooperation· between the two parties for the duration of this agreement.

(7) Measures are to be discussed to settle matters pertaining to Arab property in Israel territory by allowing the owners of such property either to enter Israel themselves or to send their representatives in order to sell such property or to deal with it as they see fit. And this is in order that they will have the right, if such solutions prove difficult to implement, to authorize the parties to the agreement to resolve the difficulties. This would apply also to Jewish property in Jordanian territory.

(8) The Special Committee will discuss measures to facilitate Israeli access to the institutions on Mt Scopus and Arab access to Bethlehem, in accordance with Article 8 of the Armistice Agreement.

Addenda to this agreement will be drawn up to determine ways and means of implementing the above resolutions.

R[euven] S[hiloah]
M[oshe] D[ayan]
F[awzi al-] M[ulqi]
S[amir al-] R[ifa'i]

Appendix D: Draft of a Peace Treaty Between Israel and Hashemite Jordan, 28 February 1950

THE STATE OF ISRAEL AND THE HASHEMITE–JORDAN KINGDOM, ON 28.2.50

WHEREAS on the third day of April, 1949, the Contracting Parties signed at Rhodes a General Armistice Agreement to remain in force until a peaceful settlement between the Parties is achieved,

AND WHEREAS the Parties now desire, in order to promote normal relations and as a further step toward a peaceful settlement to reinforce the said General Armistice Agreement and extend the scope of mutual accord between them,

HAVE THEREFORE agreed to conclude the following Agreement of Amity and Non-Aggression and have accordingly appointed as their Plenipotentiaries

The State of Israel . . . .[all dotted lines indicate text left blank in the original]

The Hashemite–Jordan Kingdom . . . .

who, after presentation of their full powers, found in good and due form, have agreed on the following provisions.

Article I

(1) Each of the Contracting Parties undertakes not to resort to war or acts of armed violence or other acts of aggression or hostility against the other, or to invade territories under the control of the other, or to permit any territory under its control to serve as a base or to be used for passage for armed attack by a third party on the other.

(2) If, on any occasion, there should arise between the Contracting Parties differences of opinion which they are unable to settle

between themselves, they undertake to have recourse to the conciliatory and arbitral procedures offered under international law for the settlement thereof, or such other means of pacific settlement as shall be agreed upon by the Parties.

Article II

For the duration of this Agreement the Armistice Demarcation Line described in the said General Armistice Agreement shall remain in force subject to any modifications agreed to by both Parties in accordance with the terms of the said General Armistice Agreement. In order to reduce possible friction, the Contracting Parties agree to eliminate the various areas of "no man's land" the continued existence of which they consider undesirable.

Article III

The Contracting Parties are agreed upon the necessity for taking joint steps in order to protect the Holy Places of all faiths in Jerusalem and to ensure freedom of access thereto and freedom of worship thereat to the adherents of all faiths. A Joint Declaration by the Contracting Parties in this regard is contained in Annex 1 to the present Agreement. The Contracting Parties further agree to offer requisite assurances to the United Nations regarding the inviolability of the Holy Places and the observance of the said Declaration.

Article IV

(1) The Contracting Parties are agreed upon the desirability of establishing economic and commercial relations between them.
(2) For the implementation of this Article economic and commercial accords shall be concluded between the Parties. Trade Delegates shall be exchanged between them not later than three months from the coming into force of this Agreement. They shall negotiate these economic and commercial accords and be responsible for their effective observance.

Article V

The Contracting Parties are agreed that all necessary steps shall be taken to ensure the resumption of the normal functioning of the cultural and humanitarian institutions on Mount Scopus and the use of the cemetery on the Mount of Olives and access thereto, as well as the free movement of traffic on the Bethlehem–Jerusalem road, in accordance with Article VIII of the said General Armistice Agreement.

Article VI

(1) Having regard to the purposes of this Agreement and in order to implement its provisions and to formulate the basis for a final peaceful settlement, the Contracting Parties hereby establish a Mixed Commission to be known as the Israel–Jordan Commission.

(2) The Israel–Jordan Commission shall inter alia:

   (a) Examine all territorial problems outstanding between the Contracting Parties.

   (b) Consider and elaborate plans for the determination of rights to financial recompense and the assessment and payment thereof in respect of immovable property in Jerusalem which was abandoned by its owners as a consequence of the armed conflict.

   (c) Examine ways and means for the settlement of the just claims for compensation of persons permanently resident in the territory of either of the Contracting Parties for property abandoned by them in the territory of the other Contracting Party.

   (d) Devote its attention to the question of the establishment of a free zone in the Port of Haifa for the Hashemite–Jordan Kingdom for commercial purposes.

   (e) Examine measures for the full resumption of operations by the Palestine Electric Corporation and by the Palestine Potash Limited.

Article VII

(1) The Commission established pursuant to Article VI hereof shall be composed of $^1/_2$ . . . representatives of each Party designated by the respective Governments.

(2) This Commission has the power to appoint such sub-commissions as it deems necessary in order to make possible the expeditious completion of its task.

(3) The Contracting Parties shall immediately nominate their representatives to the Commission, which shall hold its first meeting not later than seven days from the coming into force

of this Agreement. Subsequent meetings shall take place upon the first and fifteenth days of each month thereafter, unless such dates fall on a Friday or on a Saturday, in which event the meeting will be postponed for not more than two days.

(4) The Commission's headquarters shall be at Jerusalem.

(5) The Commission and its sub-commissions shall establish their own rules of procedures.

(6) Members of the Commission and of sub-commissions shall, while on the territory of the other of the Contracting Party, be granted the appropriate privileges and immunities.

Article VIII

The Contracting Parties agree that the Mixed Armistice Commission set up in accordance with the said General Armistice Agreement shall have no powers or functions in relation to the execution of this Agreement.

Article IX

This agreement shall enter into force immediately upon signature, and shall remain in force for a period of five years or for so long as the General Armistice Agreement signed at Rhodes on 3 April, 1949, is in force, whichever period shall be the shorter.

Article X

Nothing in the present agreement is intended to, or shall in any way prejudice the rights and obligations which devolve, or may devolve, upon either of the Contracting Parties under the Charter of the United Nations.

Article XI

A copy of this Agreement shall be communicated to the Secretary General of the United Nations for transmission to the appropriate organs of the United Nations.

IN FAITH WHEREOF THE Plenipotentiaries of the Contracting Parties have signed the present Agreement and have hereunto affixed their seals.

Done in duplicate in the Hebrew, Arabic and English languages, all
authentic, this ... day of March, 1950, corresponding to the ... day
of Adar in the year 5710 since the creation of the world, and the
... day of Jumada-j-ula in the year 1369 of the Hijra.

> For the State of Israel.........
> For Hashemite–Jordan........

ANNEX ONE: JOINT DECLARATION CONCURRING THE HOLY PLACES, RELIGIOUS BUILDINGS AND SITES IN JERUSALEM

The Governments of Israel and of the Hashemite–Jordan Kingdom,
    CONSCIOUS of their responsibilities concerning the protection
and preservation of the sanctuaries in Jerusalem of the three great
religions;
    Solemnly undertake by the provisions of the present Declaration
to guarantee the protection and preservation of and free access to
the Holy Places, religious buildings and sites of Jerusalem.

Article 1

The free exercise of all forms of worship shall be guaranteed and
ensured in accordance with the Declaration of Human Rights of 10
December, 1948, the Declaration of Independence of Israel and the
Constitution of the Hashemite–Jordan Kingdom.

Article 2

The Holy Places, religious buildings and sites which were regarded
as Holy Places, religious buildings and sites on 14 May, 1948, shall
be preserved and their sacred character protected. No act of a
nature to profane that sacred character shall be permitted.

Article 3

The rights in force on 14 May, 1948, with regard to the Holy Places,
religious buildings and sites shall remain in force.
    The Governments of the Hashemite-Jordan Kingdom and Israel
undertake in particular to assure the safety of ministers of religion,

those officiating in religious services and the members of religious orders and institutions, to allow them to exercise their ministries without hindrance, and to facilitate their communications both inside and outside the country in question with the performance of their religious duties and functions.

Article 4

The Governments of the Hashemite-Jordan Kingdom and Israel undertake to guarantee freedom of access to the Holy Places, religious buildings and sites situated in the territory placed under their authority by the final peaceful settlement between them, or, pending that settlement, in the territory at present occupied by them under armistice agreements; and, pursuant to this undertaking, will guarantee right of entry and of transit to ministers of religion, pilgrims and visitors without distinction as to nationality or faith, subject only to considerations of national security, all the above in conformity with the *status quo* prior to 14 May, 1948.

Article 5

No form of taxation shall be levied in respect of any Holy Place, religious building or site which was exempt from such taxation on 14 May, 1948.

No change in the incidence of any form of taxation shall be made which would either discriminate between the owners and occupiers of Holy Places, religious buildings and sites, or sites, or would place such owners and occupiers in a position less favourable in relation to the general incidence of that form of taxation than existed on 14 May, 1948.

Appendix E: Agreement Reached by King Hussein and Israel's Foreign Minister Shimon Peres in London, 11 April 1987

SECRET/MOST SENSITIVE

(Accord between the Government of Jordan, which has confirmed it to the United States, and the Foreign Minister of Israel, ad referendum to the Government of Israel. Parts "A" and "B", which when they become public upon agreement of the parties, will be treated as US proposals to which Jordan and Israel have agreed. Part "C" is to be treated, in great confidentiality, as commitments to the US from the Government of Jordan to be transmitted to the Government of Israel.)

A THREE-PART UNDERSTANDING BETWEEN JORDAN AND ISRAEL

A   Invitation by UN Secretary General
B   Resolutions of the International Conference
C   The Modalities Agreed Upon by Jordan-Israel

A   The Secretary General will issue invitations to the five permanent members of the Security Council and the Parties involved in the Arab–Israeli conflict in order to negotiate a peaceful settlement based on Resolutions 242 and 338 with the objects of bringing a comprehensive peace to the area, security to its states and to respond to the legitimate rights of the Palestinian people.

B   The Participants in the Conference agree that the purpose of the negotiations is the peaceful solution of the Arab–Israeli conflicts based on Resolutions 242 and 338 and a peaceful solution of the Palestinian problem in all its aspects. The Conference invites the Parties to form geographical bilateral committees to negotiate mutual issues.

C Jordan and Israel have agreed that: (I) the International Conference will not impose any solution or veto any Agreement arrived at between the Parties; (II) the negotiations will be conducted in bilateral committees directly; (III) the Palestinian issue will be dealt with in the committee of the Jordanian–Palestinian and Israeli delegations; (IV) the Palestinians' representatives will be included in the Jordanian–Palestinian delegation; (V) participation in the Conference will be based on the Parties' acceptance of Resolutions 242 and 338 and the renunciation of violence and terrorism; (VI) each committee will negotiate independently; (VII) other issues will be decided by mutual agreement between Jordan and Israel.

The above understanding is subject to approval of the respective Governments of Israel and Jordan. The text of this paper will be shown and suggested to the USA.

11/4/87
London

Appendix F: Unity (Wihda) Dam Treaty Text, 3 September 1987

AGREEMENT: THE HASHEMITE KINGDOM OF JORDAN AND THE SYRIAN REPUBLIC FOR THE UTILIZATION OF THE WATERS OF THE YARMOUK RIVER

The Government of the Hashemite Kingdom of Jordan and the Government of the Syrian Republic;

Confirming bonds of friendship and ties of Arab race existing between the two countries, and emphasizing the spirit of sincere cooperation which exists between them, and after perusal of the results of discussions which took place between their two delegations in Damascus on July 4–5, 1987 and August 9–11, 1987 for the utilization of the waters of the Yarmouk basin; and in accordance with the Agreement signed in Damascus June 4, 1953.

And appreciating the benefits which could be secured for the two countries by the proper collection and utilization of the waters of the Yarmouk basin for the purpose of securing irrigation of agricultural lands and generation of electric power;

Have resolved to conclude an Agreement and have delegated their representatives for this purpose:

For the Government of the Hashemite Kingdom of Jordan
Zaid Al-Rifai, Prime Minister
For the Government of the Syrian Republic
Dr Abdul Raouf Al-Kassem, Prime Minister

And after having examined the credentials which each holds on behalf of his Government and after being satisfied with the genuineness of these documents, these representatives have agreed on the following articles:

Article 1

In this treaty the following terms shall have the meanings as defined hereunder:

(a) "Jordan"—The Government of the Hashemite Kingdom of Jordan.

(b) "Syria"—The Government of the Syrian Republic.

(c) "Government"—Jordan or Syria as the context requires.

(d) "Jordan Valley"—The Valley of the River Jordan.

(e) "Al-Wihda (Unity) Dam and Reservoir"—A dam on the Yarmouk River for collection of water, and a reservoir for water storage to be constructed on Jordanian and Syrian Territory.

(f) "Al-Wihda Power Plant"—A plant for the generation of electricity located on the Southern bank of the Yarmouk River within the Al-Wihda Dam.

(g) "Yarmouk Project"—Al-Wihda Dam and Reservoir, the Al-Wihda Power Plant, and any other buildings and construction required by this project and the relocation of the Hejaz Railway near Maqarin Station.

(h) "The Joint Commission"—The Jordanian–Syrian Commission defined in Article 9 of this Agreement.

Article 2

The two Governments recognize that, for natural and technical reasons, it is important to obtain the additional water and the electric power which both countries need in an economical and practical way, through by construction of the Al-Wihda dam. For this purpose they agree to the construction of the following works:

(a) *The Al-Wihda Dam and Reservoir* which are a dam designed to collect river water and a reservoir to be constructed on the Yarmouk River on Jordanian and Syrian territory near Maqarin Station in Syria. This water is intended for the generation of electric power and for use in irrigating Jordanian lands and for other Jordanian schemes and for irrigating Syrian lands located downstream from the dam along the river bed up to a level of 200M above sea level.

(b) *The Hydroelectric Power Plant* which is to be constructed below the dam to generate whatever electric power is possible.

(c) *Relocation of the Hejaz Railway* where it follows the Yarmouk Valley as necessitated by the project and the construction of all buildings and works required by the project.

Article 3

Jordan agrees, subject to the provisions of Article 9 of this Agreement, to assume primary responsibility for the cost of investigations, studies, design construction, operation and maintenance.

Syria agrees to provide all necessary facilities and assistance in allowing project workers to enter Syrian territory and to carry out thereon all work relating to the project through all stages of the work until its completion, subject to the regulations in force in its Government and in accordance with this Agreement.

Article 4

Each Government will compensate the owners of the lands and properties expropriated for the Yarmouk Project in accordance with the laws in effect by both Governments. Syria will liquidate all outstanding claims within this territory relating to the referred to properties and the rights attached thereto, and for expenditure resulting from the liquidation of claims relating to water rights, and Jordan will pay all these claims paid by Syria.

Article 5

Jordanian and Syrian laborers will be employed in the building of the Yarmouk Project construction as necessary. Jordanian and Syrian supervisors and technicians shall be employed during the course of studies and execution and maintenance. Syrian public construction companies will be treated equal to Jordanian construction companies for the construction of this project.

Article 6

Jordan will carry out design and construction of the Al-Wihda Dam at a height of 100m including gated spillway for the storage of water of the Yarmouk River, after filling with water all Syrian dams listed in the attached annex. Syria has the right to hold all stored water in these dams as an integral part of their right in this agreement. Design of Al-Wihda Dam should provide for future raising of the Dam to store more water if it is found feasible, technical and economical by both Governments.

Article 7

A Syria reserves the right to dispose of the waters of all streams springing in its land in the basin of the Yarmouk and its tributaries, with the exception of waters which spring upstream of the dam below the 250 meter contour. Syria also reserves the right to utilize the waters which join the River or from these tributaries below the dam for irrigating Syrian lands situated in the lower basin of the river.

B Jordan has the right to dispose of the water released from the Reservoir and the Power Plant at the Al-Wihda Dam for the purpose of generating electric power.

C Electricity generated from the Al-Wihda Dam will be divided between Jordan and Syria in the ratio of 25 per cent to Jordan and 75 per cent to Syria.

Article 8

Syria will be responsible for the implementation of the relocation of the Hejaz Railway as necessitated by the project and the construction of all buildings and work required by the project, and Jordan will pay for all costs required to implement it.

Article 9

A Jordanian–Syrian commission, consisting of citizens of both Governments, shall be formed for the execution of the provisions of this Agreement, the regulation of rights and obligations which the two Governments have acquired and accepted therefrom, and for exercising these rights and obligations and for considering all cases which may arise from their application.

This Joint Commission shall be considered a legal body (a body possessing juristic personality), the members of which shall enjoy diplomatic privileges and rights in the Government which they do not represent. The Joint Commission shall consist of three members from each Government, with the provision that one of them shall be of the grade of Deputy-Minister, or Under-Secretary. The Joint Commission shall have the right to seek advice of experts and advisers, and to employ assistants, technicians, and employees from among the citizens of both Governments and other Governments as required for carrying out its work.

Representation of this commission to outsiders shall be by both presidents jointly and not separately.

The Joint Commission shall be the responsible body in accordance with the provisions of this agreement, and shall carry out all responsibilities entrusted to it for the completion of the project and the utilization of its benefits in the best manner possible. In the event of the inability of the Joint Commission to reach a definite agreement, the members shall immediately submit a report to this effect to their respective Governments and the two Governments shall then settle the dispute immediately by way of direct negotiations.

The Joint Commission shall set up internal regulations for organizing its work. These regulations shall be approved by the heads of both Governments.

Article 10

Employees, representatives of both Governments, members of the Joint Commission, and employees of technical organizations working on the project, who are in possession of an authorization from the Joint Commission to that effect, and who carry special identification documents, shall have the right to visit the lands on which the Al-Wihda project works are located, together with such neighboring lands as the Joint Commission may find necessary for the purpose of carrying out studies, investigations, construction work, administration, and maintenance, without being subject to procedures arising from the application of the passports or any other law or regulation in force by the two Governments provided that local laws of the two Governments shall remain in force in their own territories in all other respects.

Article 11

The two Governments agree that each within its territory, shall take all necessary measures for the prevention or minimization of silt accumulation in the Interstate Reservoir, and shall also take effective measures for erosion control, forestation, grass development, gully control and other measures which will assist in attaining the maximum benefit from the full capacity of the reservoir. The costs of these measures shall be paid by Jordan.

Article 12

The rights of the two Governments in the use of the lake in its territory, to utilize, operate and maintain for the purpose of tourism and raising fish in a way which does not interfere with the administration of the Al-Wihda Dam facilities.

Article 13

Boundaries between the two Governments shall remain unchanged as before the construction of the Al-Wihda Dam and shall be considered drawn on the surface of the water.

Article 14

This Agreement shall be ratified by the competent authorities of the two Governments and shall become valid from the date of exchange of ratification documents. Its provisions, which may be amended by annexes, shall continue in force until the treaty is nullified by another concluded between the two Governments for this purpose.

In confirmation of what is stated above, the representatives of the two Governments have signed and sealed this Agreement with their respective signatures and seals.

This Agreement is drawn up in Arabic with two original copies which are equally ruling.

Article 15

The Agreement signed between the two Governments in Damascus on June 4, 1953 for the utilization of the waters of the Yarmouk River shall be herewith cancelled.

Signed in Amman on the 3rd of September 1987

FOR THE GOVERNMENT OF THE   Zaid Rifai (sgn.)
HASHEMITE KINGDOM OF JORDAN   PRIME MINISTER

FOR THE GOVERNMENT OF   Dr Abdul Raouf Al-Kassem (sgn.)
THE SYRIAN REPUBLIC   PRIME MINISTER

ANNEX

The Table attached with the Agreement between the Hashemite Kingdom of Jordan and the Syrian Arab Republic for the Purpose of utilizing the water of the Yarmouk River.

Valley Name	Dam Name	Level of Storage m	Storage Capacity (in millions of cubic meters)
Al-Thabah:	Al-Shawah (Al-Balatah)	1100	1.00
	Rasas	1000	0.035
	Ghadeer Al-Soof	700	0.160
	Al-Gharyah Al-Sharqyah	750	5.000
	'Attman'	525	0.17
Al-Zeidi·	Al-Mata'iyah	570	1.00
	Al-Ein	1350	1.15
	Harran	1200	1.95
	Sahwat Al-Khader	1420	8.750
	Dir'a Al-Sharqi	550	15.00
Al-Aram:	Sheikh Meskeen	540	15.00
	Abta'a 1-2	500	4.50
	Tafass	450	2.10
	Adwan	425	5.675
Al-Allan:	Taseel	535	6.60
	Al-Ghor	465	5.50
	Saham Al-Joulan	440	20.00
	Al-Hajah	740	0.85
Al-Ruqad:	Al-Mantarah	945	2.30*
	- Rawaihaineh	870	1.10
	- Buraigah	775	1.80
	- Kudneh	735	30.00
	- Ghadeer Al-Bustan	590	12.00
	- Jisr Al-Ruqad	505	9.00
	- Abdeen	420	5.50

* The water of this valley pours out behind the Al-Wihda Dam

Note:
The Dams: 1—Al-Butum 2.1 million m^3; 2—Al-Room Juwaliain 6.4 million m^3. The two pouring out basins for these two dams are dead ended and do not pour out in the Yarmouk River.
The lower Yarmouk project irrigates an area of 6800 hectares
The upper Yarmouk project irrigates winter field crops of an area 10500 hectares.

Bibliography
(*cited sources only*)

Books and Dissertations

Clinton Bailey, *Jordan's Palestinian Challenge, 1948–83* (Boulder: Westview, 1984).
Uri Bar-Joseph, *The Best of Enemies: Israel and Transjordan in the War of 1948* (London: Frank Cass, 1987).
Meron Benvenisti, *The West Bank Data Project* (Washington: American Enterprise Institute, 1984).
Isaiah Bowman, *The New World: Problems in Political Geography* 4th edn (Yonkers-on-Hudson, New York: World Book Company, 1928).
E. L. M. Burns, *Between Arab and Israeli* (Beirut: Institute for Palestine Studies, 1969).
Neil Caplan, *Futile Diplomacy: Early Arab–Zionist Negotiation Attempts, 1913–1931*, vol. 1 (London: Frank Cass, 1983).
Aharon Cohen, *Israel and the Arab World* (New York: Funk & Wagnalls, 1970).
Yair Evron, *War and Intervention in Lebanon: The Israeli–Syrian Deterrence Dialogue* (Baltimore: Johns Hopkins University Press, 1987).
Ladislas Farago, *Palestine on the Eve* (London: Putnam, 1936).
Abdel Majid Farid and Hussein Sirriyeh (eds) *Israel and Arab Water: An International Symposium* (Ithaca, New York: Ithaca Press, 1985).
Adam Garfinkle, *Western Europe's Middle East Diplomacy and the United States* (Philadelphia: Foreign Policy Research Institute, 1982).
David Grossman, *The Yellow Wind* (New York: Farrar, Straus & Giroux, 1988).
Rami G. Khouri, *The Jordan Valley* (London: Longman, 1981)
Sir Alec Kirkbride, *A Crackle of Thorns* (London: J. Murray, 1956).
Aharon Klieman, *Statecraft in the Dark: Israel's Practice of Quiet Diplomacy* (Tel-Aviv: Jaffee Center, 1988).
Robert Lacey, *The Kingdom* (New York: Harcourt Brace Jovanovich, 1982).

Bruce Maddy-Weitzmann, *The Crystallization of the Arab State System: Inter-Arab Politics, 1945–1954* (Syracuse: Syracuse University Press, 1991).

Amin Abdullah Mahmoud, "King Abdallah and Palestine: An Historical Study of His Role in the Palestine Problem from the Creation of Transjordan to the Annexation of the West Bank, 1921–1950," unpublished Ph.D. dissertation, Georgetown University, 1972.

John W. McDonald, Jr, and Diane B. Bendahmane (eds) *Conflict Resolution: Track Two Diplomacy* (Washington: Foreign Service Institute, US Department of State, May 1987).

Yossi Melman and Dan Raviv, *Behind the Uprising: Israelis, Jordanians, and Palestinians* (Westport, Conn.: Greenwood Press, 1989).

Meir Merhav (ed.) *Economic Cooperation and Middle East Peace* (London: Weidenfeld & Nicolson, 1989).

Shaul Mishal, *West Bank/East Bank* (New Haven: Yale University Press, 1978).

John Norton Moore (ed.) *The Arab–Israeli Conflict: Volume III, Documents* (Princeton: Princeton University Press, 1974).

Benny Morris, *The Origins of the Palestinian Refugee Problem* (New York: Cambridge University Press, 1988).

Samir A. Mutawi, *Jordan in the 1967 War* (New York: Cambridge University Press, 1987).

Avi Plascov, *The Palestinian Refugees in Jordan* (London: Frank Cass, 1981).

Gideon Raphael, *Destination Peace* (London: Weidenfeld & Nicolson, 1981).

Yakov Salomon, *In My Own Way* (Haifa: Gille Salomon Foundation, 1982).

Ronald Sanders, *The High Walls of Jerusalem* (New York: Holt, Rinehart & Winston, 1983).

Ariel Sharon, *Warrior* (New York: Simon & Schuster, 1989).

Avi Shlaim, *Collusion Across the Jordan* (New York: Columbia University Press, 1988).

Dan Shueftan, *Yahase Yarden – Ashaf B'shelav Hadash* (Tel-Aviv: Yad Tabenkin, 1985).

Kenneth W. Stein, *The Land Question in Palestine* (Chapel Hill: University of North Carolina Press, 1986).

Georgiana Stevens, *Jordan River Partition* (Stanford: Hoover Institution, 1965).

Brian van Arkadie, *Benefits and Burdens* (New York: Carnegie Endowment, 1971).

Mary C. Wilson, *King Abdallah, Great Britain and the Making of Jordan* (New York: Cambridge University Press, 1988).

Bat Ye'or, *The Dhimmi: Jews and Christians Under Islam* (Rutherford, New Jersey: Fairleigh Dickinson University Press, 1985).

Journal Essays and Monographs

Fouad Ajami, "The King of Realism," *The New Republic* (10 April 1989).

John K. Cooley, "The War Over Water," *Foreign Policy*, No. 54 (Spring 1984).

Graham E. Fuller, "The Palestinians: The Decisive Year?" *Current History* (February 1990).

Adam Garfinkle, "The Importance of Being Hussein," in Robert O. Freedman (ed.) *The Middle East From the Iran–Contra Affair to the Intifada* (Syracuse: Syracuse University Press, 1990).

Adam Garfinkle, "Getting It Right?: U.S. Mideast Policy in the Bush Administration," *The Jerusalem Quarterly*, No. 52 (Fall 1989).

Adam Garfinkle, "U.S. Decisionmaking in the Jordan Crisis of 1970: Correcting the Record," *Political Science Quarterly* (Spring 1985).

Adam Garfinkle, "'Common Sense' About Middle East Diplomacy: Implication for U.S. Policy in the Near Term," *Middle East Review* (Winter 1984–85).

Adam Garfinkle, "Sources of the al-Fatah Mutiny," *Orbis* (Fall 1983).

Mordechai Gazit, "B'diduto shel ha-melekh Abdallah b'hatirato l'hesder im yisrael, 1949–1951," *Gesher*, 2/113 (Winter 5846, 1985).

H. Gelber, "The Negotiations Between the Jewish Agency and Transjordan, 1946–1948," *Studies in Zionism*, 6:1 (1985).

Moshe Inbar and Jacob O. Maos, "Water Resource Management in the Northern Jordan Valley," *Kidma* (April 1983).

"Interview: H.M. King Hussein," *Defense & Diplomacy* (June 1984).

"Jordan: West Bank and Gaza Trade," *MidEast Markets* (8 August 1983).

Leopold Yehuda Laufer, *Western Europe and the Palestinians: The Socio-Economic Dimension*, Jerusalem: Leonard Davis Institute, Policy Study 39 (May 1990).

Ann Mosely Lesch, *Israel's Occupation of the West Bank: The First Two Years*, Santa Monica, Ca.: Rand RM–6296–ARPA (August 1970).

Samuel Lewis, "Israel: The Peres Era and Its Legacy," *Foreign Affairs*, America and the World (1986).

"Livening Up the Dead Sea," *MidEast Markets* (8 September 1980).

Miriam Lowi, *The Politics of Water: The Jordan River and the Riparian States* (Montreal: Center for Developing Area Studies, McGill University (1984).

Ian Lustick, *Israel and Jordan: The Implications of an Adversarial Partnership*, Berkeley: Institute of International Affairs (1978).

David Mitrany, "The Functional Approach to World Organization," *International Affairs* (July 1948).

Don Peretz, "Intifadeh: The Palestinian Uprising," *Foreign Affairs* (Summer 1988).

Thomas R. Pickering, "Water Scarcity and Political Stability in the Middle East: A Lecture Before the U.S. Congress," 14 September 1989, United States Global Strategy Council.

Daniel Pipes, "Two Bus Lines to Bethlehem," *The National Interest*, No. 6 (Winter 1986/87).

Daniel Pipes, "The Unacknowledged Partnership," *The National Interest*, No. 10 (Winter 1987/88).

Daniel Pipes and Adam Garfinkle, "Is Jordan Palestine?" *Commentary* (October 1988).

David Pryce-Jones, "The Timid King," *The New Republic*, Year-End Issue (1982).

Charles E. Rittenband, "Israel and Jordan: Peaceful Coexistence," *Swiss Review of World Affairs* (August 1984).

Harold Saunders, "Comment," *Mediation in Middle East Conflicts*: Maxwell Summer Lecture Series, 1986 (Syracuse: Syracuse University, 1986).

Avraham Sela, "From Contacts to Negotiations: The Jewish Agency's and the Israeli State's Relationship with King Abdallah, 1946–1950," *Dayan Center Occasional Paper*, Tel-Aviv University (December 1985).

Thomas Stauffer, "Tightening the Squeeze on Jordan's Water," *Middle East International* (20 April 1984).

Kenneth Stein, "The Intifadah and the 1936–1939 Uprising: A Comparison of the Palestinian Arab Communities," The Carter Center of Emory University, *Occasional Paper Series*, Vol. I, No. 1 (March 1990).

Asher Susser, "Jordan," *Middle East Contemporary Survey (MECS)*, Vol. 7 (1982–83).

Shibley Telhami, "Israeli Foreign Policy: A Static Strategy in a Changing World," *Middle East Journal*, 44:3 (Summer 1990).

Moshe Zak, "A Survey of Israel's Contacts With Jordan," in
Itamar Rabinovich and Judah Reinharz (eds) *Israel in the Middle
East* (New York: Oxford University Press, 1984).
Moshe Zak, " Israeli–Jordanian Negotiations," *Washington
Quarterly* (Winter 1985).
Moshe Zak, "The Ambivalent Diplomacy of King Hussein," *Global
Affairs* (Spring 1989).

Documents

Husni 'Ayish and 'Isa Abu Shaykha, *Al Mujtama'al-'Arabi: li's-suff
ath-Thani ath-Thanawi* (al-Matba'a al-Markatiya, adopted 1987–
88).
Foreign Assistance Legislation for Fiscal Years 1988–89 (Part 2),
Hearing before the Subcommittee on Arms Control, Interna-
tional Security and Science of the Committee on Foreign Affairs,
U.S. House of Representatives, One Hundredth Congress, First
Session, Overview of Security Supporting Assistance Programs (3
March 1987) (Washington: USGPO, 1987)
The Next Generation in Four Key Arab Societies, Office of Near East
and South Asia Analysis, Office of Leadership Analysis, Central
Intelligence Agency (March 1989), chapter 4, "Jordan."
Peace: Israel's 40-Year Quest, Israeli Ministry of Foreign Affairs,
Information Division, Jerusalem (1988).
Statistical Abstract of Israel 1971, Central Bureau of Statistics,
Jerusalem (September 1971).

Middle East Media

Al-Anba (Kuwait)
Al-Bayan (Dubai)
Al-Dustur (Amman)
Al-Hamishmar (Tel-Aviv)
Al-Ittihad al-Usbu'i (Abu Dhabi)
Al-Quds (Jerusalem)
Al-Ra'y (Amman)
Al-Tali'ah (Jerusalem)
Al-Wafd (Cairo)
Amman Domestic Service
Amman Television Service
An-Nahar (Jerusalem)
Cairo Domestic Service
Davar (Tel-Aviv)

Haaretz (Tel-Aviv)
Hadashot (Tel-Aviv)
Hatzofeh (Tel-Aviv)
Israeli Defence Forces Radio
Jerusalem Domestic Service
Jerusalem Radio in Arabic
Jerusalem Television
Jerusalem Post
Jordan Times
KUNA (Kuwait)
Ma'ariv (Tel-Aviv)
Radio Monte Carlo
Sawt al-Sha'b (Amman)
WAKH (Manama)
Yedi'ot Aharonot (Tel-Aviv)

US and Other Media

Financial Times (London)
Hong Kong AFP
New York Times
Philadelphia Inquirer
Wall Street Journal
Washington Post
Wochenpresse (Vienna)

Index

El Al, 76
Elat, 52, 71, 77–80, 161
Eldar, Akiva, 89
Electrical and Mechanical
  Services (EMS), 63
electrical utilities, 2, 115, 179,
  185
Entebbe raid, 92
Environmental Protection
  Agency (US), 80
Eretz Yisrael, 36
Escondito Elementary
  School, 41
European Community (EEC,
  EC), 123–4, 130
European Jewry, 16
Ezekiel, 92

Faisal ibn Husein (Emir, King
  of Iraq), 18–20, 22, 24, 46,
  189, 191, 193–4
Farago, Ladislas, 22–3
Fatah, al', 43, 51, 71, 104, 116,
  118, 126
Fez Plan, 103
Fifi, 70
Force 17 (PLO), 128
Foreign Broadcast Information
  Service, xiv
Foreign Ministry (Israel) Guest
  House, 72, 82
Foreign Policy Research
  Institute, 112
France, 18–19, 36–7, 128
Frankfurter, Felix, 20, 193–5
Friedman, Mikha, 135
Fuller, Graham, 6
functional ties, x, 1–2, 12, 71,
  74, 77, 82, 89, 91, 99–100,
  111–13, 115, 122–4,
  129–33, 136–8, 145, 163,
  179, 185–6
functionalism, x–xi, 34, 59

Gabay, Shefi, 135–6
Galei Zahal, 87
Galilee, 35, 101
Gaza, 6–7, 10–12, 58, 72, 87,
  108, 112, 124, 128, 137,
  147, 149, 154, 176–7
Gazit, Mordecai, 82
Gazit, Sholomo, 58
Germany, xi, xviii, 16, 62, 83,
  130, 173
Givati, Haim, 61, 82
Golan disengagement accord
  (1974), 4
Great Britain, 16, 23–4, 36–7,
  45, 111, 120, 189, 191
Greater Israel, 103
Greater Syria, 21, 24
green cards, 148
Grossman, David, 58

Haaretz, 87
Haas, Ernst, x
Hadassah hospital, 69–70
Haifa, 81, 135, 159, 197, 201
Haig, Alexander M., 112
Hamad, Walid Mustafa, 115
ham radio, 87
HAMAS, 161–2
Haq, Badr abd al-, 86
Harza Engineering, 49
Ha-selah Ha-adom (The Red
  Rock), 43
Hashemite monarchy, 9, 172,
  181–2
Hashemites, 2, 9, 15–16, 19, 21,
  22, 44, 102, 107, 119, 136,
  147, 153, 155, 158, 174,
  180, 182, 184
Hassan bin Tallal (Crown
  Prince of Jordan), 82, 181
Hassan, Khalid al-, 156
Hebrew University, 29
Hebron, 115–16, 131, 159